NATIONAL GEOGRAPHIC

Field Guide to the

TREES

of North America

By Keith Rushforth and Charles Hollis

National Geographic
Washington, D.C.

CONTENTS

National Geographic's Field Guide to the Trees of North America is intended to help readers to identify more than 400 species of tree commonly encountered throughout North America–from ornamental to forest species. Hikers, birders, gardeners and backyard landscapers, and those with a general interest in trees will find the guide's more than 1,000 illustrations essential in their quest to identify the unusual, the spectacular, and the unfamiliar.

—Dr. Sharon G. Haines, Director of Sustainable Forestry and Forest Policy, International Paper

INTRODUCTION

A tree is usually defined as a woody perennial plant growing with a single stem to a height of 6 m or more, whereas a shrub rarely attains this height and usually has several stems originating at or near the ground line. Not all woody plants fall consistently into these human-made categories; some portray both tree and shrub characteristics depending on environmental and cultural influences. This guide assumes if a species occurs as a tree with more than negligible frequency, then it is included. The identification guide attempts to provide characteristics of leaves, stems, flowers and fruit for each genus such that readers may identify trees during most seasons of the year.

Points about size can only be made in general terms. This particularly concerns the bole, which increases in diameter every year — a distinctive characteristic of woody plants except palms. The girth of the trunk 1.5 m above the ground is often assumed to be an approximate method for estimating the age of a tree. Estimates of age based on girth alone, however, are usually misleading. Lawn and park trees of a given species and for a given size are often younger than their country siblings of the same size due to cultural inputs of water and fertilizer. Long-lived species slow down radial growth with advancing age, such that a few centimeters in radial growth can represent decades, whereas that same growth increment at a younger age may represent one to several years.

Some species of pines in the western United States and members of the genera *Sequoiadendron*, *Taxus* and *Taxodium* can live for several thousand years. Any measurement given in this book is expressed as the maximum for each species.

Nomenclature

Popular names of trees vary widely. This makes the use of common names unreliable, and accuracy is best served by employing the scientific name, the structure of which is governed by strict international rules. The scientific name is a Latin, Greek or Latinized binomial. The first element of the name designates the genus (a noun) to which the tree belongs. The second element is the specific epithet (an adjective). Together the genus and specific epithet designate a species. For example, the birches dwell within the genus *Betula*. River birch is known as *Betula nigra*. Genera with noticeable similarities are grouped together into families. For example, the genus *Betula* belongs in the family *Betulaceae*. According to the rules of nomenclature, the genus is a proper name and hence, capitalized. The specific epithet is an adjective and not capitalized unless it is a Latinized proper name, i.e. named for a person. For example, Douglas fir is known scientifically as *Pseudotsuga Menziesii*, which was named in honor of the Scottish naturalist A. Menzies, who discovered it in 1793. In contrast, Bigcone Douglas fir is known as *Pseudotsuga macrocarpa*, where the specific epithet refers to a very large cone size. Scientific names are italicized or underlined by convention.

The use of scientific names in this book follows the international rules, and, as many of the trees illustrated are often used as ornamentals in North America and Europe, the nomenclature and spelling followed the reference: Bailey, L. H. and E. Z. Bailey (1976) *Hortus Third: A Concise Dictionary of Cultivated Plants in the United States and Canada*. Revised and expanded: (2000) The Staff of The L. H. Bailey Hortorium, Cornell University. Barnes and Noble Press. 1293 pp. Where questions arose concerning the correct scientific names for a species, the staff of the L.H. Bailey Hortorium provided the most recent, acceptable name. [E. Cope (2003), L. H. Baily Hortorium, Cornell University, Ithaca, N.Y., Personal Communication].

Sometimes further definition is required beyond a species. A variety (indicated by "var." after the species name) is a tree that has developed slightly different characteristics from its species (or "type"). A cultivar or clone is propagated vegetatively, by grafting or rooting, from a tree that shows some unique or interesting characteristics. It is given a new name enclosed in single quotation marks and follows the species name, e.g. Autumn cherry is: *Prunus subhirtella* 'Autumnalis.' A hybrid (indicated by an "x" between the generic name and a specific epithet) is a cross between two species within the genus. Where the parentage of a hybrid is in doubt, as with many *Prunus* hybrids, a popular name replaces the specific epithet.

There is a generally accepted order in which tree families should be presented based on a presumed evolutionary sequence from the more primitive to the more advanced groups. Occasionally, this book will deviate from the accepted order to place side-by-side species that bear a strong resemblance to each other so that they may be more readily identified. Within families, the genera have been ordered purely for the sake of convenience, and their sequence does not imply any botanical significance.

How to Use This Book
The annotated illustrations, text and symbols, which are explained below, give in concise form the information necessary to identify a tree. You do not need to thumb your way through the book looking for the right species. The first step is to read the introductory pages, where the major differences between groups of trees are explained, and guidance is given on which parts of a tree to examine to narrow the choice. You can use the Identification Keys to identify the genus; from there you can proceed quickly to the species in question. Before you try to identify an unknown tree, it is a good idea to practice using the keys by working backward using a tree that is familar.

More general information will be found in the introduction to **The Conifers**, p. 27, and **The Broadleaf Trees** p. 90.

Symbols

R	Rare, usually found only in collections	Ⓦ	Needles in fascicles of 5
Ⓒ	Deciduous, leaves shed in autumn	Ⓨ	Leaves in horizontal sprays along shoot
Ⓔ	Evergreen, leaves retained into winter	Ⓓ	Found in deciduous woods
Ⓥ	Buds and leaves alternate or spiral	Ⓐ	Found in evergreen woods
Ⓨ	Buds and leaves opposite pairs	Ⓜ	Found in mixed woods
Ⓢ	leaves awl- or scale-like	Ⓖ	Common in streets, parks and gardens
Ⓡ	Leaves in rosettes on short (spur) shoots	Ⓒ	Found in open countryside
Ⓘ	Needles in fascicles of 2	Ⓦ	Found by water or on wet or moist sites
Ⓥ	Needles in fascicles of 3	♂ male ♀ female	
① ② ③ ④ ⑤ ⑥ ⑦ ⑧ ⑨ ⑩		Zones of Tree Hardiness (see p. 8)	

Tree Distribution
Trees have adapted to the wide range of conditions to be encountered in North America, from Arctic to subtropical, and climate is the main factor governing their distribution. Altitude and land mass are also important: the same trees may be found at high altitudes in the Appalachians and grow near sea level in Canada, while the Great Lakes create a climate warmer than if the region were all land. Atmospheric conditions affect habitat

locally — some trees can tolerate near-desert heat and aridity while others require heavy rainfall or high humidity. So a broad north–south scale of temperature is inadequate. In the case of the West Coast, for instance, the warm ocean and the Rocky Mountains affect temperature and rainfall so that greater hardiness is required for a tree to survive as one moves farther inland, i.e. eastward, and not southward.

Zones of Tree Hardiness

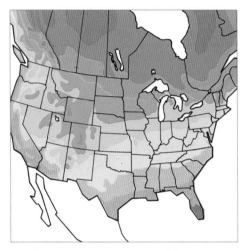

Average minimum annual temperature (°F)

Zones			Zones	
	①	below -50°		⑥	-10° to 0°
	②	-50° to -40°		⑦	0° to 10°
	③	-40° to -30°		⑧	10° to 20°
	④	-30° to -20°		⑨	20° to 30°
	⑤	-20° to -10°		⑩	30° to 40°

The widely recognized climatic zones on the map above, although not absolute, give a good indication of plant hardiness. Generally, a tree can also survive in zones warmer (higher numbered) than its own.

Abbreviations

alt	alternate	**infl**	inflorescence	**sp(p)**	species
bk	bark	**lf**	leaf		(plural)
br	branch	**lflt**	leaflet	**st**	stem
c.	about	**lvs**	leaves	**uns**	underside
cm	centimeter	**m**	meter	**ups**	upperside
fl	flower	**mm**	millimeter	**var.**	variety
flrs	flowers	**opp**	opposite	**yr**	year
fr	fruit	**sh**	shoot		

How to Identify Trees

The identification of trees is a matter of putting together all the various pieces of information provided by the plant, and not just some of them. It is very tempting to latch on to some immediately striking feature and go no further, in which case you might end up identifying a tree incorrectly, as your only piece of evidence was misleading. For instance, you might know that ashes are generally characterized by pinnate leaves, and so never entertain the possibility that the tree in front of you with single leaves is an ash, but there is an exception to the rule, the Single-leaved ash. So whenever possible, examine the foliage, buds, flowers, fruit, habit and bark, or as many as are visible at that time of the year.

The first step, before using the keys in this book, is to decide whether a tree belongs to the conifers or the broadleaf trees, something almost anybody can do. The actual difference is the conifers have exposed ovules (which develop into seeds) whereas the broadleaf trees bear their ovules in an ovary. For identification purposes, the differences indicated by the colloquial names of the groups are sufficient: the conifers bear cones and have needle-like leaves which contrast with the wider foliage of the broadleaf trees.

Besides observing as many features as possible, keep in mind a few general points. Even within the plant, leaf characteristics vary; the leaves at the top of the crown are generally smaller than those on lower branches (although poplars are a notable exception) and leaves that develop in the shade are often different in both size and shape than those growing in full sunlight. The number of lobes can decrease with the age and vigor of the shoot, as seen in some oak species. New shoots arising after pruning are more vigorous and often produce leaves of atypical proportions. As a rule, you will find more typical leaf, bud and shoot features near the middle of the crown and on the shorter shoots. Features that usually occur in pairs can occasionally be found in threes or more, depending on environment and other factors that influence tree growth.

Foliage Characteristics

Foliage should be examined thoroughly. First, important observations can be made at some distance from the tree itself, such as the color of the foliage, and whether or not it is pendent (hanging). With more detailed examination, leaves provide clues in variation of outline, and the way they are set upon the shoot. Other features to look at are the margins, the shape of the base and tip, the veins and the petiole, and the texture and hairiness.

Conifers: these trees show four types of leaf arrangement. *Fascicles* **(a)**, borne by pines, are bunches of needles growing from one bud (needle is not a scientific term but simply a descriptive alternative to leaf). Leaves set in a *pectinate row* **(b)**, such as those of the yews and firs, are arranged in ranks along opposite sides of the shoot. **Awl-shaped leaves (c)**, as borne by the junipers, are set radially around the shoot. **Scale-like leaves (d)**, set densely round the shoot, are characteristic of Lawson cypress. See also the introduction to **The Conifers**, p. 27.

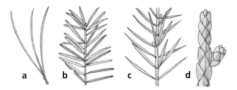

a   b   c   d

Broadleaf trees: the illustrations below show some basic leaf shapes of broadleaf trees, which have more varied foliage than the conifers. An important point to remember is these are mostly deciduous and are found in their mature form for a relatively short time.

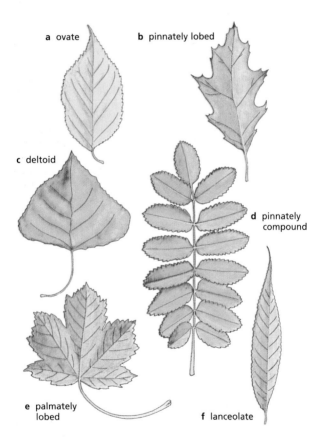

a ovate

b pinnately lobed

c deltoid

d pinnately compound

e palmately lobed

f lanceolate

Besides the basic shape, look at the *margins* (the edges of the leaf), which are serrated in **(d)**, **(e)** and **(f)**; the *apex* (the end of the leaf farthest from the shoot), which is acute (or pointed) in **(b)** and acuminate in **(a)**; and the base of the leaf, which is rounded in **(a)**, cuneate (or wedge-shaped) in **(b)** and **(f)**, truncate (or squared) in **(c)**. See also the introduction to **The Broadleaf Trees**, p. 90.

a   b   c

The *petiole* or leaf stalk (above) can provide useful clues when its shape, particularly in cross-section, is examined. It is usually round **(a)** but can also be grooved **(b)**, as in Sweet cherry, or flattened **(c)**, as in Quaking aspen. Some palms have stout, hooked spines on the petioles. There is a bud at the base of the petiole, and usually the petiole is curved around it in a crescent shape. In some species, however, the bud is completely enclosed in the enlarged petiole base; when the leaf falls, a circular scar remains.

Shoots and Buds
Shoots are the new growth that spring from the buds at the start of the new season. They usually harden into their mature wooden state by midsummer and then are ready to bear the buds for the next season's growth.

Points to look for on shoots are the color, whether they are hairy or not, and their shape. Most shoots, when seen in cross-section, are round, but they can be angled or winged in some species. Cutting down lengthwise through a shoot reveals its basic structure, which is shown in illustration **(c)** below. In the center, there is always the *pith*, sometimes a useful identification guide; it is generally a soft amorphous mass of various colors and texture, but is occasionally chambered, as in **(b)**.

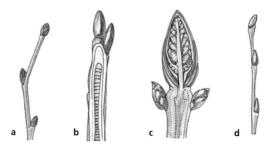

a   b   c   d

The *buds*, borne through the winter before producing the new growth, are a key identification feature. There is usually a single bud at the tip of the shoot, known as the terminal bud, from which the shoot will continue elongation growth when temperature, moisture and day length conditions are favorable. Lateral buds are arranged along the sides of the shoot and, in turn, produce new lateral shoots. The new shoots will produce the leaves and initiate buds in the axils of these leaves for the next growth cycle. The way in which lateral buds and shoots are arranged can vary considerably, and the main differences are illustrated above. They can be arranged alternately along the stem, as in **(a)**, in opposite or nearly opposite pairs, as in **(c)**, or in a spiral pattern, as in **(d)**. Some species do not produce terminal buds, the upper-most lateral functions to extend the shoot, and a peg-like vestige of the terminal growing point can be seen next to the upper most lateral, as in **(d)**.

Buds are a useful identification guide because they are set in different ways. A few trees, such as the cypresses, do not have a terminal bud in winter, while oaks are distinctive by having a cluster of buds at the shoot tips. Many trees have dormant buds covered by the bark; they remain dormant until the main shoot is damaged or more light reaches the bole, then they start growing and produce what are called epicormic shoots.

Other features to look for in buds are such obvious things as the shape, size, color, presence or absence of scales and hairs, all of which differ widely. Buds may be ovoid, globose, conical or spindle-shaped. Some species have resinous, or sticky, buds. Another key feature is the number and arrangement of scales on the outside of each bud: some may be naked and have no scales at all, just miniature leaves, as in Witch-hazel; or they may have a single cap-like scale, as in the willows; or they may have two or four opposing scales in a valvate arrangement, as in the ashes; or they may have many scales adpressed on top of each other.

Thorns
Thorns and spines are characteristic of a few species. Thorns are modified shoots, whereas spines are usually modified stipules, which occur at the base of a leaf or axillary bud. Thorns may be unbranched, as in **(a)**, or branched, as in **(c)**. Spines are unbranched, and may occur singly, or more often in pairs, as in **(b)**.

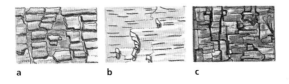

Bark
The bark, the protective outer covering of the stem, can be a useful identification feature, especially as it is available throughout the year. The young branches have smooth bark that, on the

bole, is usually split and broken as the diameter of the stem increases with age. It is the form that this breaking up takes, which can be diagnostic. The chief characteristics, such as color, are usually more pronounced in the bark higher up in the tree than in the mature bark near the base, because it has broken up more recently. Three basic types of bark are shown in the illustrations above: scaly fissures **(a)**, ridged and furrowed bark **(c)** and peeling bark **(b)**. The fissure color can be important.

Identification Keys

Do not shy away from botanical keys; they are a tried and tested aid to tree identification. As pointed out in the prior section on Nomenclature, trees are grouped into genera based on common characteristics. The keys provided on pages 14–26 list observable characteristics that will lead you to the genus of the tree in question. From the page numbers listed for the various genera, you can compare your specimen to the several species illustrated in the section for that particular genus. Obviously not all the tree species are illustrated here, but by comparing the key characteristics for related species within the genus, you can determine the major group to which your specimen belongs.

These keys are known as dichotomous keys, i.e. you are given two choices between contrasting characteristics. As you progress through the contrasts, you will notice that you are eliminating characteristics that are not common to your specimen, hence narrowing your choices to those common to species within the genus to which your specimen belongs. The characteristics listed represent the range of features visible throughout the year, i.e. leaves, flowers, fruit, bark, etc. Read each choice carefully and fully before selecting an option.

To use these keys, select a good specimen and progress through the listed options. Choose the option that best fits the characteristics of your specimen, then move on to the name or number indicated. If you find yourself at a dead end, go back to a set of choices where you were uncertain and take the alternate choice and proceed. Eventually, you will reach the genus to which your specimen belongs. In winter, there is nothing to prevent you from using fallen and dry leaves or fruit, and remember bud arrangement is the same as leaf arrangement.

Learn to use the keys with a species already familiar to you. With practice, you will find that the use of botanical keys, together with detailed observation in the field, will greatly improve your knowledge of trees and your ability to identify them. There are many good field guides and books on trees at your local library and bookstore that can help you identify more of the trees in your area.

Key to Genera

1. Leaves awl-shaped, linear, needle-like, or scale-like, visible veins one mid-vein or absent, or if present, lvs fan-shaped with dichotomous parallel venation; seeds not borne in an enclosed ovary
Gymnosperms   **Key A**
1. Leaves not as above, seeds borne in enclosed ovary, which develops into recognizable fruit at maturity
Angiosperms   ➜ **2.**

2. Leaves generally broad; venation is reticulate with pinnately or palmately arranged major veins; wood has visible pith and annual rings
Dicots   **Key B**
2. Leaves long and narrow, or palm-like; venation is parallel; flower parts in 3's or multiples of 3; wood lacks central pith and annual rings
Monocots   **Key C**

Key A — Gymnosperms

1. Lvs deciduous, fan-shaped, notched in middle, venation dichotomous and parallel; twigs have short spur shoots on which leaves are spirally arranged; producing a fleshy, yellow drupe-like seed; *Ginkgo* p. 29
1. Lvs awl-shaped, linear, needle-like or scale-like ➜ 2.

2. Seed surrounded by a fleshy red or green aril (drupaceous) or fleshy, small terminal cone ➜ 3.
2. Seeds borne in a cone ➜ 6.

3. Seed within a fleshy terminal cone-like with 3 whorls of 3 fleshy scales *Saxegothaea* p. 31
3. Not as above ➜ 4.

4. A single seed surrounded by a fleshy scarlet aril; leaves linear, 4 cm, yellowish beneath and appearing 2-ranked *Taxus* p. 30
4. Not as above ➜ 5.

5. Lvs 2-ranked, stiff and sharp-pointed to 7 cm; a terminal, single drupe-like seed covered by a green or brown fleshy aril, often with greenish or purplish striations *Torreya* p. 30
5. Lvs loosely 2-ranked or spirally arranged and clustered toward branch tips, flexible and not sharp pointed; a single seed often attached to a fleshy, brightly colored receptacle *Podocarpus* p. 31

6. Lvs or branchlets deciduous ➜ 7.
6. Lvs or branchlets evergreen ➜ 9.

7. Lvs linear, triangular in cross section, spirally arranged on short spur shoots; cone scales thin with long tipped bracts exserted beyond the scales *Larix* p. 62
7. Lvs flat and 2-ranked or awl-shaped and adpressed along branch, branchlets deciduous; cone globose with peltate scales ➜ 8.

8. Lvs spirally arranged, adpressed and awl-shaped on fertile branches, and linear 2-ranked on non-fertile branchlets; branchlets alternately arranged on stem (one species evergreen) *Taxodium* p. 46
8. Lvs flattened, 2-ranked, curved and oppositely arranged; branchlets opposite *Metasequoia* p. 47

9. Lvs linear, needle-like, or awl-shaped ➜ 10.

9. Lvs scale-like, or, if awl-shaped, both scale-like and awl-shaped leaves on same tree → 21.

10. Lvs needle-like in fascicles of 1–5 enclosed in basal sheath **Pinus** p. 73
10. Lvs linear or flattened, not in fascicles → 11.

11. Lvs whorled on short spur shoots, blue-green and flexible; cones erect **Cedrus** p. 60
11. Lvs spirally arranged or 2-ranked, not on spur shoots → 12.

12. Cones erect at maturity, cone scales deciduous leaving the erect central axis; buds often resinous, resin blisters often visible under bark of young stems **Abies** p. 51
12. Cones pendant at maturity, cone scales persistent → 13.

13. Cones with spirally arranged overlapping scales → 14.
13. Cones with peltate scales → 18.

14. Lvs broad at base, hard, sharp-pointed → 15.
14. Lvs uniformly linear, or narrower at base → 16.

15. Lvs generally as broad as long, closely overlapping; branches distinctly whorled on main stem; cones large, to 7 x 15 cm, seeds 1 per scale **Araucaria** p. 32
15. Lvs longer than broad, appearing 2-ranked with broad white bands beneath; cones globose, generally less than 5 cm in diameter with 3 seeds per scale **Cunninghamia** p. 48

16. Lvs not on peg-like projections; cones with exserted 3-lobed bracts visible between the scales; buds pointed often with reflexed scales **Pseudotsuga** p. 70
16. Lvs linear or flattened on peg-like projections; cones without exserted bracts → 17.

17. Lvs mostly linear, spirally arranged, stiff and pointed, generally 4-angled in cross section; cones generally cylindrical and longer than broad; buds not resinous **Picea** p. 64
17. Lvs mostly flattened or rounded in cross section, often loosely 2-ranked; cones terminal, ovoid, scales orbicular and thin **Tsuga** p. 71

18. Lvs long and in distinct whorls of 20 or more clustered at ends of twigs **Sciadopitys** p. 49
18. Lvs not as above → 19.

19. Lvs clasping at base, keeled, pointing forward and incurving; cones, globose to 2–3 cm, scales tipped with 2–3 appendages **Cryptomeria** p. 49
19. Lvs and cones not as above → 20.

20. Lvs on lateral branches about 2 cm long, appearing 2-ranked by twist of leaf base; cones to 3 cm, ovoid and maturing in one year, buds scaly **Sequoia** p. 46
20. Lvs on lateral branches awl-shaped, adpressed, less than 10 mm long; cones oblong-ovoid, usually greater than 5 cm long, maturing in two years; buds naked **Sequoiadendron** p. 45

21. Lvs both scale-like and awl-shaped often on same branch, scale-like leaves keeled and decussate

giving branchlet 4-angled appearance, awl-like leaves opposite and decussate; cone bluish, berry-like with fleshy peltate scales ***Juniperus*** p. 43

21. Lvs scale-like; cone not berry-like ➜ 22.

22. Lvs scale-like keeled and decussate giving branchlet 4-angled appearance; cones woody, 6–12 peltate scales, 5–20 seeds per scale ***Cupressus*** p. 33
22. Lvs scale-like, opposite and flattened giving branchlet flattened appearance ➜ 23.

23. Lvs scale-like, facial pair lacking glands; cone globose with peltate scales ***Cupressocyparis*** p. 36
23. Lvs scale-like, facial pairs glandular ➜ 24.

24. Cones globose with peltate scales with 2-3 seeds per scale in ***Chamaecyparis*** p. 37
24. Cones ovoid with ovoid or wedge-shaped scales ➜ 25.

25. Lvs scale-like, broad, diverging from branch with tips incurved, glaucous and silvery on underside; cones rounded with flattened top, blue-gray ***Thujopsis*** p. 42
25. Lvs scale-like, strongly adpressed along branch; cones ovoid ➜ 26.

26. Lvs in whorls of 4, decurrent, free at apex, facial pair flattened, lateral pair keeled and overlapping the facial pair; cones ovoid to 3 cm, pendant with 3 pairs of scales the outer pair resembles a duck's bill ***Calocedrus*** p. 43
26. Lvs in pairs, decussate; Cones erect with 3–6 pairs of woody or leathery scales ➜ 27.

27. Cones oblong-ovoid, 6–12 thin, leathery scales; branchlets flattened in single plane ***Thuja*** p. 41
27. Cones globose to ovoid, thick, green, leathery scales; branchlets often flattened in 2 planes ***Platycladus*** p. 41

Key B — Dicots

1. Trees having evergreen leaves (may be leafless for a brief period in spring prior to flowering) ➜ 2.
1. Trees having leaves deciduous over a prolonged period ➜ 32.

Evergreen trees

2. Lvs opposite, subopposite or whorled ➜ 3.
2. Lvs alternate ➜ 10.

3. Lvs compound ➜ 4.
3. Lvs simple ➜ 6.

Leaves evergreen, opposite, compound

4. Lvs pinnately compound ➜ 5.
4. Lvs palmately compound ***Tabebuia*** p. 239

5. Lvs pinnately compound ***Spathodea*** p. 238
5. Lvs bipinnately compound ***Jacaranda*** p. 237

Leaves evergreen, opposite, simple

6. Lvs scale-like, whorled; br segmented; fr a samara in cone-like structure ***Casuarina*** p. 101
6. Lvs and fruit not as above ➜ 7.

7. Lvs sub-opposite, aromatic, entire with yellow margins; fr a bluish-black berry ***Cinnamomum*** p. 153

7.   Lvs opposite   ➔ 8.

8.   Lvs ‹5 cm long, ovate, petiole short; fl clustered in leaf axils; fr a brown capsule with 3 segments ***Buxus*** p. 186

8.   Lvs ovate to lanceolate, lobed or remotely serrate near apex, ›5 cm long   ➔ 9.

9.   Lvs ovate, entire, glabrous; flrs in terminal panicles, white; fr a bluish drupe, ‹1 cm ***Ligustrum*** p. 231

9.   Lvs elliptic-lanceolate, silvery-scurfy below; fl in axillary panicles; fr a black drupe ›2 cm ***Olea*** p. 231

10.   Lvs simple   ➔ 11.

10.   Lvs compound   ➔ 29.

Leaves evergreen, alternate, simple

11.   Lvs lobed   ➔ 12.

11.   Lvs unlobed, may have prominent teeth   ➔ 14.

12.   Lvs pinnately lobed (may be obvious only on young shoots), margins often toothed; fr an acorn ***Quercus*** (in part) p. 117

12.   Lvs palmately lobed   ➔ 13.

13.   Lvs deeply cleft, typically 7 or more lobes, long petioles to 100 cm, lobes pointed; tree often has an unbranched single, green stem; fr a large berry, ›12 cm with thick skin, orange flesh and black seeds ***Carica*** p. 148

13.   Lvs lobed or unlobed, on short petiole, leathery; sap milky; fr an aggregate of individual seeds inside a fleshy pear-shaped receptacle with apical ostiole ***Ficus*** (in part) p. 144

14.   Lvs with entire margins   ➔ 15.

14.   Lvs with serrate, dentate or sharply toothed margins (occasionally margins entire)   ➔ 25.

15.   Lvs aromatic   ➔ 16.

15.   Lvs non-aromatic   ➔ 21.

16.   Fr a capsule   ➔ 17.

16.   Fr a drupe or aggregate of follicles   ➔ 18.

17.   Lvs lanceolate, may have opposite ovate lvs on juvenile shoots, fl axillary; bk exfoliating ***Eucalyptus*** p. 216

17.   Lvs elliptical to lanceolate with 5 visible veins; fl in terminal spikes, which may continue to grow as leafy shoot; bk white exfoliating in thin sheets and spongy ***Melaleuca*** p. 217

18.   Fl showy; fruit a cone-shaped aggregate of follicles with red seeds ***Magnolia*** (in part) p. 149

18.   Fl not large and showy, fr a drupe or drupaceous berry   ➔ 19.

19.   Lvs leathery; fl in terminal drooping panicles; fr an orange-red drupaceous berry; bk reddish-brown, exfoliating in thin plates revealing yellowish-pink inner bark ***Arbutus*** p. 222

19.   Lvs flexible; fl axillary; fr a green or purplish drupe ➔ 20.

20.   Fr a purplish drupe attached to a prominent calyx tube ***Persea*** p. 153

20.   Fr a greenish to purple drupe; lvs produce a strong pungent odor when bruised ***Umbellularia*** p. 154

21. Lvs and br with milky sap; fr a nut subtended by fleshy, kidney-shaped receptacle ***Anacardium*** p. 189
21. Lvs without milky sap; fr a drupe, capsule or achene → 22.

22. Lvs with silvery scales beneath; br sometimes thorny; fr a red or yellow drupe with silvery scales (some sp(p) are deciduous) ***Elaeagnus*** p. 218
22. Lvs without silvery scales; branches unarmed → 23.

23. Lvs orbicular, with red veins, leathery; fl in 25 cm long white axillary racemes; fr an achene surrounded by a purple, fleshy calyx in bunches resembling grapes ***Coccoloba*** p. 147
23. Lvs ovate or obovate without red veins; fr clusters do not resemble a bunch of grapes → 24.

24. Lvs large, to 20 cm, ovate, hairy; fl large, to 5 cm, tubular, in terminal clusters; fr drupe ***Cordia*** p. 234
24. Lvs ‹20 cm, elliptic to obovate, leathery, margins wavy; fl usually ‹3 cm; fr a 2- to 4-celled capsule ***Pittosporum*** p. 206

25. Lvs having few marginal teeth to entire with prominent spiny tip; fr red or orange drupaceous berries ***Ilex*** p. 191
25. Lvs uniformly serrate or dentate (occasionally entire); fr a nut or capsule → 26.

26. Fr a nut → 27.
26. Fr a capsule → 28.

27. Fr a nut completely enclosed in spiny involucre; lvs leathery, often entire with revolute margins ***Castanopsis*** p. 134
27. Fr a nut resembling an acorn, with shallow, hairy, cup-like involucre; lvs dentate ***Lithocarpus*** p. 133

28. Fl single, white on long axillary peduncles; lvs to 15 cm, elliptic to lanceolate, serrate ***Gordonia*** p. 214
28. Fl single or double, white, pink or red, on short axillary or terminal peduncles; lvs elliptic to ovate or obovate, margins serrate to entire ***Camellia*** p. 213

Leaves, evergreen, alternate, compound

29. Lvs fern-like, margins recurved; fl orange in 1-sided racemes to 10 cm; fr a leathery follicle ***Grevillea*** p. 145
29. Lvs and fruit not as above → 30.

30. Lvs with more than 7 obovate lflts, leathery; fl white or blue in pendulous panicles; fr a cylindrical legume constricted between the seeds ***Sophora*** p. 179
30. Lvs trifoliate or nearly so; st and br armed with stout thorns; fr a berry → 31.

31. Fr small, ‹4 cm, orange; lflts to 8 cm, elliptic ***Fortunella*** p. 194
31. Fr large, ›6 cm, orange, yellow, green or pinkish, or if small not orange-colored; lvs leathery, glandular dotted, often reduced to a single terminal elliptic to ovate lflt with subtending wing-like appendages Citrus p. 192

Deciduous trees

32. Lvs opposite → 33.

32. Lvs alternate → 43.

33. Lvs simple → 34.
33. Lvs compound → 41.

Leaves deciduous, opposite, simple

34. Lvs 3- to 5-lobed, usually ‹20 cm long; fr a double samara *Acer* p. 198
34. Lvs unlobed, or if lobed, fr not double samara → 35.

35. Lvs large, ›20 cm, cordate and palmately veined; opposite and/or whorled; fr a 2-valved capsule → 36.
35. Lvs ‹20 cm; fr a drupe, berry or 4-valved capsule → 37.

36. Fr a long, thin capsule to 40 cm *Catalpa* p. 236
36. Fr an ovoid capsule ‹4 cm long *Paulownia* p. 235

37. Lvs cordate, palmately veined; fl axillary; fr a many-seeded follicle *Cercidiphyllum* p. 146
37. Lvs elliptic or ovate; fr a drupe or 4-valved capsule → 38.

38. Lvs with finely serrated margins → 39.
38. Lvs with entire margins → 40.

39. Lvs with incurving serrations; br with prominent lenticels; fr a purplish drupe *Forestiera* p. 232
39. Lvs without incurving serrations; br winged or 4-angled; fr a scarlet 4-valved capsule *Euonymus* p. 195

40. Lvs with ciliate margins and veins arching; fl terminal subtended by 4 white or pink showy bracts; fr a 2-seeded drupaceous berry *Cornus* p. 219

40. Lvs without ciliate margins, veins not arching; fl in axillary panicles; fr a purple drupe *Chionanthus* p. 232

Leaves deciduous, opposite, compound

41. Lvs palmately compound, usually 5–7 lflts; fl in erect, showy, terminal panicles; fr a capsule with 1 or more large seeds *Aesculus* p. 207
41. Lvs pinnately compound; fr a samara → 42.

42. Lvs with typically 5 or more lflts; bud scales valvate; fr a single samara; bk corky and furrowed *Fraxinus* p. 226
42. Lvs with 3–5 lflts; bud scales overlapping, twigs green; bk smooth; fr double samara *Acer* (1 sp) p. 198

Trees with deciduous, alternate leaves

43. Lvs simple → 44.
43. Lvs compound → 90.

44. Lvs lobed → 45.
44. Lvs not lobed → 51.

Leaves deciduous, simple, alternate, lobed

45. Lvs palmately lobed → 46.
45. Lvs pinnately lobed → 47.

46. Lvs star-shaped, 5-lobed (occasionally 3 lobes); buds resinous; fr a globose head of beaked capsules *Liquidambar* p. 155
46. Lvs coarsely-toothed; buds enclosed in petiole base; bk exfoliating, mottled; fr a globose head of hairy achenes *Platanus* p. 196

47. Br armed with thorns; fr a pome ***Crataegus*** p. 158
47. Br unarmed → 48.

48. Lvs 1- to 3-lobed (occasionally unlobed) on
    same tree → 49.
48. Lvs more than 3 lobes → 50.

49. Lvs and twigs strongly aromatic, margins entire;
    fr a bluish drupe on red stalk ***Sassafras*** p. 154
49. Lvs not aromatic, margins strongly serrate to dentate;
    fr a multiple of drupes; sap milky ***Morus*** p. 142

50. Lvs 4-lobed, tulip-shaped, stipules prominent;
    terminal bud large with valvate scales; fl large,
    terminal, salmon-colored with green throat; fr an
    aggregate of samaras ***Liriodendron*** p. 152
50. Lvs not 4-lobed; buds clustered near end of twigs,
    scales imbricate; fr an acorn ***Quercus*** (in part) p. 117

51. Lvs with margins entire or nearly so → 52.
51. Lvs with margins serrate, dentate or
    strongly toothed → 65.

Leaves deciduous, alternate, unlobed, entire margins

52. Lvs cordate; fr a legume → 53.
52. Lvs not cordate; fr not a legume → 54.

53. Lvs cleft at apex; fl large, showy, regular (not
    pea-like), appearing with the leaves ***Bauhinia*** p. 177
53. Lvs acute at apex; fl small, pink, pea-like, appearing
    before the leaves ***Cercis*** p. 176

54. Sap milky → 55.
54. Sap watery → 57.

55. Br and twigs with axillary spines; fr a large (10–15 cm)
    roughened multiple of drupes ***Maclura*** p. 144
55. Br unarmed → 56.

56. Lvs rhombic-ovate, apex long; terminal buds
    absent; fr terminal 3-celled capsule with white,
    waxy seeds ***Sapium*** p. 188
56. Lvs elliptic, margins wavy (sometimes lobed);
    terminal buds present; fr an aggregate of seeds
    enclosed in fleshy receptacle with apical ostiole
    Ficus (in part) p. 144

57. Twigs with chambered or diaphragmed pith → 58.
57. Twigs with homogeneous pith → 59.

58. Terminal buds present; lvs obovate, glabrous above,
    often hairy below; fr a bluish-black drupe ***Nyssa*** p. 215
58. Terminal buds absent; lvs ovate to oblong, glaucous
    below; fr an ovoid, orange or black drupaceous
    berry with persistent calyx ***Diospyros*** p. 223

59. Lvs silvery-scaly below; br silvery-scaly and
    sometimes armed; fr a dry, yellow drupe with
    silvery scales ***Elaeagnus*** p. 218
59. Lvs and fr not as above, br not armed → 60.

60. Terminal buds present → 61.
60. Terminal buds absent → 62.

61. Lvs pubescent below; buds velvety; fl terminal,
    showy, white or pink; fr an aggregate of follicles
    bearing red seeds ***Magnolia*** p. 149

61. Lvs and buds not velvety; twigs with prominent, white lenticels; fl in loose, hairy panicles; fr a dry drupe *Cotinus* p. 189

62. Lvs linear-lanceolate, sometimes alternates, opposite and whorled on same branch; fr a long (30 cm) persistent capsule *Chilopsis* p. 237
62. Lvs and fr not as above → 63.

63. Lvs thick, wooly below, oval to oblong, 10–12 cm; twigs and buds hairy; fl showy in terminal cymes; fr a drupe with persistent calyx *Cordia* p. 234
63. Lvs stellate pubescent below or glabrous, ovate to elliptic ‹10 cm long → 64.

64. Lvs stellate pubescent below; twigs zigzag, slightly hairy; buds naked; fr a 1.5 cm drupe in persistent calyx *Styrax* p. 224
64. Lvs glabrous below, ovate to obovate; twigs with decurrent ridges below leaf; fl in long, showy terminal panicles; fr a globose capsule *Lagerstroemia* p. 225

Leaves deciduous, alternate, unlobed, with serrate, dentate or spiny margins

65. Margins toothed with distinct sharp spine or hair terminating the teeth → 66.
65. Margins serrate, or if toothed, teeth not terminating in spine or hair → 69.

66. Fr a nut partially enclosed by shallow involucre (acorn); buds clustered near shoot apex *Quercus* p. 117
66. Fr a nut completely enclosed in a spiny or scaly involucre; buds not clustered → 67.

67. Terminal buds long, ›2 cm, lance-shaped; bk smooth, gray; fr triangular nut in weakly-spined, 4-parted involucre ‹2 cm long *Fagus* p. 114
67. Terminal buds ‹1 cm long, globose or ovate; bk fissured or scaly → 68.

68. Lvs ‹10 cm elliptic to ovate; fr a nut enclosed in scaly involucre, axillary, solitary, small, ‹10 mm *Nothofagus* p. 133
68. Lvs ›20 cm, oblong-lanceolate; fr a nut enclosed in large, 4 cm, spiny involucre *Castanea* p. 134

69. Fr a nut or nutlet → 70.
69. Fr not a nut or nutlet → 74.

70. Fr a nut ›1 cm, surrounded by a hairy, leafy involucre; lvs doubly serrate-dentate, pubescent *Corylus* p. 111
70. Fr a winged or wingless nutlet ‹1 cm contained in a cone-like strobilus, or leafy involucre → 71.

71. Nutlets winged, scales of strobilus deciduous; bark thin with prominent, horizontal lenticels *Betula* p. 107
71. Nutlets winged or unwinged, scales of strobilus persistent, or in a 3-winged leafy involucre → 72.

72. Nutlets mostly unwinged, or laterally winged in persistent cone-like strobilus about 2 cm; twigs reddish, terminal bud absent, lateral buds often stalked with typically 2–3 red scales *Alnus* p. 110
72. Nutlets contained in strobilus, or a strobilus with each nutlet subtended by a 3-lobed leafy bract → 73.

73. Nutlets in a strobilus of bladder-like bracts; bk in long, stringy brown shreds **Ostrya** p. 112

73. Nutlets subtended by 3-lobed leafy bracts arranged in loose strobilus; bk smooth, dark gray with prominent, sinewy ridges **Carpinus** p. 113

74. Fr fleshy, a pome, drupe or berry-like drupe ➜ 75.

74. Fr dry, a capsule or samara ➜ 84.

75. Lvs finely serrate, hairy below, veins impressed, oblong-ovate; twigs slender, terminal buds absent, pith chambered; fr a nut-like drupe with 4 wings about 3–4 cm long **Halesia** p. 225

75. Lvs serrate, crenate or dentate; pith homogeneous; fruit an unwinged drupe or berry-like drupe ➜ 76.

76. Lvs crenate toward the apex, or toothed; twigs green turning to tan or brown with warty protuberances; fr a red, persistent drupaceous berry containing 2–8 bony seeds **Ilex** p. 191

76. Lvs prominently serrate; twigs and fruit not as above ➜ 77.

77. Lvs broadly ovate to 15 cm, coarsely serrate, dark green, glabrous, unequal at base; twigs reddish-brown, terminal bud absent, lateral buds offset above petiole with 2–3 visible red-brown scales; fr a dry drupe in cymes suspended below a finger-like, persistent leafy bract **Tilia** p. 209

77. Lvs narrowly ovate to lanceolate, serrate; fr not in cymes suspended from a leafy bract ➜ 78.

78. Lvs ovate with acute to acuminate tips, coarsely to finely serrate, unequal at base, appearing 2-ranked; twigs with terminal bud absent; bk smooth, gray with corky or warty protuberances; fr a drupe **Celtis** p. 142

78. Lvs ovate to lanceolate with mostly equal bases, not appearing 2-ranked; fr a drupe or pome ➜ 79.

79. Lvs pendulous, oblong-ovate, acuminate, margins sharply toothed, cupped, with 8–14 prominent pinnate veins, pubescent below; bk gray with orange lenticels; fr a small, asymmetrical, green drupe **Zelkova** p. 141

79. Lvs not sharply toothed or cupped with prominent pinnate venation ➜ 80.

80. Lvs mostly lanceolate, finely doubly serrate, petiole often glandular at base of leaf; twigs reddish brown, with prominent horizontal lenticels, spur-like shoots, sometimes resembling thorns often present; bk thin, scaly often in horizontal curls; fr a fleshy drupe **Prunus** p. 165

80. Lvs ovate to lanceolate, finely serrate to dentate; st without horizontal lenticels; fr a pome ➜ 81.

81. Lvs serrate to coarsley dentate; twigs armed with stout thorns; fr a small reddish pome ‹2 cm, often persistent **Crataegus** p. 158

81. Lvs finely serrate, occasionally entire, ovate to lanceolate; twigs unarmed, or occasionally with weak flexible spines; fr a pome ➜ 82.

82. Lvs ovate, finely serrate; fl white, showy in conical upright racemes; fr a small, purplish berry-like pome ‹1 cm **Amelanchier** p. 157

82. Lvs ovate to lanceolate; fr a pome ›2 cm ➜ 83.

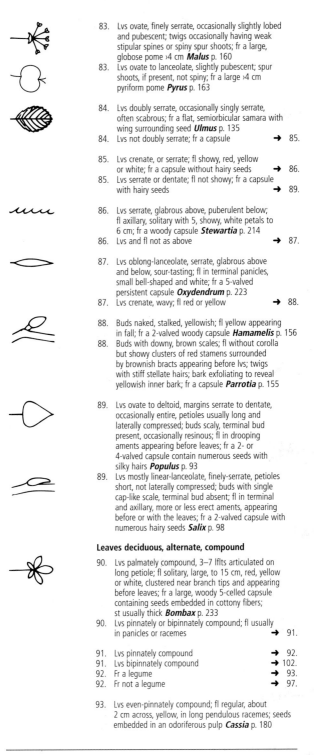

83. Lvs ovate, finely serrate, occasionally slightly lobed and pubescent; twigs occasionally having weak stipular spines or spiny spur shoots; fr a large, globose pome >4 cm **Malus** p. 160
83. Lvs ovate to lanceolate, slightly pubescent; spur shoots, if present, not spiny; fr a large >4 cm pyriform pome **Pyrus** p. 163

84. Lvs doubly serrate, occasionally singly serrate, often scabrous; fr a flat, semiorbicular samara with wing surrounding seed **Ulmus** p. 135
84. Lvs not doubly serrate; fr a capsule → 85.

85. Lvs crenate, or serrate; fl showy, red, yellow or white; fr a capsule without hairy seeds → 86.
85. Lvs serrate or dentate; fl not showy; fr a capsule with hairy seeds → 89.

86. Lvs serrate, glabrous above, puberulent below; fl axillary, solitary with 5, showy, white petals to 6 cm; fr a woody capsule **Stewartia** p. 214
86. Lvs and fl not as above → 87.

87. Lvs oblong-lanceolate, serrate, glabrous above and below, sour-tasting; fl in terminal panicles, small bell-shaped and white; fr a 5-valved persistent capsule **Oxydendrum** p. 223
87. Lvs crenate, wavy; fl red or yellow → 88.

88. Buds naked, stalked, yellowish; fl yellow appearing in fall; fr a 2-valved woody capsule **Hamamelis** p. 156
88. Buds with downy, brown scales; fl without corolla but showy clusters of red stamens surrounded by brownish bracts appearing before lvs; twigs with stiff stellate hairs; bark exfoliating to reveal yellowish inner bark; fr a capsule **Parrotia** p. 155

89. Lvs ovate to deltoid, margins serrate to dentate, occasionally entire, petioles usually long and laterally compressed; buds scaly, terminal bud present, occasionally resinous; fl in drooping aments appearing before leaves; fr a 2- or 4-valved capsule contain numerous seeds with silky hairs **Populus** p. 93
89. Lvs mostly linear-lanceolate, finely-serrate, petioles short, not laterally compressed; buds with single cap-like scale, terminal bud absent; fl in terminal and axillary, more or less erect aments, appearing before or with the leaves; fr a 2-valved capsule with numerous hairy seeds **Salix** p. 98

Leaves deciduous, alternate, compound

90. Lvs palmately compound, 3–7 lflts articulated on long petiole; fl solitary, large, to 15 cm, red, yellow or white, clustered near branch tips and appearing before leaves; fr a large, woody 5-celled capsule containing seeds embedded in cottony fibers; st usually thick **Bombax** p. 233
90. Lvs pinnately or bipinnately compound; fl usually in panicles or racemes → 91.

91. Lvs pinnately compound → 92.
91. Lvs bipinnately compound → 102.
92. Fr a legume → 93.
92. Fr not a legume → 97.

93. Lvs even-pinnately compound; fl regular, about 2 cm across, yellow, in long pendulous racemes; seeds embedded in an odoriferous pulp **Cassia** p. 180

93. Lvs odd-pinnately compound; fl and fruits
not as above ➜ 94.

94. Lvs with 3 lflts; fl pea-like, yellow, in long,
pendulous racemes; fr a flat legume to 6 cm; twigs
and buds hairy; bark smooth, greenish with
prominent lenticular ridges **Laburnum** p. 184

94. Lvs with more than 3 lflts ➜ 95.

95. Twigs armed with paired stipular spines, buds hairy,
embedded below petiole; fl pea-like, white to pink, in
pendulous racemes; fr a compressed legume
Robinia p. 178

95. Twigs unarmed ➜ 96.

96. Lflts 8–10 cm long, obovate, margins entire,
apex acute; fl pea-like, white in axillary panicles;
fr a compressed legume **Cladrastis** p. 183

96. Lflts 2–6 cm long, elliptic to obovate (some species
lvs are persistent); fl pea-like, white or blue
in pendulous racemes; fr a cylindrical legume
constricted between the seeds **Sophora** p. 179

97. Fr a drupe-like nut ➜ 98.
97. Fr a drupe, pome or samara ➜ 99.

98. Lvs with ›10 lflts; twigs with superposed buds and
chambered pith; fr an ovoid or globose nut encased
in an indehiscent, semi-woody husk, nuts with
rugose surface **Juglans** p. 102

98. Lvs with ‹10 lflts per lf; twigs with solitary buds, pith
homogeneous; fr an ovoid to globose drupaceous
nut encased in a dehiscent or partially dehiscent
husk with 4 sutures; nuts with smooth or 4-ridged
surface **Carya** p. 104

99. Fr a fleshy, or small, woody drupe ➜ 100.
99. Fr a pome or samara ➜ 101.

100. Lvs with 3–19 ovate to obovate lflts, often hairy,
margins entire; fr a small, woody, red or blue drupe
in erect panicles **Pistacia** p. 190

100. Lvs with 3–31 elliptic to lanceolate lflts, margins
usually serrate; fl mostly in dense, erect, terminal
panicles; fr a persistent, red, hairy (occasionally
white) drupe **Rhus** p. 190

101. Lvs ›50 cm, lflts glandular and coarsely-toothed;
twigs velvety, terminal bud absent; fr a samara, to
3 cm, with seed embedded in center and occurring
in dense clusters **Ailanthus** p. 185

101. Lvs ‹20 cm long; lflts serrate but not glandular;
twigs puberlous to smooth, terminal bud present;
fl white in terminal corymbs appearing after leaves;
fr a red or yellow 1 cm pome **Sorbus** p. 159

102. Fr a capsule or berry in persistent panicles ➜ 103.
102. Fr a legume ➜ 104.

103. Lvs 20–40 cm long, coarsely-toothed or lobed lflts;
fl yellow in large cascading panicles; fr a bladder-like
capsule; twigs zigzag **Koelreuteria** p. 213

103. Lvs to 60 cm long, lflts dark green, serrate; fl blue
to purple in axillary panicles; fr a persistent, globose,
yellow berry (often mistakenly called a drupe); crown
dense and umbrella-like **Melia** p. 187

104. Twigs and branches armed with spines or thorns ➜ 105.
104. Twigs and branches unarmed ➜ 108.

105. Twigs and branches armed with stout thorns, usually branched; lvs both pinnately and bipinnately compound on same tree, ‹30 cm long; fl small, greenish, in axillary racemes; fr a 20–50 cm leathery, flat, twisted legume, constricted between seeds that appear arrayed on one side **Gleditsia** p. 178

105. Twigs and branches armed with spines or unbranched thorns; lvs bipinnately compound ‹106.

106. Fl small, greenish-yellow, regular, in axillary spikes ‹10 cm long; lvs evenly doubly pinnate, often appearing as a pair of pinnae terminating a long petiole, lflts glandular; fr a cylindrical to slightly compressed legume slightly constricted between seeds **Prosopis** p. 181

106. Fl large and showy, mostly yellow or yellow with red-tinged petals, usually in heads or panicles; twigs usually prickly with stipular spines → 107.

107. Lvs with fewer than 10 pairs of pinnae, lflts oblong to 2 cm; twigs spiny (some species unarmed); fl large, to 5 cm, petals yellow-tinged with red, often turning red with age, stamens 10 and exserted; fr a broad, flat legume to 10 cm. **Caesalpinia** p. 182

107. Lvs with more than 10 pairs of pinnae, lflts narrow, linear 1 cm; twigs often armed with stipular spines; fl yellow, in panicles, petals ‹1 cm across, stamens many; fr a linear, oval legume, sometimes constricted **Acacia** p. 179

108. Fl not showy, small, greenish, in racemes appearing after leaves; twigs stout, with reddish hairs and large leaf scars; lvs to 1 m long and 60 cm broad, generally evenly pinnately-compound, lflts ovate, 6 cm long; fl in loose panicles; fr a broad, flat legume to 25 cm, constricted about 6–9 large seeds **Gymnocladus** p. 183

108. Fl large, showy, in heads or corymbs → 109.

109. Fl in corymbs emerging before leaves, scarlet to 10 cm across, petals 5, clawed, stamens 10 and no longer than petals; fr a broad, flat legume to 10 cm **Delonix** p. 181

109. Fl in globose heads, mostly near ends of branches, corolla short, stamens, numerous, exserted and pink or white, united into a tube at their base; fr a flat legume to 15 cm not constricted about seeds **Albizia** p. 180

Key C — Monocots

1. Lvs linear or sword-shaped → 2.
1. Lvs palmate or pinnate → 3.

2. Lvs dagger-like, to 40 cm, broad at base, margins finely toothed, apex terminating in spine; fl large, numerous, white, in erect panicles; fr a 10 cm 3-valved capsule **Yucca** p. 246

2. Lvs lanceolate, narrow, to 90 cm, crowded near top of branches; fl white in terminal panicles; fr a 3-celled bluish berry **Cordyline** p. 246

3. Lvs palmate or fan-shaped → 4.
3. Lvs pinnately shaped → 8.

4. Petioles not armed with stout teeth → 5.
4. Petioles armed with stout teeth → 6.

5. Lvs orbicular, whitish below, folds divided nearly to the center, petiole with winged margin; leaf sheath persistent on slender bole; fr small, white, drupaceous **Thrinax** p. 245

5. Lvs fan-shaped to semi-orbicular to 1.5 m, folded segments commonly divided to less than half the blade; leaf sheaths only persistent near base of live crown; fr a 1 cm bluish drupe **Sabal** p. 245

6. Bole not covered with fibers and leaf bases, except for dead leaves near base of crown; bk gray, finely-furrowed with visible leaf scars **Washingtonia** p. 244

6. Bole covered by fibers and persistent leaf bases ➜ 7.

7. Lvs fan-shaped to 50 cm with 12–15 acute segments divided nearly to base, petiole to 1 m, semi-circular in cross-section, armed with slender forward-pointing spines; fr a fleshy drupe **Chamaerops** p. 243

7. Lvs fan-shaped to orbicular with 40–60 1.5 m long segments divided almost to base, petioles finely-toothed along margins; fr an oblong-reniform, bluish seed about 1.5 cm wide **Trachycarpus** p. 240

8. Petiole armed with 2 stout spines at base of pinnae; lvs to 7 m, drooping; leaf bases persisting on bole; lflts folded and without midrib; fr dense panicles of ovoid drupes **Phoenix** p. 241

8. Petioles unarmed ➜ 9.

9. Lvs arching to give a globose appearance to crown, leaf sheath clasping at top of crown to form a ›1 m green column; lflts tapering in length toward apex of leaf, midrib prominent and many veins; bole swollen near middle; fr a blue drupe **Roystonea** p. 241

9. Lvs stiff with prominent midrib, leaf sheath fibrous and persistent at base of crown; bole swollen at base, roughened by prominent leaf scars; fr large, to 50 cm, elliptical, dry drupe with single, large, thick seed encased in a fibrous husk **Cocos** p. 243

THE CONIFERS

The *Gymnospermae*, known as the conifers, contain three botanical groups: the Ginkgo, Yew and true conifers. Some 50 genera of conifers include over 600 species; many of these are native to North America, and other conifers have been introduced from Europe and Asia.

The fundamental botanical difference between conifers and all others plants is that their ovules, which develop into seeds, are carried naked. This gives the group their scientific name, the *Gymnospermae*, and distinguishes them from the *Angiospermae*, or "enclosed ovule" trees, known as broadleaf trees. The ovules are borne on the scales of the female flower, an immature cone, which closes its scales after fertilization.

This is of little help with identification, however, and it is far better to examine other characteristics of growth, habit and fruit. Conifers in general have a strongly monopodal growth habit, with a single stem and much lighter, smaller side branches. Some do not maintain this character into old age and, particularly in European larch and some of the firs, one or two very heavy horizontal side branches may turn up at the ends and form competing leaders. Some of the yews also have a tendency to heavier branching; forking often occurs and one of the stems outpaces and suppresses the other.

a   b   c

The illustrations above show some points to look for when examining similar needles. The spruce needle **(a)** has a pointed apex, is squarish in cross section and is similar in appearance above and below. The Silver fir needle is notched at the apex **(b)**, much flatter and has white bands on the underside **(c)**. Conifer leaves are generally arranged helically along the shoot, although this is sometimes disguised when the leaves are twisted at the base and appear to be arranged pectinately, spreading along either side of the shoot. In some species, the leaves may be arranged on short shoots. Although still in a helix, the leaves are compressed and appear to be a whorl with a central bud.

The seeds ripen in autumn six or eighteen months after fertilization, and the cone scales usually open, in dry weather, to release them on the wind. The seeds are tucked between the fertile and bract scales (left).

They are usually winged to assist in their distribution. The number of seeds per scale can vary from one to as many as 20. In some conifers, the seeds remain attached to the scales, which themselves separate from the cone and fall.

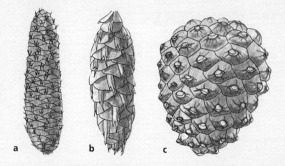

a   b   c

The colloquial name of the conifers derives from the cones, the hard woody structures with overlapping scales which bear their seeds. They vary from one genus to another, and are perhaps the best means of identification; the illustrations on this page show some points to look for. The fir cone **(a)** always sits erect on the shoot and is long and cylindrical. It is also distinctive because of the bracts, which are reflexed and stand out from the body of the cone. These cones are rarely found whole on the ground because their scales are deciduous, falling to the ground and leaving a long bare stalk or "candle" on the tree. The Douglas fir cone **(b)** is distinctive in its growth as it always hangs from the shoot. It is also shorter and more ovoid in shape and has prominent bracts, which are three-pointed. The pine cone **(c)**, with its rounded base, pointed tip and triangular scales, is often imagined to be typical of all cones, although it only reaches this form after 18 months. A blunt projection known as an umbo is borne on the outside of each scale. Pine cones are often asymmetrical.

d   e   f

The Juniper cone **(d)** differs from other conifers in that it resembles a soft fleshy berry. As the cone takes one, two or three years to ripen, the green immature fruit and the ripe blue ones can usually be found on the same tree. The female cones begin life like all other conifers, as open scales, but they mature into hard round berry-like cones, recognizable by the scars and blunt points left from what were their scales. Western red cedar cone **(e)** is unusual in not having overlapping scales but ones which separate from the base. The center of the cone is leathery and ovoid, visible behind the few spreading scales. The cone of California redwood **(f)** is much smaller and very knobbly, with the scales presenting a diamond-shaped surface. These scales each have a central hollow, and as they ripen from green to brown, they shrink and separate. The seeds, which can be obtained by shaking a newly-ripened cone, vary in size and appearance.

Ginkgo Family *Ginkgoaceae*

The Ginkgo family has but a single genus and single species. It is one of the few deciduous members of the *Gymnospermae* and widely used as an ornamental. The species is probably extinct in the wild.

GINKGO
Ginkgo biloba

Height 30 m.
Crown columnar, broadening with age.
Branches short, numerous, dipping when old.
Bark ridged, fissured.

Buds set spirally around shoots.

Leaves variable, from 6–12 cm; set in whorls of 2–5 on short, slow-growing, older shoots; larger, set singly on new shoots.
Blades open pale yellow-green, golden in autumn.

Leaf dichotomously veined, divided into two or more lobes on short shoots; those on long shoots may be undivided.

Veins straight, parallel, dichotomous veins divided by twos.

Ginkgo is the only survivor of a group of trees that flourished some 200 million years ago. Its primitive ancestry shows in its regular, dichotomous (forked) venation and the rudimentary method by which its ovule is fertilized. As in the ferns, this is by free-swimming sperm cells, and fertilization often occurs after its ovoid, yellow fruit, found only on female trees, has fallen. The fruit emits a putrid stench once its fleshy coat begins to rot. Ginkgo is only native to a remote part of China where it was adopted as a sacred tree by Buddhist monks who carried it to Japan. From there, it was introduced to Europe and America in the 18th century. Specimens planted then still survive, and a resistance to air pollution, most pests and diseases makes Ginkgo ideal for towns. Its name, "Maidenhair tree," is based on the similarity of its leaves to those of the Maidenhair fern.

29

Yew Family *Taxaceae*

Yews are usually dioecious; females produce solitary seeds in a fleshy aril. Leaves are set spirally or in pectinate ranks.

ENGLISH YEW
Taxus baccata

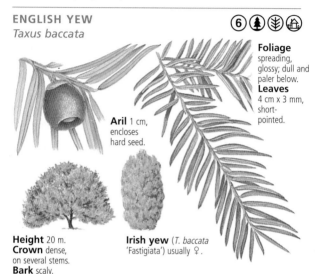

Foliage spreading, glossy; dull and paler below.
Leaves 4 cm x 3 mm, short-pointed.

Aril 1 cm, encloses hard seed.

Height 20 m.
Crown dense, on several stems.
Bark scaly.

Irish yew (*T. baccata* 'Fastigiata') usually ♀.

A long-lived ornamental evergreen, English yew is widely grown except from New England northward, where it is not hardy. There, it is replaced by its hybrid *T. x media*, with sparser, longer foliage, and 'Hicksii,' a small tree similar to Irish yew in habit. The Pacific Yew (*T. brevifolia*), a native to western North America, is a source for Taxol®, a modern anti-cancer drug. Yews are long-lived with recorded specimens over 4,000 years old.

CALIFORNIA NUTMEG
Torreya californica

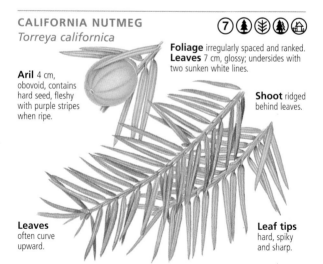

Foliage irregularly spaced and ranked.
Leaves 7 cm, glossy; undersides with two sunken white lines.

Aril 4 cm, obovoid, contains hard seed, fleshy with purple stripes when ripe.

Shoot ridged behind leaves.

Leaves often curve upward.

Leaf tips hard, spiky and sharp.

An open-crowned tree with spreading branches and stout shoots, this species can reach 25 m and has seeds resembling those of the true nutmeg. Japanese nutmeg (*T. nucifera*) has shorter and decurrent needles.

Podocarp Family *Podocarpaceae*

These species come mainly from the Southern Hemisphere and carry cones with fleshy scales and less regular foliage than the Yew family. Male and female cones may appear on the same tree.

PRINCE ALBERT YEW
Saxegothaea conspicua

⑧ Ⓡ 🌲 🌿 🏠

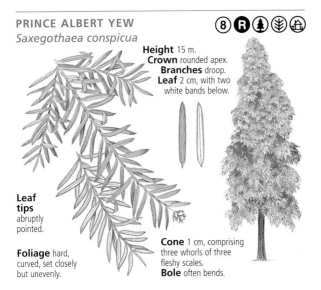

Height 15 m.
Crown rounded apex.
Branches droop.
Leaf 2 cm, with two white bands below.

Leaf tips abruptly pointed.

Foliage hard, curved, set closely but unevenly.

Cone 1 cm, comprising three whorls of three fleshy scales.
Bole often bends.

A Chilean tree named after Queen Victoria's consort, this tree differs from English yew in its cone, irregular foliage and leaf undersides while its less dense, pendulous shoots distinguish it from *P. andinus*.

CHILE YEW
Podocarpus andinus

⑧ Ⓡ 🌲 🌿 🏠

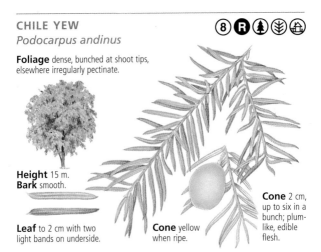

Foliage dense, bunched at shoot tips, elsewhere irregularly pectinate.

Height 15 m.
Bark smooth.

Leaf to 2 cm with two light bands on underside.

Cone yellow when ripe.

Cone 2 cm, up to six in a bunch; plum-like, edible flesh.

Chile yew is a small tree of variable habit, which is sometimes confused with Prince Albert yew (above). Large-leaf podocarp (*P. macrophylla*), native to China and Japan, has 5–10 cm leaves, up to 1 cm broad, and a gray, shallowly fissured shredding bark.

Chile Pine Family *Araucariaceae*

This family comprises three genera and 37 species, all natives of the Southern Hemisphere. Trees are either male or female. The female trees carry globose or ovoid cones containing many scales, each with one seed. Leaves are hard with parallel venation and are usually broad and arranged spirally.

MONKEY PUZZLE
Araucaria araucana

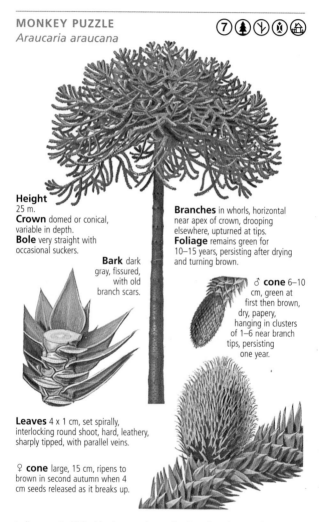

Height 25 m.
Crown domed or conical, variable in depth.
Bole very straight with occasional suckers.

Bark dark gray, fissured, with old branch scars.

Branches in whorls, horizontal near apex of crown, drooping elsewhere, upturned at tips.
Foliage remains green for 10–15 years, persisting after drying and turning brown.

♂ **cone** 6–10 cm, green at first then brown, dry, papery, hanging in clusters of 1–6 near branch tips, persisting one year.

Leaves 4 x 1 cm, set spirally, interlocking round shoot, hard, leathery, sharply tipped, with parallel veins.

♀ **cone** large, 15 cm, ripens to brown in second autumn when 4 cm seeds released as it breaks up.

Indigenous to Chile, Monkey puzzle was first introduced to America in 1795 and its common name, alluding to the problems its sharp foliage would give potential climbers, was first used in 1834. The seeds, once an important food source of the Araucano tribe, are tasty if roasted like chestnuts. Norfolk Island pine (*A. heterophylla*) has softer, awl-shaped leaves. It can grow in the open in warm areas, but is more common as an indoor plant.

Cypress Family *Cupressaceae*

Trees in the Cypress family are distinguished from other conifers, except *Metasequoia*, by their paired or ternate leaves. Those of juvenile plants are always awl-shaped, a condition retained by many special cultivars. Adult leaves are mostly small, scale-like and adpressed. Members of *Cupressaceae* carry male and female cones on the same or separate trees and three types of cone are produced: those of *Cupressus* and *Chamaecyparis* are globose or ellipsoid with peltate scales; *Juniperus* cones have unique, fleshy scales which are fused together. All other Cypress genera — including *Thuja*, *Thujopsis* and *Calocedrus* — have larger cones with woody scales hinged at their bases.

MONTEREY CYPRESS
Cupressus macrocarpa

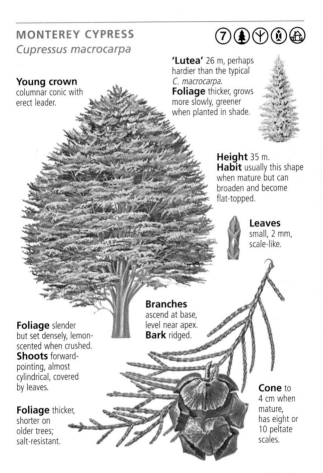

'Lutea' 26 m, perhaps hardier than the typical *C. macrocarpa*.
Foliage thicker, grows more slowly, greener when planted in shade.

Young crown columnar conic with erect leader.

Height 35 m.
Habit usually this shape when mature but can broaden and become flat-topped.

Leaves small, 2 mm, scale-like.

Branches ascend at base, level near apex.
Bark ridged.

Foliage slender but set densely, lemon-scented when crushed.
Shoots forward-pointing, almost cylindrical, covered by leaves.

Foliage thicker, shorter on older trees; salt-resistant.

Cone to 4 cm when mature, has eight or 10 peltate scales.

This species is found wild on the coast of California and was widely planted as a hedge tree, although it has now been largely superseded in that role by the hardier and faster growing Leyland cypress. A fungus, *Seiridium (Coryneum) cardinale*, attacks Monterey cypress as well as Italian cypress, and can prove fatal.

ITALIAN CYPRESS
Cupressus sempervirens

⑦ 🌲 🌱 🈂 🏠

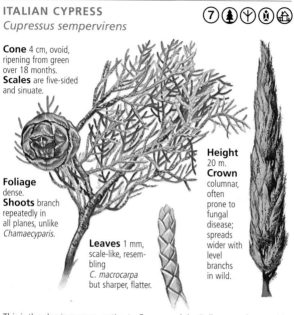

Cone 4 cm, ovoid, ripening from green over 18 months.
Scales are five-sided and sinuate.

Foliage dense.
Shoots branch repeatedly in all planes, unlike *Chamaecyparis*.

Leaves 1 mm, scale-like, resembling *C. macrocarpa* but sharper, flatter.

Height 20 m.
Crown columnar, often prone to fungal disease; spreads wider with level branchs in wild.

This is the classic cypress, native to Greece and the Balkans, and now wide-ly distributed throughout Mediterranean countries. Cedar of Goa (*C. lusi-tanica*), from Mexico and Central America, has a broader crown, smaller, glaucous cones and spreading, pointed leaves.

SMOOTH CYPRESS
Cupressus glabra

⑦ 🌲 🌱 🈂 🌲 🏠

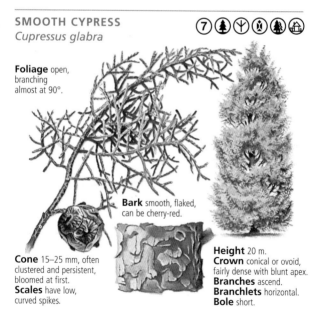

Foliage open, branching almost at 90°.

Bark smooth, flaked, can be cherry-red.

Cone 15–25 mm, often clustered and persistent, bloomed at first.
Scales have low, curved spikes.

Height 20 m.
Crown conical or ovoid, fairly dense with blunt apex.
Branches ascend.
Branchlets horizontal.
Bole short.

Distinguished by its bark, this tree is increasingly being planted as an orna-mental. It was once classified as a cultivar of Arizona cypress (*C. arizonica*), whose bark is much rougher.

ARIZONA CYPRESS
Cupressus arizonica

Leaves are pale green and persist for several years.

Bark reddish-brown, smooth when young, turning to dark brown at maturity, scaly and ridged.

Branches irregularly arranged and appear four-sided near the branch tips, particularly where there are leaves.

Trees monoecious; male strobili are small, oblong and yellowish, typically at the ends of branchlets; female conelets are small and globose.

♀ **cone** globose cone 2 to 3 cm wide; the 6-8 scales are woody, peltate each with a short point; cones mature in two years.

Leaves evergreen, scale-like, flattened and adpressed in four rows; about 2 mm long and pointed at the tip.

This native of the American Southwest is a small- to medium-sized tree to 15 m. Its pyramidal crown and fine-textured, evergreen foliage have made this an attractive tree for windbreaks.

LEYLAND CYPRESS
Cupressocyparis x Leylandii

⑧ 🌲 🍸 ⚙ 🏠

Cone (when present) 3 cm, globular, brown.

Foliage dark green or gray, in irregular, flattish planes (with neither the truly flat sprays of *Chamaecyparis* nor the more radial arrangement of *Cupressus*); less dense near leader.
Shoots branch repeatedly.
Leaves slightly incurved with rigid glands.
Growth fast, can exceed 1 m a year.

Height 40 m.
Crown dense, columnar with conic or rounded conic apex.
Branches ascend steeply.
Leader leans slightly, not drooping as in Lawson cypress.
Bark initially smooth, then rigid becoming fibrous.

'Castlewellan' is extremely vigorous and its foliage, arranged in plumes, turns bronze-green in winter.

Leyland cypress is a naturally occurring hybrid of Monterey cypress and Alaska cedar, and the qualities inherited from its parents — the vigorous growth rate of the first and the adaptable durability of the second — have made this tree unbeatable as a hedge conifer. Several clones are now marketed. The most popular, 'Haggerston Grey,' was first raised in 1888, but two recently introduced golden forms, 'Castlewellan' and 'Robinson's Gold,' are becoming increasingly acceptable. Leyland cypress rarely sets viable seed, but plants are easily raised from cuttings.

HINOKI CYPRESS
Chamaecyparis obtusa

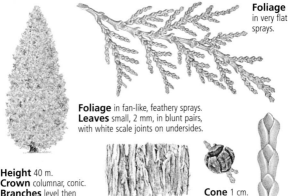

Foliage in very flat sprays.

Foliage in fan-like, feathery sprays.
Leaves small, 2 mm, in blunt pairs, with white scale joints on undersides.

Height 40 m.
Crown columnar, conic.
Branches level then ascending.
Bole straight.

Bark fissured.

Cone 1 cm.

This native of Japan can be distinguished from other "false" cypresses by its blunt, incurved leaves and larger, round cones. 'Crippsii,' a popular cultivar, has bright, golden-yellow foliage which darkens to green inside the crown.

SAWARA CYPRESS
Chamaecyparis pisifera

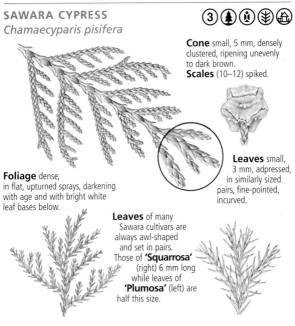

Cone small, 5 mm, densely clustered, ripening unevenly to dark brown.
Scales (10–12) spiked.

Leaves small, 3 mm, adpressed, in similarly sized pairs, fine-pointed, incurved.

Foliage dense, in flat, upturned sprays, darkening with age and with bright white leaf bases below.

Leaves of many Sawara cultivars are always awl-shaped and set in pairs. Those of **'Squarrosa'** (right) 6 mm long while leaves of **'Plumosa'** (left) are half this size.

Native to Japan, this tree has distinctively small cones and, as the type, is far less common than its numerous cultivars. These can be divided into those with pendulous foliage, such as 'Filifera,' and those whose awl-shaped leaves are set at about 45°, like 'Plumosa,' or approximately at right angles, as on 'Squarrosa.'

ALASKA CEDAR
Chamaecyparis nootkatensis

Leading shoot leans.
Crown extremely regular.

Cone 1 cm, globular, with large scale spikes, green with blue bloom, ripens brown over two years.

Foliage very pendulous, in thick, flat, alternate sprays.
Leaves 2–3 mm, hard, in equal-sized pairs.

Height 30 m.
Bark stringy, peels.

One of the parents of Leyland cypress, Alaska cedar, native from Alaska southward, is recognized by its hanging branchlets and the hooked spines of its cones. Its 'Pendula' form has very pendulous foliage, shorter, upturned branches and 2 cm cones. Some dendrologists classify Alaska cedar as *Cupressus nootkatensis*.

ATLANTIC WHITE CEDAR
Chamaecyparis thyoides

Height 20 m.
Crown columnar or broad conic.

Foliage very slender, 1 mm, short, fern-like, angular green or bluish-gray sprays.
Cones set on small branchlets.

Branches short.
Bark fibrous. It is dark brown-red in color.
Cone 6 mm, glaucous blue-purple ripening brown.

Leaves often have central resin glands and carry prominent white marks near bases, particularly on undersides.

Leaves very small, down to 1 mm, acutely pointed, incurved and close-pressed but freer on vigorous growth.
Shoot becomes brown in second year.

This slow-growing white cedar is native to swamps along the eastern American seaboard. Its wood is so durable, trees buried for decades have proved sufficiently strong to use for making roof shingles. Its botanical name comes from a resemblance to *Thuja*, and its common name from the paleness of its foliage.

LAWSON CYPRESS
Chamaecyparis Lawsoniana

Height 20–35 m, to 50 m in wild.
Crown regular in young trees, less so in mature ones.
Stem often forked.
Foliage dense, pendulous, becoming spaced in old trees.
Leader and new shoots always droop.
Terminals wispy, unbranched near tips.

♀ cones
8 mm, globose, ripening from green or blue-green to dark brown.
Scales (8) have short central spikes.

Bark
smooth, ridged then scaly, dark red-brown, purplish on older trees.

♂ cones
terminate weakest branchlets.

Foliage flat, fern-like.
Leaves grouped in pairs: lateral ones keel-shaped, facing pairs smaller, adpressed. Each leaf has central translucent gland. Between leaf scales, stomata form thin, white lines. Especially clear on foliage underside; give best identification.

The Lawson cypress is native to a small area on the Oregon-California border and, as a forest species, is characterized by a uniform crown of dense, pendent foliage. An expedition sponsored by the Scottish nurseryman Peter Lawson discovered it there in 1854, and the vast array of hardy and easily propagated cultivars raised since then — some 250 — have made this "false" cypress one of the most common ornamental conifers. Its varieties can be divided into a group with vivid foliage, one with distinctly shaped habits and a third whose long, awl-like leaves resemble the juvenile leaves of the seedling.

Some cultivars of Lawson cypress

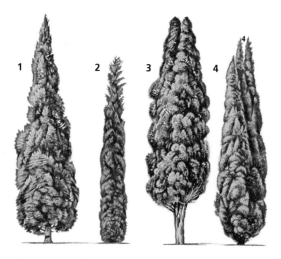

1 *'Allumii'*: Height 20 m; compact habit, soft foliage. **2** *'Columnaris'*: Height 10 m; dense, consistently narrow crown. **3** *'Erecta'*: Height 25 m; first Lawson cypress cultivar, raised in 1855 from seeds of a Californian type; much-forked crown. **4** *'Fletcherii'*: Height 16 m; juvenile foliage, often on several stems; multiple leaders.

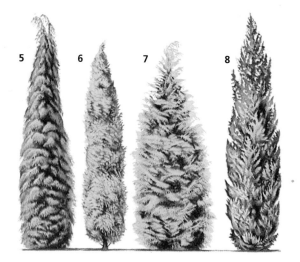

5 *'Intertexta'*: Height 25 m; foliage sparse, dark and bloomed, sprays pendent. **6** *'Lutea'*: Height 16 m; short, pendulous branchlets; older interior foliage darker. **7** *'Stewartii'*: Height 16 m; ascending branches with sprays decurved below shoot. **8** *'Wisselii'*: Height 25 m; spaced foliage arranged in dense, radiating "spires."

WESTERN RED CEDAR
Thuja plicata

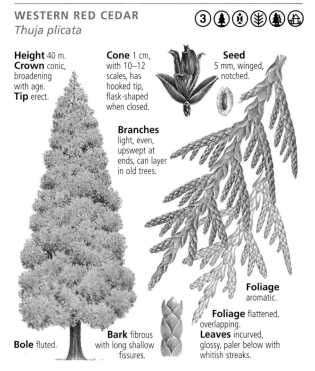

Height 40 m.
Crown conic, broadening with age.
Tip erect.

Cone 1 cm, with 10–12 scales, has hooked tip, flask-shaped when closed.

Seed 5 mm, winged, notched.

Branches light, even, upswept at ends, can layer in old trees.

Foliage aromatic.

Foliage flattened, overlapping.
Leaves incurved, glossy, paler below with whitish streaks.

Bark fibrous with long shallow fissures.

Bole fluted.

Also called Giant arborvitae, this majestic tree from the Pacific Coast has a light, but very even crown and is planted for its light and durable timber. Japanese arborvitae (*T. Standishii*) has lighter, blunt, glanded leaves which smell like lemons.

CHINESE ARBORVITAE
Platycladus orientalis

Height 15 m.
Crown on several ascending stems, less dense at base.

Cone 1.5 cm.
Foliage in flat, erect sprays.

Leaves same green below.

Bark dull, fissured, stringy.

Seed 6 mm, rounded, wingless.

This species is often included in the *Thuja* genus and, although its foliage bears some resemblance to that of the true *Thujas*, it differs from them in its broader, glaucous cones, which have fewer, strongly hooked scales and large, round, wingless seeds.

NORTHERN WHITE CEDAR
Thuja occidentalis

③ 🌲 🌲 🌿 🌲 🏠

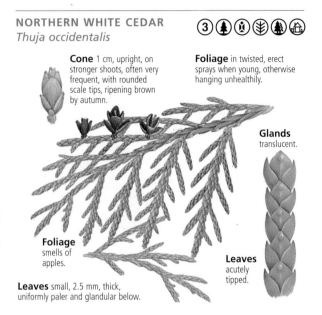

Cone 1 cm, upright, on stronger shoots, often very frequent, with rounded scale tips, ripening brown by autumn.

Foliage in twisted, erect sprays when young, otherwise hanging unhealthily.

Glands translucent.

Foliage smells of apples.

Leaves acutely tipped.

Leaves small, 2.5 mm, thick, uniformly paler and glandular below.

Small and slow-growing, Northern white cedar, or Arborvitae, is native from eastern Canada to the Appalachians. Its smooth cones and foliage underside are distinctive. 'Lutea' has a denser crown and stronger branches whose tips bear golden leaves.

HIBA
Thujopsis dolabrata

⑥ Ⓡ 🌲 🌲 🌿

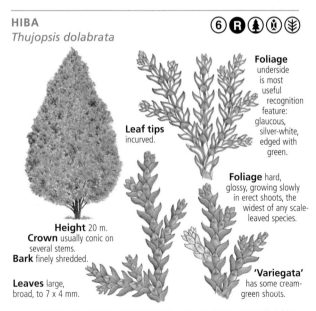

Foliage underside is most useful recognition feature: glaucous, silver-white, edged with green.

Leaf tips incurved.

Foliage hard, glossy, growing slowly in erect shoots, the widest of any scale-leaved species.

Height 20 m. **Crown** usually conic on several stems. **Bark** finely shredded.

Leaves large, broad, to 7 x 4 mm.

'Variegata' has some cream-green shoots.

This Japanese tree rarely grows on a single stem and carries rounded, blue-gray cones. The leaf undersides of Korean arborvitae (*Thuja koraiensis*) are also — sometimes completely — silvery glaucous, but its foliage is softer and it has typical *Thuja* cones.

INCENSE CEDAR
Calocedrus decurrens

④ 🌲 🔾 🌿 🌲 🏠

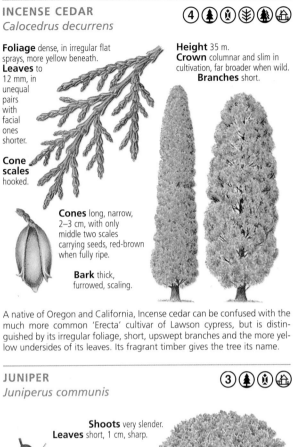

Foliage dense, in irregular flat sprays, more yellow beneath.
Leaves to 12 mm, in unequal pairs with facial ones shorter.

Cone scales hooked.

Cones long, narrow, 2–3 cm, with only middle two scales carrying seeds, red-brown when fully ripe.

Bark thick, furrowed, scaling.

Height 35 m.
Crown columnar and slim in cultivation, far broader when wild.
Branches short.

A native of Oregon and California, Incense cedar can be confused with the much more common 'Erecta' cultivar of Lawson cypress, but is distinguished by its irregular foliage, short, upswept branches and the more yellow undersides of its leaves. Its fragrant timber gives the tree its name.

JUNIPER
Juniperus communis

③ 🌲 🔾 🏠

Shoots very slender.
Leaves short, 1 cm, sharp.

Height 8 m.

Crown small, usually spreading, shrubby, but cultivars very variable.

Leaves concave, set in whorls of three.

Leaves glaucous white on inner surfaces.
Cone 1 cm, green for two to three years, blue-black when ripe.

Juniper will grow on both acid and alkaline sites and has a very wide distribution throughout the Northern Hemisphere. The bright green leaves of Temple juniper (*J. rigida*) are softer and longer while Alerce (*Fitzroya cuppressoides*) has spreading blue-green leaves with two silver bands on each side.

EASTERN RED CEDAR
Juniperus virginiana

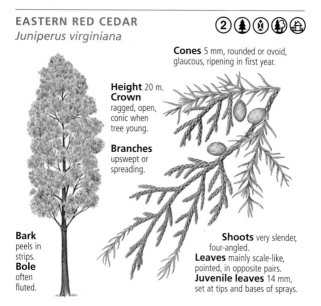

Cones 5 mm, rounded or ovoid, glaucous, ripening in first year.

Height 20 m.
Crown ragged, open, conic when tree young.

Branches upswept or spreading.

Bark peels in strips.
Bole often fluted.

Shoots very slender, four-angled.
Leaves mainly scale-like, pointed, in opposite pairs.
Juvenile leaves 14 mm, set at tips and bases of sprays.

Eastern red cedar, or Pencil cedar, native to the eastern United States, is the tallest of the junipers and provides useful timber, especially for pencils. Alligator juniper (*J. Deppeana*), from the southwest United States, has distinctive bark, up to 10 cm thick, deeply fissured into 5 cm squares like an alligator's skin. Its foliage is blue-green.

CHINESE JUNIPER
Juniperus chinensis

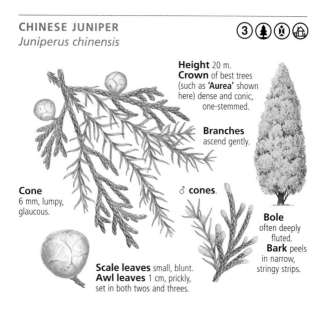

Height 20 m.
Crown of best trees (such as **'Aurea'** shown here) dense and conic, one-stemmed.

Branches ascend gently.

Cone 6 mm, lumpy, glaucous.

♂ **cones**.

Bole often deeply fluted.
Bark peels in narrow, stringy strips.

Scale leaves small, blunt.
Awl leaves 1 cm, prickly, set in both twos and threes.

'Aurea' is the most popular of the named varieties of Chinese juniper. Many of the varieties are shrubs and produce masses of cones. Western juniper (*J. occidentalis*) has glandular and scaly bark while Rocky Mountain juniper (*J. scopulorum*) has glandular leaves, often glaucous.

This ancient group of large, beautiful trees comprises 10 genera from North America, eastern Asia and Tasmania. Its members usually have evergreen leaves, which are flat, linear or awl-shaped and set spirally along the shoot, and globular woody cones, whose peltate scales are also arranged spirally. All redwoods are monoecious and have thick, red-brown, fibrous bark. Some genera are deciduous.

GIANT SEQUOIA
Sequoiadendron giganteum

Leaves small, to 7 mm, awl-shaped, hard, dotted with white stomata.

Foliage blue-gray when young then shiny, dark green on older shoots.

Shoot stout, initially covered by leaves, later developing gray-brown fissures.

Cone large, 6 cm, 35–40 scales, green for two years, then brown.

Branches have tips upswept.

Height 50 m.
Crown often has rounded apex.
Bole tapers, fluted.
Bark often dimpled by Tree-creepers using it for winter roosting.

Bark very thick, to 60 cm, soft and resilient, can withstand punching.

Giant sequoia is the world's largest (though not the tallest) living tree and is native to 72 groves on the high, western slopes of the Californian Sierra Nevada where it was first discovered in 1833, but then rediscovered in 1852. The largest individual there, named "General Sherman," is 83 m tall, has a trunk diameter of 10 m and weighs 1,000 tons, yet must have developed over the centuries from a seed weighing a mere 5 milligrams. Such specimens may live for 4,000 years, although the average age of native species is only a quarter of this. In Europe, growth rates have exceeded 50 m in a century. Giant sequoias have deep roots to withstand long, dry summers and their thick bark gives protection against forest fires.

CALIFORNIA REDWOOD
Sequoia sempervirens

⑧ 🌲 🌱 🌿 🌲 🏠

Shoot green.
Strong shoot leaves small, 6–8 mm, scale-like, awl-shaped, adpressed around stem with tips incurved.

Side-shoot leaves 1–2 cm, tapering to hard apexes with two white bands below, set in flat sprays.

Cone 3 cm. **Scales** (15–20) ripen in first season.

Bark, to 35 cm thick, very soft, fibrous; bright red-brown on young trees, darker and fissured on old ones.

Height 50 m. **Crown** thin, columnar conic, becoming flat-topped. **Bole** straight, tapering.

The redwood is one of the tallest trees in the world, reaching 112 m (the height of St. Paul's Cathedral, London) in its native California where it thrives in the damp atmosphere of the narrow, coastal "fogbelt." It is similar to Giant sequoia but has softer bark, flatter foliage, cones ripening the first year and it can coppice when cut down.

BALD CYPRESS
Taxodium distichum

⑤ 🌳 🌱 🌿 🌲 🏠 🌳

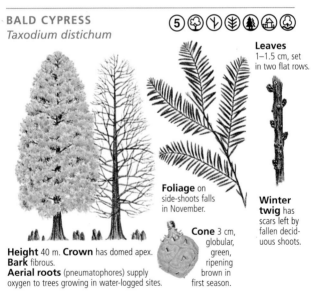

Leaves 1–1.5 cm, set in two flat rows.

Foliage on side-shoots falls in November.

Winter twig has scars left by fallen deciduous shoots.

Cone 3 cm, globular, green, ripening brown in first season.

Height 40 m. **Crown** has domed apex. **Bark** fibrous. **Aerial roots** (pneumatophores) supply oxygen to trees growing in water-logged sites.

Sometimes confused with *Metasequoia*, from which it can be distinguished by its alternate foliage, this tree from the southern United States prefers waterside sites but grows well on any fairly moist soil. The closely related Pond cypress (*T. ascendens*) has erect, spiky shoots of shorter, radially arranged leaves.

DAWN REDWOOD
Metasequoia glyptostroboides

Foliage fern-like, bright yellow-green then darkening.

Shoots opposite, deciduous when not bearing buds.

Leaves 2–4 cm x 2 mm, opposite, soft, curved, in flat sprays.

Bole shown in cross-section below very deeply fluted, tapering.

Bark bright orange or red-brown, fissured.

Height 30 m.
Crown sparse, narrow conic becoming columnar.
Branches ascend.
Foliage assumes exquisite autumnal hues.

Long thought to be extinct, this fine tree was located in southeastern China as recently as 1941. Its hardiness, the ease with which it propagates and a growth rate which can average a meter per annum have made it a popular ornamental. Its botanical name indicates affinities with Sequoia and the rare, deciduous Chinese swamp cypress (*Glyptostrobus lineatus*), but it is more easily confused with Bald cypress, whose similar foliage is also deciduous. The leaves and lateral shoots of Dawn redwood, however, are longer and opposite. It is unique in carrying its side-buds below its shoots and not in their axils.

Cone monoecious, male strobili in terminal clusters.

Leaves evergreen, stiff linear lanceolate, 3–7 x 3 cm with a sharp, pointed apex and finely toothed margins; spirally arranged on the branch but those on the upper and lower sides are twisted to produce a horizontally pectinate appearance; dark green above and whitish beneath.

Shoot tapering with a pronounced pyramidal habit, drooping branches and a ragged appearance as the tree gets older.
Bark thin, brown and scaling off in long thin strips revealing a reddish inner bark.

♀ **cone** 3–5 cm, thin-scaled, spine-tipped, globose and terminal, often several together.

This native of China was introduced to the West in the early 19th century. In the milder climates, it can be seen as a specimen tree. The leaves remain green for five or more years, but persist for several years more and are mostly shed with the dead branches. A large tree, 30 m or more in height, it loses some of its fir-like charm as it gets older. The wood is light and durable, strongly resistant to rot and termites. It is one of the few which will coppice, or regrow from the stump, if cut down.

JAPANESE CEDAR
Cryptomeria japonica

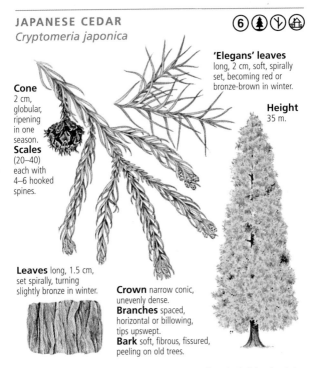

Cone
2 cm, globular, ripening in one season.
Scales (20–40) each with 4–6 hooked spines.

'Elegans' leaves
long, 2 cm, soft, spirally set, becoming red or bronze-brown in winter.

Height
35 m.

Leaves long, 1.5 cm, set spirally, turning slightly bronze in winter.

Crown narrow conic, unevenly dense.
Branches spaced, horizontal or billowing, tips upswept.
Bark soft, fibrous, fissured, peeling on old trees.

As an introduced ornamental, this tree never reaches the heights it attains in its native China and Japan. The Tasmanian *Athrotaxis* species has similar cones but shorter leaves; King William pine (*A. selaginoides*) has hard, shiny leaves of 1 cm; Summit cedar (*A. laxifolia*) awl-like leaves to 2 mm; and Tasmanian cedar (*A. cupressoides*) addressed scale leaves.

UMBRELLA PINE
Sciadopitys verticillata

Leaves very long, 10–15 cm, fused in grooved pairs which are glossy above and bright yellow below.

Height 20 m.
Crown narrow to to broad conic.
Branches short, upturned and spreading.
Bark dark red-brown, peeling in strips.

Foliage set round shoots in whorls.

Native to the mountains of Japan where it is an important timber tree, this ornamental species grows very slowly in parks and large gardens. Its distinctive foliage of long and whorled, glossy "double" leaves distinguishes it from all other conifers and offers immediate identification.

Pine Family *Pinaceae*

The Pine family is the most varied of all those groups of trees that bear cones. Besides the genus *Pinus* itself, the family also includes *Abies*, *Picea*, *Tsuga*, *Pseudotsuga* and *Larix* as well as *Pseudolarix*, *Cathaya* and *Keteleeria*. (These latter three are fairly obscure Chinese genera and, because they are so seldom found elsewhere, are not included in this book.)

Pinaceae comprise well over 250 species, all of which are native to the Northern Hemisphere. They all have woody cones with spirally arranged scales and linear or flat leaves (usually called needles) which are attached to the shoot in a variety of different ways.

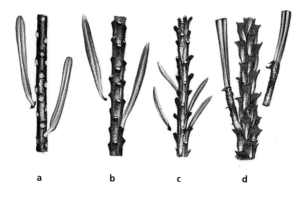

a   b   c   d

The illustrations above demonstrate these differences. The leaves of the firs (*Abies*) leave a depressed or concave scar **(a)** while a slightly raised scar, together with a minutely stalked leaf **(b)** shows the tree is almost certainly a Douglas fir (*Pseudotsuga*). Spruces (*Picea*) are immediately notable for the prominent woody peg (*pulvinus*) that is left where the leaf **(c)** is pulled away or falls from it naturally. The leaves of pines (*Pinus*) are set in fascicles of one, two, three or five and bound by a basal sheath by which they are attached to the shoot **(d)**. These fascicles are extensions of short or spur shoots and, despite the number of their leaves, can always be brought together to make up a simple, but divided cylinder.

The length of the shoot can also be a guide to genus identification; while all the family produce long shoots, some genera, namely the pines, larches (*Larix*) and cedars (*Cedrus*) also produce much shorter or spur shoots. These grow from a bud in the axil of a needle on a long shoot, and eventually a new whorl of needles is formed. The bud in the center of this new whorl may either be the starting point for subsequent growth or may remain dormant for years. The shorter shoots of the larches grow for several years and have many deciduous needles, a feature unique in this family.

The majority of trees in Pinaceae grow pendent cones but *Abies*, Cedrus and *Larix* have cones which remain erect after the female cones have been fertilized. Those of larches, firs, spruces and hemlocks ripen over one season; those of the pines and cedars take longer. In true firs (*Abies*) and cedars (*Cedrus*), the cone scales are deciduous and break apart to release the seeds. The central core of fir cones, a long spike or "candle," is left standing on the shoot.

All other genera have pendent cones whose scales remain attached to their central axis and eventually fall to the ground intact, having released their seeds.

Firs *Abies*

Most firs have short leaves set in flat ranks which become more assurgent in the upper crown; silver firs are so called because of the whitish under-side of their foliage. Their deciduous cones develop at the top of the tree. About 40 species exist.

SILVER FIR
Abies alba

Cone 10–15 cm, green ripening brown.
Bracts pointed, reflexed.

Leaves 2.5 cm, with white stomata below.

Foliage well parted on dark, pubescent shoot.

Height 50 m.
Crown slender and open.

Branches spreading, whorled.
Bole long.

Silver fir is an important forest tree in its native area, the mountains of central Europe. It has thick leaves with notched tips, and non-resinous buds. King Boris fir (*A. Borisii-regis*) has denser foliage, narrower leaves to 3 cm and pale-haired twigs.

CAUCASIAN FIR
Abies Nordmanniana

Cone to 15 cm.
Bracts exserted.

Leaves 3 cm, tip notched, grooved, banded below.

Foliage forward-pointing.

Height 45 m.
Crown dense, conic.

This fir has a more luxuriant crown than *A. alba* and its forward-pointing foliage persists for about six to eight years. Bornmüller fir (*A. Bornmuellerana*) has longer leaves with spots of stomata by the upperside tips, shiny red-brown shoots and sticky buds.

SPANISH FIR
Abies Pinsapo

Shoot brownish, becoming orange in second year.

Bud 3–5 mm, resinous.

Leaves all around shoot.

Leaves 1–2 cm, thick, blunt.

Leaves have stomata on both sides.
Cones 10–15 cm, cylindrical, clustered near top of tree, ripen brown.

Foliage crowded, set radially around shoot. **Crown** dense, often on several stems, becoming rugged.

Bark dark gray, becoming black, in small plates.

Spanish fir only occurs wild in southern Spain but is fairly widely planted in Europe. It is also called Hedgehog fir because of its stiff foliage; that of Algerian fir (*A. numidica*) is parted below and has a prominent band of stomata at its leaf tips.

GREEK FIR
Abies cephalonica

Height 40 m.

Cone to 15 cm.
Bracts exserted, reflexed.

Cones numerous on upper branches.

Buds sticky.

Crown conic.
Bark fissured.

Leaves to 3 cm, tips spiny.
Foliage glossy above, silver-white below, set radially, less dense below.

With a massive bole and heavy branches which sometimes rise as secondary leaders, Greek fir is often the bulkiest of the firs. *A. cephalonica var. apollonis* has denser, blunter, forward-pointing leaves, mostly arranged above the shoot.

WHITE FIR / LOW'S FIR

⑤ 🌲 🌿 🌿 🌲 🏠

Abies concolor /
A. concolor var. Lowiana

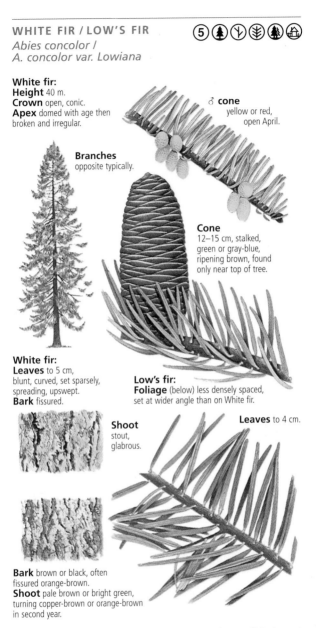

White fir:
Height 40 m.
Crown open, conic.
Apex domed with age then
broken and irregular.

♂ **cone**
yellow or red,
open April.

Branches
opposite typically.

Cone
12–15 cm, stalked,
green or gray-blue,
ripening brown, found
only near top of tree.

White fir:
Leaves to 5 cm,
blunt, curved, set sparsely,
spreading, upswept.
Bark fissured.

Low's fir:
Foliage (below) less densely spaced,
set at wider angle than on White fir.

Shoot
stout,
glabrous.

Leaves to 4 cm.

Bark brown or black, often
fissured orange-brown.
Shoot pale brown or bright green,
turning copper-brown or orange-brown
in second year.

White fir grows wild in the western United States and parts of Mexico and is recognizable by its long, assurgent, bluish leaves, which smell of lemons when crushed. Low's fir, from Oregon and California, has longer leaves which either spread flat along the shoot or rise on both sides to form a wide U-shaped "groove." Therefore, it combines several features of White fir, which grows to the south of its range, with several of Grand fir, which is native farther north. Low's fir is ultimately distinguishable from other firs by the unique combination of lax, bluish leaves with a fissured bark usually resembling that of Douglas fir.

GRAND FIR
Abies grandis

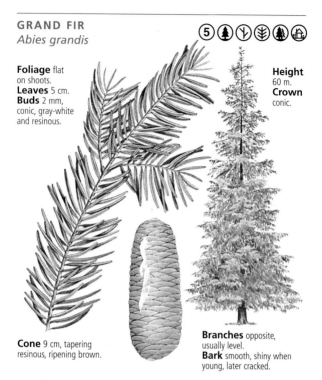

Foliage flat on shoots.
Leaves 5 cm.
Buds 2 mm, conic, gray-white and resinous.

Height 60 m.
Crown conic.

Cone 9 cm, tapering resinous, ripening brown.

Branches opposite, usually level.
Bark smooth, shiny when young, later cracked.

A very fast-growing species, Grand fir is an important forest tree in western North America, identified by its flat foliage, which becomes more assurgent in the upper crown. West Himalayan fir (*A. Pindrow*) has large globular buds and longer leaves to 9 cm, spreading down at the sides of its glabrous, ash-gray shoots.

PACIFIC FIR
Abies amabilis

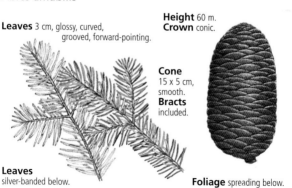

Leaves 3 cm, glossy, curved, grooved, forward-pointing.

Height 60 m.
Crown conic.

Cone 15 x 5 cm, smooth.
Bracts included.

Leaves silver-banded below.

Foliage spreading below.

The shapely crown and rich foliage of this fir justify its specific name which may be translated as "lovely." It is native from British Columbia to California. Maries fir (*A. Mariesii*) is its closest relative and its 2 cm leaves are glossier. Its shoot has dense orange-red, not light brown, pubescence.

NOBLE FIR
Abies procera

Bark smooth, may have blisters of resin when young, later having several deep fissures and many fine cracks.

Bark can be gray, silver-gray or purplish.

Leaves to 3 cm, four-sided, grooved, not notched.

Seeds 1 cm, in 2.5 cm wings.

Cone 25 cm, cylindrical, resinous, set at summit of the tree, often produced on young trees only 5 m high.

Bracts with 1 cm reflexed tips, set spirally, almost covering the cone.

Shoot densely haired, reddish.

Foliage assurgent.

Foliage dense.

Noble fir is remarkable for the size of its cones, which may contain up to 1,000 seeds, and for its silvery, fissured, mature bark. Its lower branches carry many crimson male cones in the spring.

RED FIR
Abies magnifica

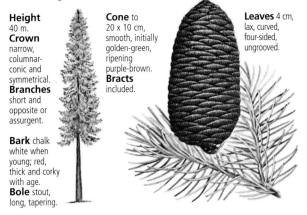

Height 40 m.
Crown narrow, columnar-conic and symmetrical.
Branches short and opposite or assurgent.

Bark chalk white when young; red, thick and corky with age.
Bole stout, long, tapering.

Cone to 20 x 10 cm, smooth, initially golden-green, ripening purple-brown.
Bracts included.

Leaves 4 cm, lax, curved, four-sided, ungrooved.

This fir is native to Oregon and California and, while closely related to Noble fir, has ungrooved, longer and less densely set foliage. Its name comes from the red bark of mature trees. The cones of Shasta fir (*A. magnifica var. shastensis*) have exserted bracts.

VEITCH FIR
Abies Veitchii

⑤ 🌲 🌿 🌾 🏠

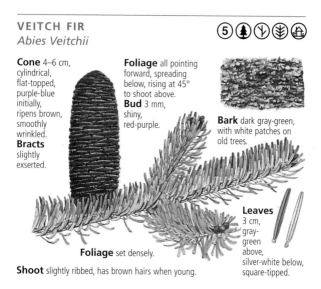

Cone 4–6 cm, cylindrical, flat-topped, purple-blue initially, ripens brown, smoothly wrinkled.
Bracts slightly exserted.

Foliage all pointing forward, spreading below, rising at 45° to shoot above.
Bud 3 mm, shiny, red-purple.

Bark dark gray-green, with white patches on old trees.

Leaves 3 cm, gray-green above, silver-white below, square-tipped.

Foliage set densely.

Shoot slightly ribbed, has brown hairs when young.

Veitch firs form trees to 20 m with tapered, flat-topped crowns. On trees whose crowns reach the ground, the lowest branches are very upswept revealing the silver underside of their foliage. It is a native of Japan, as is Sakhalin fir (*A. sachalinensis*), with longer, narrower, bright green leaves to 3.5 cm.

KOREAN FIR
Abies koreana

⑤ 🌲 🌿 🌾 🏠

Height 15 m.
Crown conic with slightly ascending branches.
Leaves spreading below shoot, curving upward above.

Leaves 1–1.5 cm, glossy green or yellow-green above, tips often white.

Bark shiny, dark brown to black, smooth, spotted conspicuously with lenticels.
Leaves vividly white underneath, rather radial and spaced along shoot.

Shoot fawn.
Buds small, globular, initially pale brown but soon covered with white resin.

Cone 7 cm, pointed, purple, ripening brown.
Bracts reflexed, very exserted.

This silver fir, first discovered in 1907 on an island off Korea, usually only manages to grow to 10 m in 40 years. It is very free in producing its small, violet cones, often as a young tree less than 1 m tall. The strongly exserted and reflexed bracts show clearly how the cone scales in the Pine family are radially arranged.

BALSAM FIR
Abies balsamea

Leaves 4 cm, two rows spreading at right angles below, narrow, parted above, very aromatic.
Apex notched.
Buds 6 mm, purplish, resinous.

Shoot has fine, blackish hairs.
Bracts hidden.

Leaves shiny dark green above, with two narrow whitish-gray bands of stomata below.

Bark on young trees smooth with many resin blisters, broken into scaly plates.

Cone 10 cm, cylindrical, erect, purple, ripens brown.

Often used as a Christmas tree, Balsam fir, from eastern Canada and northern New England, reaches 15 m, with a spire-like crown. The cones of the closely related Fraser fir (*A. Fraseri*), from the Appalachians, have strongly exserted and reflexed bracts.

SUBALPINE FIR
Abies lasiocarpa

Leaves 4.5 cm x 1 mm, flat, dense, spreading below, pointing forward above and at sides, gray-green, white bands on both sides.

Buds 5 mm, resinous.

Shoot stout, with dense reddish-brown hairs, later gray-brown, shiny.

Height 30 m.
Crown narrow spire, dense, furnished with branches to the ground, lower ones pendulous, the rest horizontal.
Bark smooth, gray, with resin blisters, later fissured, scaly.

Cone 10 cm, cylindrical, erect, numerous on topmost branches, dark purple-gray at first, ripening brown, soon disintegrating.
Bracts included.
Scales hairy.

Subalpine fir is often the last tree before the treeline in its native Rockies, and, at higher altitudes, has a less regular habit. In the southern part if its range, it becomes Arizona or Cork fir (*A. lasiocarpa var. arizonica*), with bluish foliage and corky bark.

Abies Delavayi var. Forrestii /
A. Delavayi var. Georgei

Forrest fir cone (right) is 7–12 cm long, cylindrical or barrel-shaped, top dimpled, violet, ripening brown over winter.
Bracts exserted, often reflexed with very prominent awl-like cusps to 5 mm.

George fir cone (right) often larger, occasionally to 15 cm.
Bracts exserted, with cusps up to 1 cm, pointing upright except near base of cone.
Bract edges well exposed, bright blue-purple with light brown edges.

Forrest fir shoot (below) stout, red-brown, usually glabrous and finely roughened; in second year deeper color with pale fissures.
Foliage may be radial.

George fir shoot (above) brownish-orange, with a dense, short pubescence of the same color.
Leaves close more over top of shoot.
Foliage short, perpendicular.

George fir leaves (left) shorter, to 2.5 cm, off-white below, gray bloomed above.

Forrest fir foliage (left) to 4 cm, spreading around shoot, often lax below, dense and may be parted.
Leaves green above, white below.

These two firs were discovered in China and introduced into gardens by George Forrest, after whom they are named. George fir is chiefly distinguished by the densely pubescent shoots and longer cusps, and, although both trees grow to 25 m, George fir has a more columnar and denser crown than Forrest fir. Related species from the Himalayas and west China include: Himalayan fir (*A. spectabilis*), which has ash-gray or light brown shoots pubescent in deep grooves; and Delavay fir (*A. Delavayi*), which has bright violet narrow cones, maroon shoots, orange buds and inrolled leaf margins, which make the leaves narrow and square-tipped; and Farges fir (*A. Fargesii*) has stout 2.5 cm needles on glossy, purple shoots and conic, purple buds.

Abies homolepis

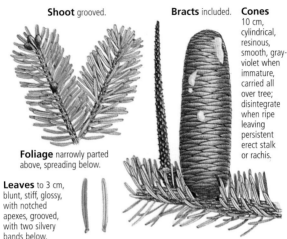

Shoot grooved.

Bracts included.

Cones 10 cm, cylindrical, resinous, smooth, gray-violet when immature, carried all over tree; disintegrate when ripe leaving persistent erect stalk or rachis.

Foliage narrowly parted above, spreading below.

Leaves to 3 cm, blunt, stiff, glossy, with notched apexes, grooved, with two silvery bands below.

Nikko fir, tolerant of urban pollution, has strongly ridged and grooved glabrous shoots. Min fir (*A. recurvata*) has smooth shoots, more ovoid, 8 cm cones, and bluntly pointed needles, green on both surfaces, that may point backward.

SANTA LUCIA FIR

Abies bracteata

Foliage parted, forward-pointing, widely spaced.
Shoot stout, glabrous, almost shiny, green-purple to dark brown.

Cones 8 cm, ovoid, uncommon.
Bracts remarkable for erect or spreading cusps that reach 3 cm, and often carry large blobs of resin.
Bud to 2 cm, spindle-shaped, sharply pointed, not resinous, pale brown.

Leaves to 5 cm, leathery, hard, very sharp, spiny tips, persist for up to five years, and closely resemble those of California nutmeg.

Leaves white-banded below.

Unique in its cones, its beech-like buds and its foliage, this rare fir grows wild in the Santa Lucia Mountains of California. Manchurian fir (*A. holophylla*) has similar assurgent foliage but ovoid-conic, resinous buds.

True Cedars *Cedrus*

True cedars develop two types of foliage and have deciduous cones which ripen over two years and disintegrate *in situ* to release triangular-winged seeds. "Atlas — ascending, Deodar — drooping, Lebanon — level" can be a useful mnemonic for identifying cedars by their growing branch tips.

CEDAR OF LEBANON
Cedrus libani ⑦ 🌲 ❀ 🏠

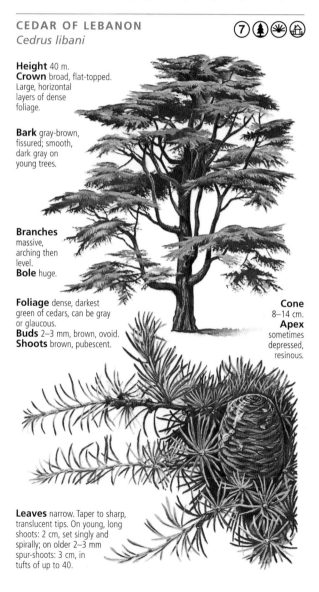

Height 40 m.
Crown broad, flat-topped. Large, horizontal layers of dense foliage.

Bark gray-brown, fissured; smooth, dark gray on young trees.

Branches massive, arching then level.
Bole huge.

Foliage dense, darkest green of cedars, can be gray or glaucous.
Buds 2–3 mm, brown, ovoid.
Shoots brown, pubescent.

Cone 8–14 cm.
Apex sometimes depressed, resinous.

Leaves narrow. Taper to sharp, translucent tips. On young, long shoots: 2 cm, set singly and spirally; on older 2–3 mm spur-shoots: 3 cm, in tufts of up to 40.

Cedar of Lebanon grows naturally in Asia Minor and has become a familiar ornamental in parks in the South. Cyprus cedar (*C. brevifolia*) is less common and has shorter leaves, narrower, more ovoid cones and a more conical crown.

ATLAS CEDAR
Cedrus atlantica

(5) 🌲 🍃 🏠

Cone 8 cm, usually depressed.

♂ **cones** reach 5 cm by September when pollen is shed and dispersed by wind.

Height 40 m.
Crown broad, conic.
Branches widely spaced.
Leaves 2.5 cm on long shoots; 2 cm, in tufts of up to 30 on 1–2 cm spur-shoots.
Buds ovoid, 2–3 cm.

Native to the mountains of north Africa, wild Atlas cedars are found in both green and glaucous forms. The very blue 'Glauca' clone shown here is the one most commonly encountered as an ornamental and derives its color from the wax coating of its leaves.

DEODAR CEDAR
Cedrus Deodara

(7) 🌲 🍃 🏠

Crown broad, columnar, conic.
Leader and long shoots always droop.
Stem single. Young trees blue-gray.

Height 50 m.

Cone 10 cm broad, egg-shaped, ripening dark brown.

Foliage dark blue-green, bright green when new.
Leaves 5 cm on long shoots, 3.5 cm in tufts of up to 30 on short shoots.
Buds only 1 mm.

In the western Himalayas where they grow wild, Deodars can reach 70 m. Pendulous branchlets on spreading and slightly downswept branches are their most distinctive features.

Larch *Larix*

Some leaves of these deciduous conifers are set singly on long shoots, but most foliage is set in whorls on short, spur-like shoots. The small, erect, persistent cones and the short and long shoots are the key identifying features.

EUROPEAN LARCH / HYBRID LARCH
Larix decidua / Larix x eurolepsis

Shoot straw yellow, glabrous.
Cones to 4 cm, narrow, blunt erect scales.

Leaves 3 cm, set in whorls of 20–30, blunt.

Leaves not banded below, on short 1 mm pegs.

♀ **cones** 1 cm, erect.
♂ **cones** pendent, whitish.

Height 45 m.
Crown open, conic.

Hybrid shoot (below) orange-brown.

Hybrid leaves to 5 cm.

Hybrid cones (above) have scales more reflexed.

Bark smooth initially, later scaly, ridged, fissured, dark pink.

Foliage pendulous.
Bole very upright.

Lower branches more drooping.
Shoots long, pendulous.

Native to the mountains of northern and central Europe, European larch is the only European conifer to shed all its leaves annually. Hybrid, or Dunkeld, larch is a natural cross between European and Japanese larch, identifiable by shoots and cones. Some dendrologists refer to Hybrid larch as *L. Marschlinsii*. Western larch (*L. occidentalis*), from the northern Rockies, differs in its stout shoots and 5 cm cones with long exserted bracts.

JAPANESE LARCH
Larix Kaempferi

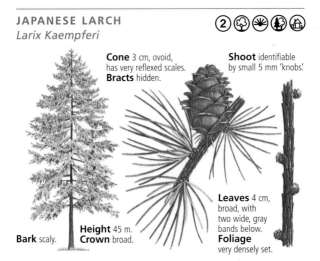

Cone 3 cm, ovoid, has very reflexed scales. **Bracts** hidden.

Shoot identifiable by small 5 mm 'knobs'.

Leaves 4 cm, broad, with two wide, gray bands below. **Foliage** very densely set.

Bark scaly. **Height** 45 m. **Crown** broad.

This species, native to Mount Fuji, is more vigorous than European larch and forms a shorter, stouter tree with heavier branches. It can be distinguished by its purplish-red shoots, wider leaves and squatter cones with scales reflexed like rose petals.

TAMARACK/AMERICAN LARCH
Larix laricina

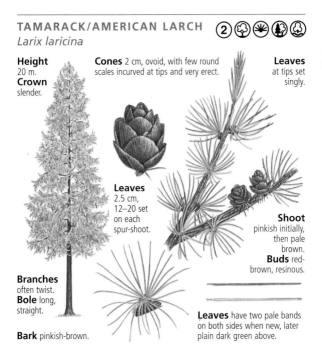

Height 20 m. **Crown** slender.

Cones 2 cm, ovoid, with few round scales incurved at tips and very erect.

Leaves at tips set singly.

Leaves 2.5 cm, 12–20 set on each spur-shoot.

Shoot pinkish initially, then pale brown. **Buds** red-brown, resinous.

Branches often twist. **Bole** long, straight.

Bark pinkish-brown.

Leaves have two pale bands on both sides when new, later plain dark green above.

Tamarack is the most widely distributed conifer in North America, growing across Canada from Alaska to the Atlantic and as far south as Pennsylvania. It grows in anything from swamps to sub-Arctic conditions. Dahurian larch (*L. Gmelinii*) has a gaunt crown and smaller leaves.

Spruces *Picea*

Spruces have single, pointed needles that are set on a *pulvinus*, an extension of the shoot. When the needles fall, they leave behind a short peg, making the bare shoots prickly.

NORWAY SPRUCE
Picea Abies

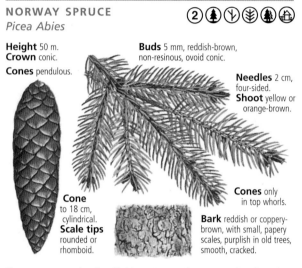

Height 50 m.
Crown conic.
Cones pendulous.

Buds 5 mm, reddish-brown, non-resinous, ovoid conic.

Needles 2 cm, four-sided.
Shoot yellow or orange-brown.

Cone to 18 cm, cylindrical.
Scale tips rounded or rhomboid.

Cones only in top whorls.

Bark reddish or coppery-brown, with small, papery scales, purplish in old trees, smooth, cracked.

Norway spruce, a familiar Christmas tree, native to central and northern Europe, has longer needles and longer, less woody cones than Siberian spruce (*P. obovata*), from northern Eurasia, and Wilson spruce (*P. Wilsonii*), which also has ash-gray shoots.

CAUCASIAN SPRUCE
Picea orientalis

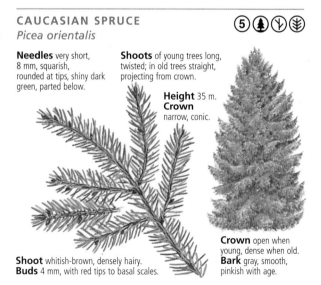

Needles very short, 8 mm, squarish, rounded at tips, shiny dark green, parted below.

Shoots of young trees long, twisted; in old trees straight, projecting from crown.

Height 35 m.
Crown narrow, conic.

Crown open when young, dense when old.
Bark gray, smooth, pinkish with age.

Shoot whitish-brown, densely hairy.
Buds 4 mm, with red tips to basal scales.

Caucasian spruce is unique in its short needles and has spindle-shaped, often curved cones that grow to 7 cm. Likiang spruce (*P. likiangensis*) has buff shoots, blue-gray needles and papery purple cones to 15 cm.

SERBIAN SPRUCE
Picea Omorika

(5) (🌲) (🍂) (🌿) (🏠)

Height
35 m.
Crown
narrow
spire.

Needles 2 cm, broad, flat,
bluish-green above, glaucous
white below.
Shoot pale buff,
pubescent.
Buds ovoid,
tips acute.

Cone
6 cm,
spindle-
shaped.

Cone scales
rounded, finely
toothed.

Cone purple-blue, ripens brown.

Native to a single Bosnian river valley but widely planted throughout Europe, this spruce owes its spire-like habit not to the branches being short, but to their recumbent position down the stem before curving out. This adaptation prevents snow damage.

SITKA SPRUCE
Picea sitchensis

(7) (🌲) (🍂) (🌿) (🌲)

Shoot glabrous, whitish, grooved.
Buds ovoid, slightly
resinous purple.

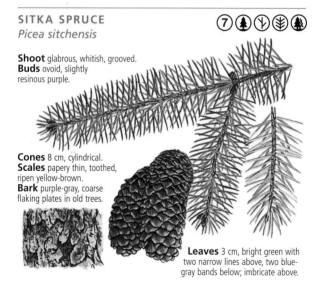

Cones 8 cm, cylindrical.
Scales papery thin, toothed,
ripen yellow-brown.
Bark purple-gray, coarse
flaking plates in old trees.

Leaves 3 cm, bright green with
two narrow lines above, two blue-
gray bands below; imbricate above.

An important timber tree, Sitka spruce is native along the west coast of North America, where it can grow to 80 m, making it the tallest of the spruces. Jezo spruce (*P. jezoensis*), from northeastern Asia, has denser, assurgent, blunt, leathery needles to 1.5 cm, and a gaunt habit. Sargent spruce (*P. brachytyla*), from western China, has leaves to 1.5 cm which are silver-white below and curve down at the sides. Its 13 cm cones are conical.

WHITE SPRUCE
Picea glauca

①②③④⑤

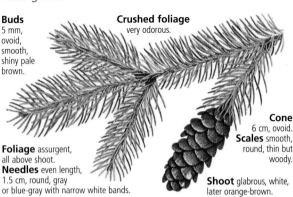

Buds
5 mm, ovoid, smooth, shiny pale brown.

Crushed foliage
very odorous.

Cone
6 cm, ovoid.
Scales smooth, round, thin but woody.

Foliage assurgent, all above shoot.
Needles even length, 1.5 cm, round, gray or blue-gray with narrow white bands.

Shoot glabrous, white, later orange-brown.

White spruce, which has a wide range across Canada and northern United States, grows to 40 m usually with a narrow conic crown. Engelmann spruce (*P. Engelmannii*) differs in its longer, softer, 2.5 cm needles, hairy shoots and papery scales. Native to the eastern Rockies, it has a red-brown, not gray, bark.

COLORADO BLUE SPRUCE
Picea pungens 'Glauca'

②②③④⑤

Height
40 m.
Crown
columnar-conic, dense.

Needles 3 cm, arranged radially but upswept below; four-sided, stiff, sharp.
Buds 1 cm, with long slender scales at base.

Cone 12 cm, cylindrical.
Scales thin, papery.
Margins wavy.

Branches level, later pendent with tips upswept.
Bark thick, purplish-brown, coarse and flaking.

This form of the normally blue-green foliaged Colorado spruce is the one usually cultivated. Dragon spruce (*P. asperata*) has gray, exfoliating, papery bark and lacks a ring of scales at the base of the bud; its cones have round woody scales. Tigertail spruce (*P. Torana*) has viciously sharp, shiny, dark green radial leaves and cones with rounded scales.

ENGELMANN SPRUCE
Picea Engelmannii

Leaves bluish-green, linear, acute, not sharp, flexible, about 3 cm, emit a fetid odor when crushed, crowded toward the upper side of the branch.

Bark dark purplish-brown, thin with large, loose scales.

Twigs orange-brown and finely pubescent.
Buds broadly ovoid, 5 mm with adpressed scales.

♀ **cone** about 5 cm long with thin wedge-shaped scales having eroded margins.
Seeds are black with a 10 mm long wing.

Cones borne separately in catkins.
♂ **catkins** are purplish, female strobili are reddish.

Englemann spruce is one of the major timber species of the mountainous regions of western North America. It is a large tree, to 50 m, and long-lived with specimens over 852 years recorded. Spruces can retain previous leaves for up to seven years, giving the branches and crown a dense foliated appearance. Spruce cones are produced in the upper part of the crown at the ends of twigs. Unlike true firs, spruce cones are pendent at maturity and retain their scales.

BLACK SPRUCE
Picea mariana

① ② ③ ④ ⑤ ⑥

Height 20 m.
Crown conic, sometimes very narrow, appears dark blue-gray from distance.

Leaves 1.5 cm, dark blue-green with two bluish-white bands below; spreading around shoot, looser below and pressed down above.

Leaves stiff, four-sided.
Shoot densely hairy.

Branches horizontal or slightly pendent, reach to ground; when pressed there by snow for long periods they frequently layer.

Cone 3.5 cm, ovoid, pendent, often curved, grows profusely even on young trees.

Bark gray, flaky. **Bud** ovoid, hairy, red-brown.
Cone persistent, clustered in crown.

Black spruce, so called because of the dark appearance of its foliage from afar, grows across Canada and in New England and is often the last tree before the tundra in the North. It occurs in wet sites. Because of layering, saplings may occur in rings.

RED SPRUCE
Picea rubens

② ③ ④ ⑤ ⑥

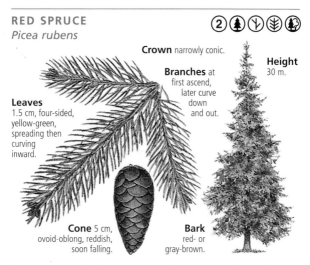

Crown narrowly conic.

Branches at first ascend, later curve down and out.

Height 30 m.

Leaves 1.5 cm, four-sided, yellow-green, spreading then curving inward.

Cone 5 cm, ovoid-oblong, reddish, soon falling.

Bark red- or gray-brown.

Red spruce is related to Black spruce but grows only in southeastern Canada and New England, and is distinguishable by the redness of its cones and its inner bark, which, unlike the outer bark, is always red-brown. Its ovoid, acute buds are hairy.

BREWER SPRUCE
Picea Brewerana

Shoot hairy, slender.

Cone 12 cm, reddish, cylindrical, often patched with resin.
Scales round, woody, flexible.

Height 40 m.
Crown broad conic, or columnar.
Cones on upper branches pendulous.

Bud 7 mm, blunt.

Branches initially ascending, later down curving; side branches droop in curtains.
Leaves 3.5 cm, radial on pendulous shoots, flat, apex blunt, two blue-white lines below.

A native of Oregon and California, this fine weeping tree has branchlets drooping vertically either side of the main branches. Sikkim spruce (*P. spinulosa*) has white glabrous shoots on an open, less pendent crown, and its leaves are not as flat.

MORINDA SPRUCE
Picea Smithiana

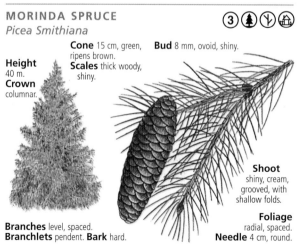

Cone 15 cm, green, ripens brown.
Scales thick woody, shiny.

Bud 8 mm, ovoid, shiny.

Height 40 m.
Crown columnar.

Shoot shiny, cream, grooved, with shallow folds.

Foliage radial, spaced.
Needle 4 cm, round.

Branches level, spaced.
Branchlets pendent. **Bark** hard.

Morinda spruce is native from Afghanistan to Nepal and has the largest cones of the genus, up to 20 x 5 cm, borne throughout the upper crown. Schrenk spruce (*P. Schrenkiana*) is similar, but has less weeping branchlets, gray-green leaves less radially arranged and long pale buds. It is native to central Asia.

DOUGLAS FIR
Pseudotsuga Menziesii

Douglas foliage densely set, parted above (left), spreads below, emits powerful sweet aroma, can be any shade of green.

Leaves to 2.5 cm, with bands below.

Height 90 m.
Crown columnar.

Buds 7 mm, conic, not resinous.
Leaves have blunt apexes.

Blue Douglas foliage (below) set more radially.
Leaves blue-gray, thick, stand above the shoot in first year, produce little scent.
Apexes are rounder.

Habit slender, grows ragged later.
Foliage in pendent masses.

Bracts point forward.

Branches whorled, upswept when young, later heavy, level.

Blue Douglas cone (right) smaller 5 cm.
Bracts three-pronged, exserted, spreading or reflexed, sometimes bent back.

Douglas cone (above) 8 cm, green when young.

Bark smooth, gray when young, later thick, ridged, corky, fissured.

The genus Pseudotsuga was named after its resemblance to the hemlocks but it also shows an affinity with Abies. Douglas fir is native to the western side of the Rockies, but Blue Douglas fir (*P. Menziesii var. glauca*), recognizable by its cones and its blunt foliage, grows wild on the drier eastern side between Montana and Mexico. Large-coned Douglas fir (*P. macrocarpa*) is a California species with longer needles to 5 cm with bony acuminate tips and 10–15 cm cones with less exserted bracts.

Hemlocks *Tsuga*

Hemlocks are a small group of conifers differing from spruces in their flattened needles, usually notched at the apex, and the slender branchlets which lack the prominent *pulvini* of the *Picea*. Except in the Mountain hemlock, the cones are less than 3.5 cm.

WESTERN HEMLOCK
Tsuga heterophylla

Cone 3 cm, pendulous, ovoid, scales rounded, entire.

Needles 2 cm at side but only 1 cm above, tip rounded.

Shoots slender, ribbed, cream-brown, hairs brown.
Buds small, ovoid, non-resinous.

Leaves have white bands below.

Height 50 m.
Crown conic, broader on old trees, dense, pendulous tips to straight branches ascending at 45°, low branches droop.

Young tree (right) has leading shoot which arches over to form hanging curtain.
Foliage spreading below, parted above.

Bark thin, smooth, fissured and ridged in older trees.
Bole straight, fluted; single stem straight from ground to tip of tree.

Western hemlock, a native of the western half of North America, is a fast-growing tree with attractive foliage, extremely tolerant of shade condition. The specific name refers to the irregular foliage arrangement. This is also a feature of Japanese hemlock (*T. diversifolia*), which has entire leaf margins, shorter leaves that are vividly white below and orange shoots.

CANADA HEMLOCK
Tsuga canadensis

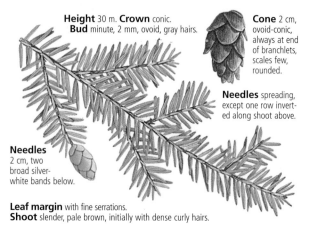

Height 30 m. **Crown** conic.
Bud minute, 2 mm, ovoid, gray hairs.

Cone 2 cm, ovoid-conic, always at end of branchlets, scales few, rounded.

Needles spreading, except one row inverted along shoot above.

Needles 2 cm, two broad silver-white bands below.

Leaf margin with fine serrations.
Shoot slender, pale brown, initially with dense curly hairs.

Canada hemlock grows in the eastern half of North America and is commonly associated with eastern hardwoods. Carolina hemlock (*T. carolinensis*), from the southeastern United States, has entire margined needles on shiny orange shoots and larger long-ovoid cones to 3.5 cm with thin rounded scales.

MOUNTAIN HEMLOCK
Tsuga Mertensiana

Needles 2.5 cm, slender, stomata on both sides.

Leaves dense, green or gray.

Leaves set all around shoot.
Shoot hairy, shiny, pale brown.
Bark deeply furrowed with rounded ridges, rough on younger trees and more orange.

Height 30 m. **Crown** spire-like, tip nodding.

Cone 8 cm, cylindrical, tapers at both ends, scales rounded, reflexed when cone open.

Mountain hemlock is distinguishable by the petiole-like base of its needle. It is used for timber and has a similar though higher distribution than Western hemlock.

Pines *Pinus*

The members of this genus can be identified by their leaf groupings and divided into hard pines (Diploxylon) such as Scotch pine and soft pines (Haploxylon) like Blue pine. The former have leaves in fascicles of two or three, rough bark and cones whose woody scales have central umbos; the latter have leaves in fives and softer cones with umbos at their scale tips.

SCOTCH PINE
Pinus sylvestris

Height 35 m.
Crown rounded on old trees, conical when young.
Branches short, horizontal or slightly ascending.

Buds resinous, short-pointed, cylindrical.

Cone 8 cm, ovoid, green in first year. **Scales** not spined.
Bark in upper crown orange, flaking, heavily fissured gray-brown at base.

Shoot glabrous, ridged.

Leaves 8 cm (15 cm on young trees), broad, stout, twisted.

This hard pine has a wide natural range across Europe and Asia from the Atlantic to the Pacific; in America, it has naturalized locally in other areas from upstate New York across to the West Coast. Its change in bark color and texture is distinctive, as is its gray-green to bright blue-green foliage; that of 'Aurea' is golden in winter. It is the main species cultivated for Christmas trees.

AUSTRIAN PINE · CORSICAN PINE
*Pinus nigra ssp. nigra ·
P. nigra ssp. lariciv*

④ 🌲 🍃 🍃

Foliage dense, in forward-pointing bunches. **Shoot** ridged and shiny.

Leaves 15 cm, stiff, curved in second year. **Sheaths** 1 cm, persistent.

Buds long, 12 mm.

Bark coarse, deeply furrowed. **Corsican pine** (below): **Height** 45 m. **Crown** sparsely branched.

Cones (both trees) 8 cm.

Corsican foliage slender, spreading, twisted.

Leaves 18 cm, in spaced fascicles. **Bud** resinous.

This hard pine is widely distributed throughout the Mediterranean, Black pine (*P. nigra*) occurs in several forms, two of which are shown here: Austrian pine is a hardy, densely crowned tree, usually growing on several stems to 30 m and Corsican pine is more vigorous and often planted for its timber. Their cones are identical but they can usually be identified by their shoots, buds and leaves. Bosnian pine (*P. leucodermis*) has similarly dense foliage but cobalt blue, unripe cones and bloomed shoots.

SHORE PINE · LODGEPOLE PINE
Pinus contorta var. contorta ·
P. contorta var. latifolia

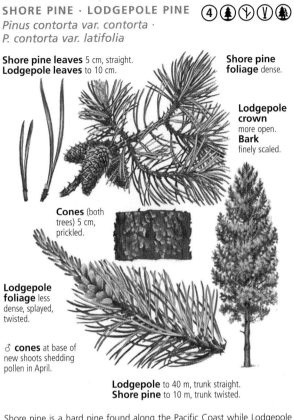

Shore pine leaves 5 cm, straight.
Lodgepole leaves to 10 cm.

Shore pine foliage dense.

Lodgepole crown more open.
Bark finely scaled.

Cones (both trees) 5 cm, prickled.

Lodgepole foliage less dense, splayed, twisted.

♂ **cones** at base of new shoots shedding pollen in April.

Lodgepole to 40 m, trunk straight.
Shore pine to 10 m, trunk twisted.

Shore pine is a hard pine found along the Pacific Coast while Lodgepole pine's range extends inland, hybridizing with Jack pine in some areas. Both of these pines are short-lived and regenerate after fires.

STONE PINE
Pinus pinea

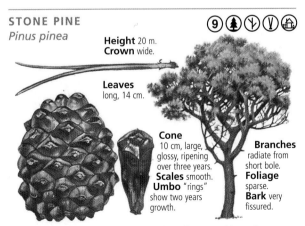

Height 20 m.
Crown wide.

Leaves long, 14 cm.

Cone 10 cm, large, glossy, ripening over three years.
Scales smooth.
Umbo "rings" show two years growth.

Branches radiate from short bole.
Foliage sparse.
Bark very fissured.

Instantly recognizable by its umbrella-shaped crown, this Mediterranean species has large, 2 cm, wingless seeds, which have been a culinary delicacy since the time of the Romans.

JACK PINE
Pinus Banksiana

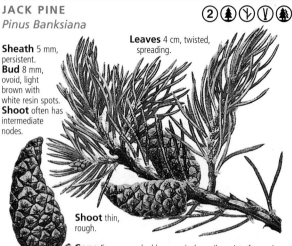

Sheath 5 mm, persistent.
Bud 8 mm, ovoid, light brown with white resin spots.
Shoot often has intermediate nodes.

Leaves 4 cm, twisted, spreading.

Shoot thin, rough.

Cone 5 cm, curved, oblong-conical, sessile, points forward or spreads from shoot. **Umbo** flat or a minute prickle.

Jack pine, an often ragged tree to 25 m, is found across Canada east of the Rockies and is unique in its forward-pointing cones. Table mountain pine (*P. pungens*), from the Appalachians, has similar foliage to 9 cm and cones with sharp hooked umbos.

VIRGINIA PINE
Pinus virginiana

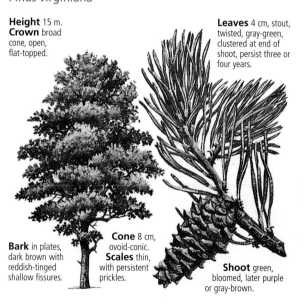

Height 15 m.
Crown broad cone, open, flat-topped.

Leaves 4 cm, stout, twisted, gray-green, clustered at end of shoot, persist three or four years.

Bark in plates, dark brown with reddish-tinged shallow fissures.

Cone 8 cm, ovoid-conic.
Scales thin, with persistent prickles.

Shoot green, bloomed, later purple or gray-brown.

Virginia, or Scrub pine, is distinguished from Jack pine by its cones and is found in the Appalachians and the Atlantic states. Spruce pine (*P. glabra*), from southeastern United States, has slender, flexible leaves, globose cones to 5 cm and a gray, furrowed bark.

BISHOP PINE
Pinus muricata

⑦ 🌲 🖖 🖖

Leaves 15 cm, stiff, spreading, crowded, yellowish near base.

Leaves green-gray.

Cones 8 cm, ovoid, oblique, sessile, often persist unopened clustered on shoot.
Scales on outer basal side larger, protrude, end in stout prickle.

Sheath 2 cm, persists.
Bud 1.5 cm, red-brown, cylindric, acute.

Umbo spined.

Shoot rough, glabrous.

Bishop pine forms a tree to 30 m with a domed crown and usually heavy branching, often profusely covered with closed cones. In its seven coastal and island sites in California, it shows some variation, including a northern form which has a narrowly conic crown and darker, bluish-gray leaves.

SHORTLEAF PINE
Pinus echinata

⑥ 🌲 🖖 🖖 🌲 🌲

Leaves 12 cm, in both twos and threes, slender, flexible.
Bud 1 cm, gray-brown, slightly resinous.

Height 30 m.
Crown narrow conic, later spreading.

Cone 6 cm, ovoid to oblong-conic.
Scales thin, prickly.

Cone sessile or short-stalked.
Umbos sharp, often deciduous.

Bark red-brown, scaly with resin pockets.

Shortleaf pine is a major lumber tree in the southeastern United States and may have sprouts on its branches.

RED PINE
Pinus resinosa

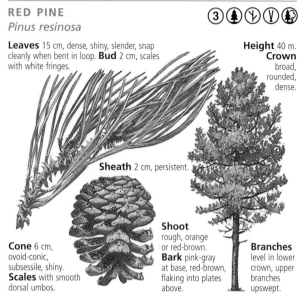

Leaves 15 cm, dense, shiny, slender, snap cleanly when bent in loop. **Bud** 2 cm, scales with white fringes.

Height 40 m. **Crown** broad, rounded, dense.

Sheath 2 cm, persistent.

Cone 6 cm, ovoid-conic, subsessile, shiny. **Scales** with smooth dorsal umbos.

Shoot rough, orange or red-brown. **Bark** pink-gray at base, red-brown, flaking into plates above.

Branches level in lower crown, upper branches upswept.

Red pine is also misleadingly called Norway pine, though it is native from New England to Minnesota. It resembles Scotch pine in its flaking, red-brown bark in the upper crown, but its whorled, brittle foliage and its lemon-scented resin are distinctive.

ALEPPO PINE
Pinus halepensis

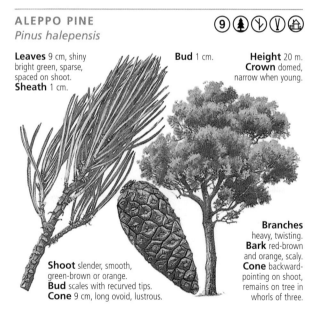

Leaves 9 cm, shiny bright green, sparse, spaced on shoot. **Sheath** 1 cm.

Bud 1 cm.

Height 20 m. **Crown** domed, narrow when young.

Branches heavy, twisting. **Bark** red-brown and orange, scaly. **Cone** backward-pointing on shoot, remains on tree in whorls of three.

Shoot slender, smooth, green-brown or orange. **Bud** scales with recurved tips. **Cone** 9 cm, long ovoid, lustrous.

This Mediterranean species, tolerant of dry sites with a very low summer rainfall, is frequently planted in California. Mondell pine (*P. eldarica*), native to Iran, Pakistan and Afghanistan, has forward-pointing cones on stout shoots with stiffer dark leaves.

MARITIME PINE
Pinus Pinaster

Umbos upcurved.

Bark deeply fissured.

Bud 2 cm, with scales at tips recurved.

Height 30 m.
Stem sinuous.

Cone to 20 cm, often clustered and persisting unopened.
Leaves very long, to 25 cm, stout with rough margins.

This tree thrives on poor, sandy sites and is widely planted in Mediterranean countries for its resin. This is tapped by longitudinal wounds made in the bark and is used in turpentine manufacturing. Its leaves are the longest and stoutest of any European pine.

PINYON
Pinus edulis

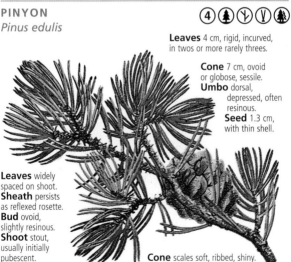

Leaves 4 cm, rigid, incurved, in twos or more rarely threes.

Cone 7 cm, ovoid or globose, sessile.
Umbo dorsal, depressed, often resinous.
Seed 1.3 cm, with thin shell.

Leaves widely spaced on shoot.
Sheath persists as reflexed rosette.
Bud ovoid, slightly resinous.
Shoot stout, usually initially pubescent.

Cone scales soft, ribbed, shiny.
Seed edible, almost wingless.

The pinyons are a group of soft pines from the semi-arid regions of the southwestern United States with several characteristics of the hard pines, such as dorsal umbos and nearly persistent sheaths. They form small, bushy trees to 20 m with rounded crowns and their edible seeds, known as pine nuts, are harvested commercially. Single-leaf pinyon (*P. monophylla*) bears single, round, gray-green leaves to 6 cm with white lines of stomata.

PITCH PINE
Pinus rigida

⑤ 🌲 🌿 🌿 🌲

Bud 2 cm, cylindric.

Leaves 13 cm, rigid, stout, twisted, often at right angle to shoot.

Height 20 m.
Crown open, irregular.

Cone 8 cm, subsessile, ovoid-conic.

Bark red-brown, coarsely fissured into plates.

Bole bears epicormic shoots.

Shoot stout, rough, gray-brown.

Umbo a curved prickle.

Pitch pine, from the northeastern United States, is unusual among pines due to its sprouting epicormic shoots from its bole. Pond pine (*P. serotina*), from the southeastern United States, differs in having flexible needles to 20 cm, globose cones and thickly resinous buds.

LOBLOLLY PINE
Pinus taeda

⑦ 🌲 🌿 🌿 🌲

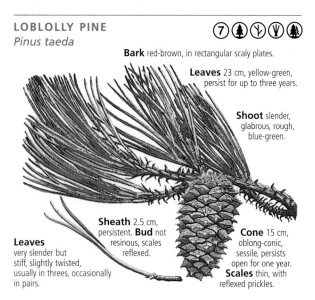

Bark red-brown, in rectangular scaly plates.

Leaves 23 cm, yellow-green, persist for up to three years.

Shoot slender, glabrous, rough, blue-green.

Sheath 2.5 cm, persistent. **Bud** not resinous, scales reflexed.

Leaves very slender but stiff, slightly twisted, usually in threes, occasionally in pairs.

Cone 15 cm, oblong-conic, sessile, persists open for one year.
Scales thin, with reflexed prickles.

Loblolly pine is a densely crowned tree to 35 m in the southeastern United States, where it covers several million acres. It is better suited to wet sites than most pines, and its name is derived from 'loblollies' — moist depressions. It is one of a group of southern pines raised for lumber, plywood and pulp.

SLASH PINE
Pinus Elliottii

(8) (🌲) (🌱) (🌿) (🌲) (🏠)

Cones ♂ catkins in clusters at base of new shoots, purplish when emerging, more abundant near crown base.
♀ **strobili** solitary, globose.

♀ **cone** woody, on short stalk, broadly ovoid and chestnut-brown when open with an umbo terminated by a short, stout prickle.
Cones 15–20 cm, shedding after opening, maturing second year.

Leaves
in fascicles of twos and threes, dark green, 15–30 cm, coarse, stiff, persist into the second year.

Bark grayish-brown, coarsely fissured into broad, irregular platelets.

Fascicle sheath greater than 2.5 cm.
Branches multinodal, slightly horizontal, stout and brittle.
Buds conical, resinous, slightly reflexed scales.

Slash pine is one of the more important commercial conifers of the lower Atlantic and Gulf Coast regions of the United States. Commonly found in wet, sandy flatwoods, it is a source of gum turpentine and rosins. This tree grows to 30 m.

LONGLEAF PINE
Pinus palustris

(8) (🌲) (🌱) (🌿) (🌲)

Shoot stout, shiny, rough with long scales beneath fascicles.
Bud 3 cm, covered with silver-white fringed scales.
Cone opens as soon as it is ripe, then falls leaving few basal scales on shoot.

Cone 25 cm, narrow conic, sessile.
Umbo incurved.
Scales thin, end in prickle.

Bark scaly, silver-purple with orange-brown fissures.

Leaves 45 cm.

Leaves slender, flexible, clustered at end of shoot.

Height 40 m.
Crown open.

Sheath 4 cm, persistent.

This species, native to the southeastern United States, has the longest needles of any conifer, and can be recognized by its conspicuous buds, which appear to be covered with cobwebs. It thrives on dry, sandy sites and is grown for its timber and resin.

MONTEREY PINE
Pinus radiata

⑦ 🌲 🌿 🌿 🌲

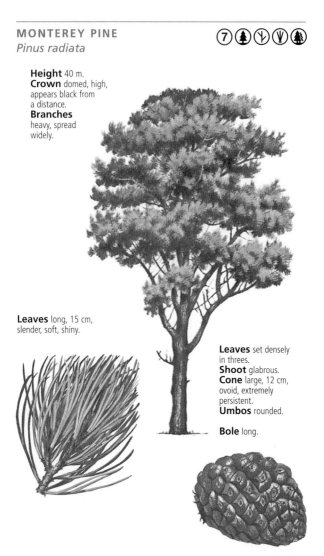

Height 40 m.
Crown domed, high, appears black from a distance.
Branches heavy, spread widely.

Leaves long, 15 cm, slender, soft, shiny.

Leaves set densely in threes.
Shoot glabrous.
Cone large, 12 cm, ovoid, extremely persistent.
Umbos rounded.

Bole long.

Native to California, Monterey pine's oblique cones may persist for over 20 years. Knobcone pine (*P. attenuata*) has asymmetrical, ovoid-conic cones, thin bark, smooth shoots and yellow-green leaves.

PONDEROSA PINE
Pinus ponderosa

Leaves to 22 cm.

Height 40 m.
Crown, variable fairly open.
Bole long, straight.

Leaves dense, stout, usually in fascicles of three.
Sheath 2 cm.

Cone 12 cm, when falls, base left behind.
Scales ridged, prickled.

This tree grows at varying altitudes and on dry sites throughout western North America. Its foliage is quite variable — even on the same tree, leaves may be set in fascicles of both twos and threes.

JEFFREY PINE
Pinus Jeffreyi

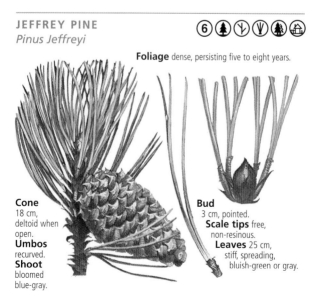

Foliage dense, persisting five to eight years.

Cone 18 cm, deltoid when open.
Umbos recurved.
Shoot bloomed blue-gray.

Bud 3 cm, pointed.
Scale tips free, non-resinous.
Leaves 25 cm, stiff, spreading, bluish-green or gray.

Native to Oregon and California and rarely exceeding 35 m, Jeffrey pine is smaller than Ponderosa pine but can grow at higher elevations. Its distinguishing features are its bloomed shoot, and, when available, its larger, broad-based cones that may reach 30 cm in length.

COULTER PINE
Pinus Coulteri

Height 20 m.
Bark dark brown, almost black.

Cone huge, 35 cm, weighs up to 2.5 kg.
Seeds 20 mm. **Scales** thick.
Umbos sharp.

Foliage stout, rigid, spaced, not densely set, becomes crinkled in second year.

Shoot stout, glabrous.

Leaves 30 cm.
Sheath 2.5 cm.

While closely related to Ponderosa and Jeffrey pines, Coulter pine can be recognized by the size of its cones, normally set at the summit, or its longer hanging leaves. Digger pine (*P. Sabiniana*) holds its 25 cm leaves level.

LACEBARK PINE
Pinus Bungeana

Height 25 m.
Foliage not set densely on shoot.

Bark smooth, flaking through white, yellow, olive and purple to gray-green.

Leaves 8 cm, slender, smooth, finely toothed, in close fascicles.
Sheath deciduous.

Cone 6 cm, on 2 cm stalk.
Umbos dorsal, spined.

This species has a low, usually bushy crown and is cultivated for the splendor of its bark. The bark is initially smooth and gray-green and then flakes away to leave rounded white patches which turn through yellow, green, red and purple to purple-brown. In its native China, the bark of old trees becomes even more chalk white.

SWISS STONE PINE
Pinus Cembra

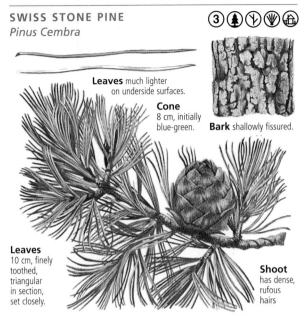

Leaves much lighter on underside surfaces.

Cone 8 cm, initially blue-green.

Bark shallowly fissured.

Leaves 10 cm, finely toothed, triangular in section, set closely.

Shoot has dense, rufous hairs

A soft pine, Swiss stone, or Arolla pine, grows wild at high altitudes in the mountains of central Europe. The crown, to 25 m, is broad and dense. Korean pine (*P. koraiensis*) has longer 12 cm needles, a more open crown and 15 cm cones with thick, fleshy scales.

MACEDONIAN PINE
Pinus peuce

Height 35 m.
Crown dense.

Leaves 12 cm, dense, rigid.

Umbos incurved.

Branches whorled, very upswept in upper crown.

Cone 15 cm, stalked.
Scales thin, convex.

Rarely planted for timber outside its native Albania, Bulgaria and Bosnia, this attractive tree is similar to Blue pine but has finer shoots, more curved cones and leaves, which are shorter, denser, rigid and more forward-pointing.

BLUE PINE
Pinus Wallichiana

③ 🌲 🜉 🌿 🏠

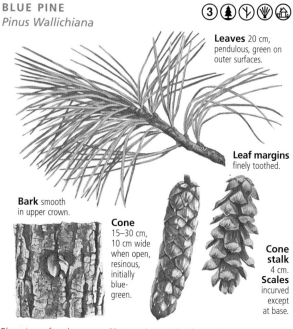

Leaves 20 cm, pendulous, green on outer surfaces.

Leaf margins finely toothed.

Bark smooth in upper crown.

Cone 15–30 cm, 10 cm wide when open, resinous, initially blue-green.

Cone stalk 4 cm. **Scales** incurved except at base.

Blue pine, often known as Bhutan pine or Himalayan pine, is indigenous throughout the Himalayas. It has been widely planted as an ornamental and forms a broad, heavily branched tree to 50 m, with stout, glabrous shoots and curved leaves. Mexican white pine (*P. Ayacahuite*) has straight needles and more tapered cones.

ARMAND PINE
Pinus Armandii

④ Ⓡ 🌲 🜉 🌿 🏠

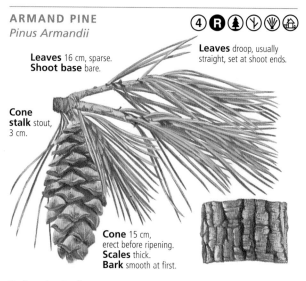

Leaves 16 cm, sparse. **Shoot base** bare.

Leaves droop, usually straight, set at shoot ends.

Cone stalk stout, 3 cm.

Cone 15 cm, erect before ripening. **Scales** thick. **Bark** smooth at first.

Dedicated to its discoverer, Père Armand David, this soft pine has a very wide distribution across China and Burma. It resembles Blue pine but has finer shoots and barrel-shaped cones.

LIMBER PINE
Pinus flexilis

Cone 15 cm, sub-cylindric, short-stalked, green or purplish at maturity.
Scales thick.   **Umbo** terminal.

Seed 1 cm, dark red-brown and black, wing short or absent.
Bud 1 cm, ovoid, pointed.
Foliage spaced.

Shoot stout, softly pubescent at first.
Bark initially gray, later dark brown, fissured.

Leaves 8 cm, firm, stout, stomata on all surfaces, tight in bundles for first year.
Sheath soon shed.

A broad-crowned tree to 20 m, Limber pine is native at elevations of up to 3,500 m on both sides of the Rocky Mountains from Canada to Mexico. The similar Whitebark pine (*P. albicaulis*) has ovoid cones to 7 cm, which do not open but fall and disintegrate.

SUGAR PINE
Pinus Lambertiana

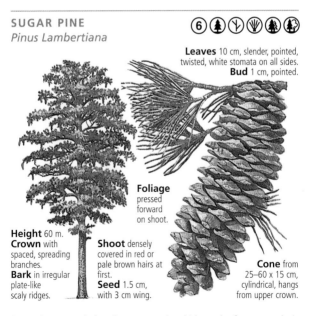

Leaves 10 cm, slender, pointed, twisted, white stomata on all sides.
Bud 1 cm, pointed.

Foliage pressed forward on shoot.

Height 60 m.
Crown with spaced, spreading branches.
Bark in irregular plate-like scaly ridges.

Shoot densely covered in red or pale brown hairs at first.
Seed 1.5 cm, with 3 cm wing.

Cone from 25–60 x 15 cm, cylindrical, hangs from upper crown.

Sugar pine, named after the sugary resin which exudes from wounds, is the tallest pine and produces the largest cones, although they are lighter than those of Coulter pine. It is restricted to Oregon and California, and is prone to blister rust.

JAPANESE WHITE PINE
Pinus parviflora

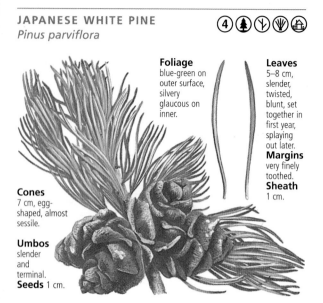

Foliage
blue-green on outer surface, silvery glaucous on inner.

Leaves
5–8 cm, slender, twisted, blunt, set together in first year, splaying out later.
Margins very finely toothed.
Sheath 1 cm.

Cones
7 cm, egg-shaped, almost sessile.

Umbos
slender and terminal.
Seeds 1 cm.

In its wild form, this species grows to a height of 25 m, but is more usually encountered as a lower, slow-growing tree that rarely reaches 10 m. It has a wide crown and tiered branches and was probably developed for Japanese ornamental gardens. The leaves of both types are the most twisting of any pine.

WESTERN WHITE PINE
Pinus monticola

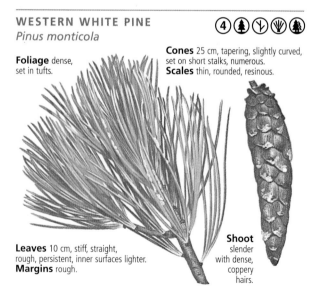

Foliage dense, set in tufts.

Cones 25 cm, tapering, slightly curved, set on short stalks, numerous.
Scales thin, rounded, resinous.

Leaves 10 cm, stiff, straight, rough, persistent, inner surfaces lighter.
Margins rough.

Shoot slender with dense, coppery hairs.

Native to the Pacific Coast and in mountains as far inland as Montana, *P. monticola* has a dense crown and can reach heights over 50 m. Like all soft pines, the bark of young trees and the bark high up on old trees is smooth and gray-green and often attacked by blister rust, a fungal disease which affects all American white pines and kills many old trees.

EASTERN WHITE PINE
Pinus strobus

Leaves 12 cm, paler on inner surfaces.

Shoot ridged behind leaves, only hairy on ridges.

Cone 15 cm, narrow, pointed.

Scales convex.

Height 40 m.
Crown conic when young, later flat-topped.
Bark narrowly fissured.

Native to the forests of the eastern United States, Eastern white pine forms a tree to 40 m and differs from Western white pine in its glabrous shoots and shorter, pointed cones, which are only 15 cm long. The leaves are stiffer and only persist for two seasons. It is susceptible to white pine blister rust.

BRISTLECONE PINE
Pinus aristata

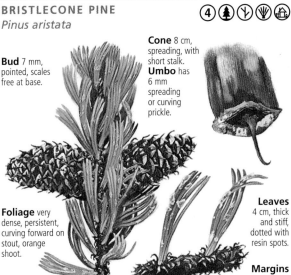

Bud 7 mm, pointed, scales free at base.

Cone 8 cm, spreading, with short stalk.
Umbo has 6 mm spreading or curving prickle.

Foliage very dense, persistent, curving forward on stout, orange shoot.

Leaves 4 cm, thick and stiff, dotted with resin spots.

Margins entire.

This is the most common of the three trees from the southwestern United States known as "foxtail pines" because of their persistent, dense foliage. Foxtail pine (*P. Balfouriana*) has longer, unspotted leaves, tight buds and 13 cm cones with minute umbos while Ancient pine (*P. longaeva*) has foxtail foliage and Bristlecone cones. Bristlecone pines are among the oldest recorded living species.

THE BROADLEAF TREES

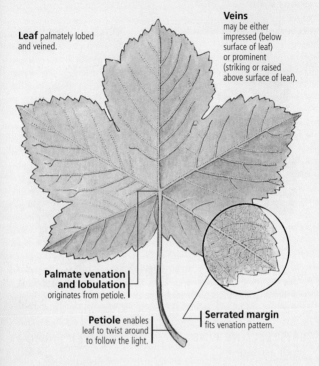

Leaf palmately lobed and veined.

Veins may be either impressed (below surface of leaf) or prominent (striking or raised above surface of leaf).

Palmate venation and lobulation originates from petiole.

Petiole enables leaf to twist around to follow the light.

Serrated margin fits venation pattern.

The trees known as the broadleaf trees, because their leaves have broad blades, are more properly classified as the *Angiospermae*, so called because their seeds develop from ovules which are enclosed in an ovary. Many can be classified as *Dicotyledonae*, because their seedlings have two seed leaves, but some are *Monocotyledonae*, with one seed leaf, which goes on to produce leaves with long unbranched veins and less complexly branched crown than the *Dicotyledonae*.

The shape of the leaf, the best feature for identification purposes, is governed by its composition and function, a vital element being the venation system, illustrated above in a Planetree, or Sycamore, maple leaf. The veins strengthen the thin blade, and the many complex patterns they form are useful for identification. The main function of the leaf is to produce energy by photosynthesis — the fixing (i.e., turning into solid form) of carbon from the air. This process has to take place in daylight and needs water, which is transported up from the root system to spread across the surface of the leaf blade through the network of veins. The veins are two-way channels; they transport water and nutrients to the leaf, and carry the sugar sap, the end product of photosynthesis, to the rest of the tree.

The excess water not used in photosynthesis is transpired or evaporated into the atmosphere. Temperate broadleaf trees are nearly all deciduous, dropping all their leaves each winter. Once the temperature drops, the tree cannot extract from the cold soil enough water to maintain transpiration, and freezing temperatures would damage the leaves. The nutrient material is withdrawn from the leaves before they wither and die.

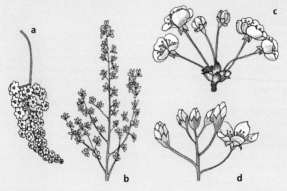

Flowers

The broadleaf trees flower for a relatively short time, but these flowers are very useful in identification. While conifers transfer the pollen from the male to the female cones on the wind, many broadleaves are insect pollinated and their flowers have brightly colored petals and strong scents to attract the insects. Flowers may be perfect, i.e., having both male and female parts within the same floret, or imperfect, i.e. having male and female parts in separate flowers. Four types of flower arrangement are illustrated above. A **raceme (a)** is a simple group of stalked flowers on a long single rachis. A **panicle (b)** is a looser compound or branched flower cluster. An **umbel (c)** is an inflorescence with pedicles all rising from the same point. A **corymb (d)** is a flat-topped flower cluster in which the individual stalks grow upward from various points along the main stem to about the same height. The outermost flowers often open first.

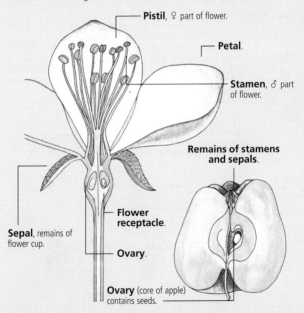

Pistil, ♀ part of flower.

Petal.

Stamen, ♂ part of flower.

Remains of stamens and sepals.

Flower receptacle.

Sepal, remains of flower cup.

Ovary.

Ovary (core of apple) contains seeds.

One mode of the transition from flower to fruit is illustrated with the apple above. The flesh develops from the flower receptacle, and, once the petals have dropped, the stamens and sepals wither until their remains are at the top of the fruit. What was the ovary becomes the core of the apple, which contains the seeds.

Fruit

The basic functions of the fruit are to protect the seeds as they develop and to disperse these seeds to propagate the species. Fruits may be less numerous than the flowers, either because some of the flowers did not develop or because the majority of the inflorescence was male. There are several different types of fruit: the apple illustrated on the previous page is a **pome**, which has a fleshy covering around one or more seeds in several fused cells; and some other examples are illustrated below. A **capsule (a)**, as borne by eucalyptus trees, is a hard woody pod which releases many small seeds through one or more lines of dehiscence. A **drupe (b)**, such as a cherry for example, has a fleshy exterior around a stone which contains one or more seeds. A **cone-like structure (c)**, as borne by the alders, has spirally or oppositely arranged scales that each carry two or more seeds. A **samara (d)**, as borne by ashes, has a single seed in a case on the end of a long wing. A **nut (e)**, such as the acorn, bears its seeds inside a hard shell; the acorn is set in a cup called an involucre or cupule.

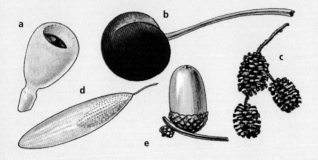

Seed Germination

The seeds which alight on suitable ground can lie dormant for a few months to several years before germination. They are gradually softened by moisture from the soil, and eventually a tiny root is produced by cell division, which breaks through the seed coat and penetrates the ground. It next develops tiny hairs to extract water and nutrients from the earth; these are renewed every year throughout its life. Sometimes two seed leaves withdraw from the withered seed casing as the seedling, the first plant, is formed. In the Horse chestnut, illustrated below, they remain inside.

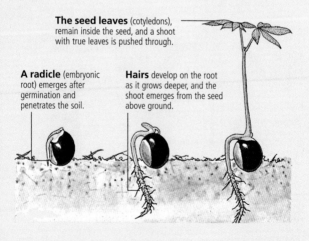

The seed leaves (cotyledons), remain inside the seed, and a shoot with true leaves is pushed through.

A radicle (embryonic root) emerges after germination and penetrates the soil.

Hairs develop on the root as it grows deeper, and the shoot emerges from the seed above ground.

Willow Family *Salicaceae*

This family has 350 or so species of willows and poplars, which are mainly natives of the Northern Hemisphere. The chief feature uniting them all is their flowers. These have neither petals nor sepals and are borne in catkins that usually appear with or before their tree's new leaves. Trees in this family are dioecious. Only one type is usually carried. Both willows and poplars prefer moist sites and hybridize so easily that positive identification is sometimes difficult.

Poplars *Populus*

Poplars have wind-pollinated catkins and leaves whose broad blades have long petioles which may be flattened at one end. Their shoots bear terminal buds, and all their buds have overlapping scales. Trees that have hybridized grow more vigorously and provide better timber than their parents.

WHITE POPLAR
Populus alba

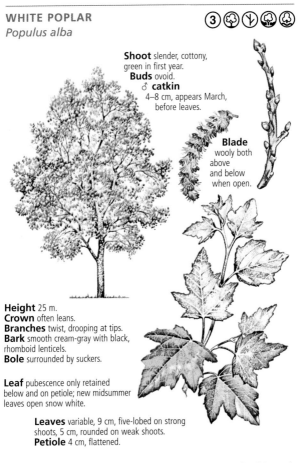

Shoot slender, cottony, green in first year.
Buds ovoid.
♂ catkin 4–8 cm, appears March, before leaves.

Blade wooly both above and below when open.

Height 25 m.
Crown often leans.
Branches twist, drooping at tips.
Bark smooth cream-gray with black, rhomboid lenticels.
Bole surrounded by suckers.

Leaf pubescence only retained below and on petiole; new midsummer leaves open snow white.

Leaves variable, 9 cm, five-lobed on strong shoots, 5 cm, rounded on weak shoots.
Petiole 4 cm, flattened.

White poplar is native to central and southern Europe, north Africa and central Asia and, with Quaking aspen, belongs to a group of poplars with smooth barks and lobed or coarsely serrate leaves. 'Pyramidis' is a fastigiate clone, broader than Lombardy poplar; 'Richardii' has golden yellow leaves.

BALSAM POPLARS
P. trichocarpa · P. balsamifera
P. x candicans

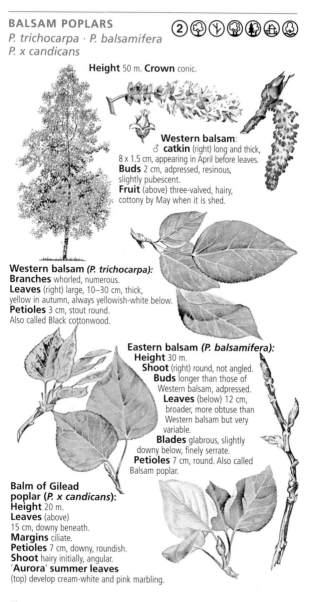

Height 50 m. **Crown** conic.

Western balsam:
♂ **catkin** (right) long and thick,
8 x 1.5 cm, appearing in April before leaves.
Buds 2 cm, adpressed, resinous,
slightly pubescent.
Fruit (above) three-valved, hairy,
cottony by May when it is shed.

Western balsam (*P. trichocarpa*):
Branches whorled, numerous.
Leaves (right) large, 10–30 cm, thick,
yellow in autumn, always yellowish-white below.
Petioles 3 cm, stout round.
Also called Black cottonwood.

Eastern balsam (*P. balsamifera*):
Height 30 m.
Shoot (right) round, not angled.
Buds longer than those of
Western balsam, adpressed.
Leaves (below) 12 cm,
broader, more obtuse than
Western balsam but very
variable.
Blades glabrous, slightly
downy below, finely serrate.
Petioles 7 cm, round. Also called
Balsam poplar.

**Balm of Gilead
poplar (*P. x candicans*):**
Height 20 m.
Leaves (above)
15 cm, downy beneath.
Margins ciliate.
Petioles 7 cm, downy, roundish.
Shoot hairy initially, angular.
'Aurora' summer leaves
(top) develop cream-white and pink marbling.

These trees are recognizable by the balsamiferous odor pervaded by their
large, resinous buds and new foliage in early summer. Their leaves are
always yellow-white below and have neither flattened leaf stalks nor
translucent margins. Western and Eastern balsams are both native to
North America and are fast-growing, the latter putting out suckers around
its bole. Balm of Gilead poplar, presumed a hybrid between *P. balsamifera*
and *P. deltoides*, produces these so easily and profusely that they soon
become a nuisance, and since its trunk is also prone to bacterial canker, its
planting is not recommended; the 'Aurora' form, with variegated foliage,
is preferable. The Chinese balsam poplar (*P. szechuanica*) is notable for its
very large leaves whose undersides are initially downy and purple.

QUAKING ASPEN
Populus tremuloides

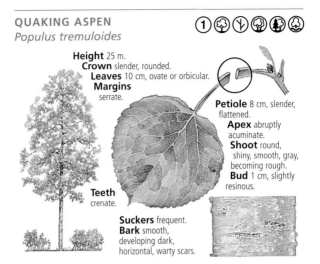

Height 25 m.
Crown slender, rounded.
Leaves 10 cm, ovate or orbicular.
Margins serrate.
Petiole 8 cm, slender, flattened.
Apex abruptly acuminate.
Shoot round, shiny, smooth, gray, becoming rough.
Bud 1 cm, slightly resinous.
Teeth crenate.
Suckers frequent.
Bark smooth, developing dark, horizontal, warty scars.

Named after the way its leaves flutter on their long petioles in even the slightest breeze, Quaking aspen is found across northern North America and down the Rockies. Flowers and fruit are borne in pendent, 10 cm catkins. Big-tooth aspen (*P. grandidentata*), from the Northeast, has coarsely toothed, 15 cm leaves and hairy buds.

EASTERN COTTONWOOD
Populus deltoides

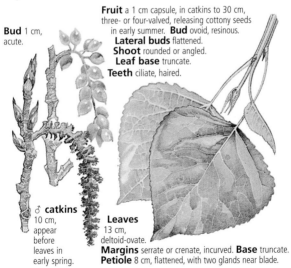

Fruit a 1 cm capsule, in catkins to 30 cm, three- or four-valved, releasing cottony seeds in early summer. **Bud** ovoid, resinous.
Bud 1 cm, acute.
Lateral buds flattened.
Shoot rounded or angled.
Leaf base truncate.
Teeth ciliate, haired.
♂ **catkins** 10 cm, appear before leaves in early spring.
Leaves 13 cm, deltoid-ovate.
Margins serrate or crenate, incurved. **Base** truncate.
Petiole 8 cm, flattened, with two glands near blade.

Growing to 40 m, with a spreading crown and gray-brown, deeply furrowed bark, Eastern cottonwood is found throughout eastern North America, and, with *P. nigra* is a parent of most of the hybrid Black poplars. Plains cottonwood (*P. Sargentii*) has slightly hairy buds and smaller, coarsely toothed leaves while Swamp cottonwood (*P. heterophylla*), from the East Coast and the Mississippi basin, has shaggy bark and cordate ovate leaves.

BLACK POPLAR
Populus nigra

③ 🌳 🌱 🏠 🍂

Buds (of both trees) to 8 mm.

P. nigra var. betulifolia:
Height 30 m.
Crown spreading and densely leaved, twiggy in winter.
Bole often burred.

P. nigra 'Italica':
Height 35 m.
Crown fastigiate.
Bole burred, often with epicormic shoots.

♂ **catkins** (of both trees) 5 cm, opening in March.

Shoot smooth; gray by third year.

Petioles (of both trees) 5-8 cm always flattened.

'Italica' leaf more deltoid, glabrous.

Leaves (of both trees) 8 cm, yellow in autumn.
Teeth forward curved.
Margins thick, translucent.

The black poplar normally encountered in western Europe is *P. nigra* var. *betulifolia* and differs from its rarer continental type (*P. nigra*) in having birch-like leaves and initially downy twigs and leaf stalks. Its burred bole is diagnostic. The more common Lombardy poplar (*P. nigra* 'Italica') may have arisen in central Asia rather than northern Italy as its name implies. The similar 'Plantierensis' clone has a leafier, slightly broader crown and initially pubescent petioles and shoots, nearly glabrous by midsummer. *Pemphigus bursarinus* aphids often attack these poplars and produce distinctively spiralled galls on their leaf stalks.

HYBRID POPLARS
Populus x 'Androscoggin'
'Strathglass' · 'Eugenii'

④ 🌳 🌿 🏠 🌲

P. x 'Androscoggin' leaves (above) 13 cm, ovate or elliptic, dark green above, oily white below.
Apex twisted, short acuminate.
Margins finely serrate.
Teeth crenate, ciliate.
Veins shallowly impressed on upper surface.
Bud 1.4 cm, resinous.

Shoot round, slightly ridged near tip on vigorous shoots.

Apex acuminate.

Lenticels linear.
Shoot glossy pale brown, slender.

Veins impressed.

P. x 'Strathglass' leaves (right) 6 cm, ovate to elliptic, smooth, lustrous above, whitish green below.
Petiole 5 cm, slightly flattened, pale yellowish green.
Margins slightly wavy, serrate.
Teeth crenate, more coarsely so on young or vigorous shoots, often more so toward apex.

Bud 1 cm, acute, lanceolate, slightly resinous.
Shoot angled near tip on strong shoots.

Petiole pinkish above, flattened toward blade.

P. x 'Eugenii' leaves (left) 10 cm, broad ovate, shiny on both surfaces, getting thicker toward apex.
Shoot slender, round, angled on vigorous shoots, marked with elliptic or round lenticels to 2 mm.
Bud 5 mm, ovoid, acute, adpressed, slightly resinous.

Margins serrate.
Teeth gland-tipped, crenate, coarser toward apex.

P. x 'Androscoggin,' a fast-growing tree which soon attains 30 m and has an open, rather gaunt crown, is a hybrid between Western balsam and the Asiatic *P. Maximowiczii*, which gives it the broad leaves with impressed veins. *P. x* 'Strathglass' makes a denser tree with pendent lower branches — its parents are Black poplar and the Siberian *P. laurifolia*. *P. x* 'Eugenii,' a hybrid of Black poplar with Eastern cottonwood, has a narrow crown with stiff, ascending branches.

Willows *Salix*

Willows include about 300 species and are particularly difficult to identify due to both extensive hybridization and variablity. Unlike poplars, willows are insect-pollinated, having stiffer, nectar-bearing catkins as well as longer and narrower stipulate leaves, shorter petioles and single-scaled buds. Their shoots lack terminal buds and growth occurs laterally behind the tips.

WHITE WILLOW · SILVER WILLOW ③ 🌳 🍃 🌼 🌰
Salix alba · S. alba 'Sericea'

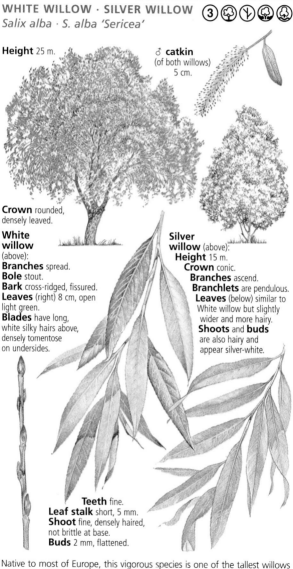

Height 25 m.

♂ **catkin**
(of both willows)
5 cm.

Crown rounded, densely leaved.

White willow (above):
Branches spread.
Bole stout.
Bark cross-ridged, fissured.
Leaves (right) 8 cm, open light green.
Blades have long, white silky hairs above, densely tomentose on undersides.

Silver willow (above):
Height 15 m.
Crown conic.
Branches ascend.
Branchlets are pendulous.
Leaves (below) similar to White willow but slightly wider and more hairy.
Shoots and **buds** are also hairy and appear silver-white.

Teeth fine.
Leaf stalk short, 5 mm.
Shoot fine, densely haired, not brittle at base.
Buds 2 mm, flattened.

Native to most of Europe, this vigorous species is one of the tallest willows and, while sometimes confused with Crack willow (*S. fragilis*), can be distinguished by its less fragile twigs and less deeply fissured bark. It is often pollarded to produce pliant shoots, which are used for basketry. The widely distributed 'Sericea' is readily identified by its coloring and more hairy foliage.

WEEPING WILLOW
Salix x chrysocoma

Height 20 m.
Crown broad.
Branches arching.
Shoots very pendulous, long, slender, yellow, becoming brighter in late winter.

Leaves 10 x 1.5 cm, glossy, glaucous below, finely haired on both surfaces, opening in early April.

Catkins 8 cm, often curving up, usually ♂.

This tree is attractive beside water toward which its foliage tends to bend. Weeping willow is a hybrid of White willow and Chinese weeping willow (*S. babylonica*), which is far less common and has pendulous, brown shoots and leaves with fewer teeth.

CORKSCREW WILLOW
Salix Matsudana 'Tortuosa'

Leaves open in March.

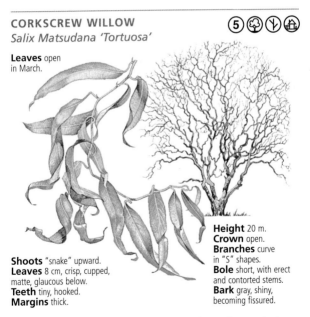

Shoots "snake" upward.
Leaves 8 cm, crisp, cupped, matte, glaucous below.
Teeth tiny, hooked.
Margins thick.

Height 20 m.
Crown open.
Branches curve in "S" shapes.
Bole short, with erect and contorted stems.
Bark gray, shiny, becoming fissured.

Useful on dry soils, this willow makes an attractive garden tree. Its leaves are among the first to appear and the last to fall. In winter, its distinctively contorted crown, which can only be confused with that of the Corkscrew hazel, is very striking.

SCOULER WILLOW
Salix Scoulerana

Leaves 15 cm, obovate to elliptic, dark green and glabrous or nearly so above, whitish and hairy below.

Margins variable, either entire or toothed. **Apex** and **Base** broadly cuneate.

Bud 6 mm, ovoid, round or slightly flattened.

Shoot initially pale pubescent, with yellow lenticels.

♀ **catkins** 5 cm, erect, before leaves, furry, silky, become yellow. **Fruit** 1 cm, oblong-ovoid, pale, pubescent, light brown capsules.

♂ **catkins** 2.5 x 1.5 cm, oblong-cylindric, stout, sessile or very short-stalked.

This species is the tallest-growing of the 'Pussy willow' group, attaining 15 m at times even though it is often used as a shrub. It is a native of the Rockies and the Pacific Coast in differing forms. The male trees are very showy in flower.

BLACK WILLOW
Salix nigra

Catkins terminal on current year's leafy shoots.
Height 40 m, but sometimes a shrub.
Crown broad, on divided bole.

Shoot red-brown, initially pubescent, soon glabrous, dull below, snaps easily at joints if bent.

Bole twisted.

Leaves green both sides.

Branches very upright.
Bark black or dark brown, rigid, deeply furrowed into scaly ridges.
Leaves on short petiole.

Leaves 15 x 2 cm, lanceolate, shiny above, dull below.
Apex long-pointed.
Margins serrate.

This is the largest of the willows and is found throughout the eastern United States. The fruit is a 1 cm green capsule. Pacific willow (*S. lasiandra*), from the West, has shorter leaves, gray-green below, and broad ovate 6 mm buds.

Casuarina Family *Casuarinaceae*

Casuarinaceae, the Casuarina family, has but a single genus native to Australia and the South Pacific. Several species are commonly planted as street trees in frost-free areas of Florida and California. Members of this family can be used as windbreaks and for dune stabilization. The wood is an important source of fuel in the tropics.

SHE OAK / AUSTRALIAN PINE / HORSETAIL TREE
Casuarina equisetifolia

Flowers dioecious, inconspicuous, ♀ flowers in dense heads, each subtended by a bract which becomes woody to enclose the fruit.

Fruit a samara, about 5 mm long enclosed in a cluster that resembles a cone about 20 x 15 mm in diameter.

Leaves inconspicuous, whorled, scale-like with 6-7 leaves about 1 mm long and persistent and forming a toothed sheath at each node.

Branches thin, about 1 mm in diameter, jointed and striate, resembling the true horsetail and evergreen, often drooping.

This species was introduced into southern Florida and California from northeastern Australia. Commonly used as a windbreak, it tolerates droughty, sandy and often brackish or alkaline soils. The tree grows to 20 m and is commonly regarded around the world as the best firewood. Related species (*C. Cunninghamiana* and *C. glauca*) are found in the same areas and often hybridize within these species.

Walnut Family *Juglandaceae*

This is a group of large trees with pinnate leaves and pendent male catkins. The fruit, usually edible, is a drupe or nut and, in *Juglans* and *Pterocarya*, the pith is chambered.

ENGLISH WALNUT / PERSIAN WALNUT ⑧ 🌳 🌱 🏠
Juglans regia

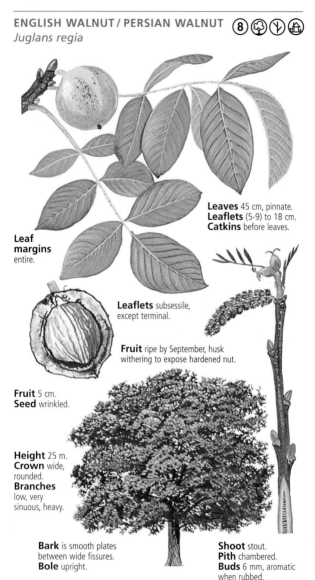

Leaves 45 cm, pinnate.
Leaflets (5-9) to 18 cm.
Catkins before leaves.

Leaf margins entire.

Leaflets subsessile, except terminal.

Fruit ripe by September, husk withering to expose hardened nut.

Fruit 5 cm.
Seed wrinkled.

Height 25 m.
Crown wide, rounded.
Branches low, very sinuous, heavy.

Bark is smooth plates between wide fissures.
Bole upright.

Shoot stout.
Pith chambered.
Buds 6 mm, aromatic when rubbed.

English, or Persian, walnut has become naturalized in Europe and across Asia and has long been cultivated, although its exact origin is unknown. Large orchards of it exist in France and California. The fruit is either picked for pickling before the end of July when still fleshy or left until autumn when it has hardened. *J. regia* is the only walnut with entire leaflets.

BLACK WALNUT
Juglans nigra

④ 🌳 🌿 🌳 🌲 🏠

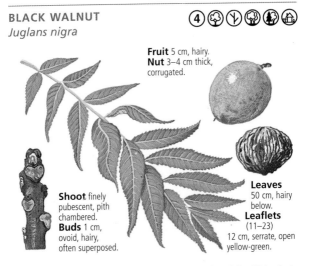

Fruit 5 cm, hairy.
Nut 3–4 cm thick, corrugated.

Shoot finely pubescent, pith chambered.
Buds 1 cm, ovoid, hairy, often superposed.

Leaves 50 cm, hairy below.
Leaflets (11–23) 12 cm, serrate, open yellow-green.

Black walnut, native to the eastern United States where it is widely planted for its timber and nuts, grows to 30 m with a broad, open crown and dark brown or black, cross-furrowed bark. It is distinguishable by its many leaflets, often without a terminal.

BUTTERNUT
Juglans cinerea

⑤ 🌳 🌿 🌳

Fruit in racemes of 1–5.
Fruit 6 cm, ovoid, pointed, husks with clammy matted hairs and two or four sutures.
Seed 6 cm, oily, deeply ribbed.

Leaves 75–60 cm.
Leaflets 11–17, to 7.5 x 5 cm, lanceolate, finely serrate, pointed, sessile.

Leaflets, finely pubescent below.
Pith chambered.

Rachis stout, downy.

Shoot stout, with reddish hairs at first; ridge of hairs remains above leaf. **Terminal bud** 2 cm, flattened.

Height 30 m.
Crown broad, open dome. **Bole** short.
Bark thick, light gray, furrowed.

The sweet, oily kernel that gives Butternut its name soon goes rancid, but is edible if picked early. This species grows in the eastern United States and into Canada, and it is distinguished from Black walnut by its larger leaves and its clustered ovoid fruits.

Hickories *Carya*

Hickories, restricted to North America and China, differ from walnuts in having a solid pith, catkins in threes on a common peduncle and a fruit with a four-valved husk and a smooth seed.

PECAN
Carya illinoinensis

Leaves to 55 cm.
Leaflets 9–17, to 20 cm, falcate, lanceolate, sessile, glabrous above, hairy below.

Margins serrated, often doubly so.

Veins prominent.

Height 30 m.

Fruit 8 cm, in clusters of 3–10, narrow.
Husk four-valved, thin, red-brown.

Crown broad, rounded, narrower in woodland.
Bark pale gray-brown, deeply fissured.
Shoots pubescent.
Fruit husk splits but persists.

Pecan is native to the Mississippi Valley, but its range has been extended by widespread cultivation in the southern United States, where its nuts are an important commercial crop. Pruning often alters the shape of the crown. It occasionally grows to over 40 m.

MOCKERNUT HICKORY
Carya tomentosa

Leaves 30 cm.

Leaflets 7–9, 20 cm, lanceolate, serrate, subsessile, densely hairy below.

Rachis hairy.

Fruit 5 cm, globose, ripens brown. **Husk** thick, with four deep grooves.
Nut ovoid, four-ribbed.

Bud 2 cm, ovoid, red-brown, hairy.

Flowers before leaves.

♂ **catkins** slender, drooping in threes on single stalk, pale yellow in summer.

Mockernut, a native of the southeastern United States, forms a tree to 25 m with a broad open crown, distinguished by its fragrant foliage. Black hickory (*C. texana*) has black bark, five to seven dark green leaflets and acuminate terminal buds never longer than 12 mm.

BITTERNUT HICKORY
Carya cordiformis

Leaflets 7–9, 15 cm, serrate.

Height 25 m. **Crown** more open in older trees.

Branches slender. **Bark** gray, fissured.

Shoot slender with white lenticels. **Buds** to 2.5 cm, slender, yellow, pubescent.

Leaves 25 cm. **Fruit** 4 cm, encloses four-ribbed nut.

A species with a wide natural range throughout the eastern North America, this hickory can grow to 50 m and is identifiable by the taste of its seeds and its yellow winter buds. Its leaves have up to 11 leaflets that are paler below and turn yellow in autumn.

SHAGBARK HICKORY
Carya ovata

Bark has long vertical plates peeling at ends, smooth when young.

Leaves to 65 cm. **Leaflets** to 30 cm; terminal on stout, 4 cm petiole.

Fruit 5 cm, with four-lobed husk, set in twos or threes on stout pedicel. **Nut** smooth, four-ribbed, sweet.

Leaflets usually in fives; thick, hard, oily.

Rachis stout.

This species is instantly identifiable by the nature of its bark, which begins to flake into long, curling plates when the tree is about 25 years old. Shellbark hickory (*C. laciniosa*) has similar mature bark but its leaves have seven leaflets with downy undersides.

PIGNUT HICKORY
Carya glabra

Leaves alternate, deciduous, odd pinnately compound, to 30 cm long, with typically five oblong-obovate, dark green, glabrous (except on veins).

Terminal leaflets usually two-thirds larger than the basal pair, the latter are sharply toothed.

Buds ovoid to 15 mm; 2–3 visible, overlapping, glabrous scales; outer scales often dehiscent at bud maturity; terminal buds present.

Bark smooth, grayish on young trees and branches, dark, fissured into irregular diamond shapes with rounded ridges at maturity.

Flowers staminate in drooping, three branched catkins appearing with emerging leaves, pistillate in few, terminal spikes, monoecious.

Fruit subglobose nut to 30 mm with hard, bony shell encased in a thin, usually unridged, husk that persists at maturity.

Shoots branches slender, smooth and glabrous.

Pignut hickory is a common, large tree to 20 m, found from southern Ontario to Florida and westward to Mississippi along the hillsides and ridges. It is an important source of wood for tool handles. The nuts are bitter and not very edible.

Birch Family *Betulaceae*

A group of trees and shrubs comprising about 50 species, the members of this family carry male and female catkins on the same tree, the females being small, initially erect when flowering and held above the males. In *Betula*, *Alnus* and *Corylus*, the males develop in autumn and are carried over winter, opening to release their pollen before, or when, the leaves appear in spring. Those of *Carpinus*, although preformed, are hidden in the winter buds.

EUROPEAN WHITE BIRCH
Betula pendula

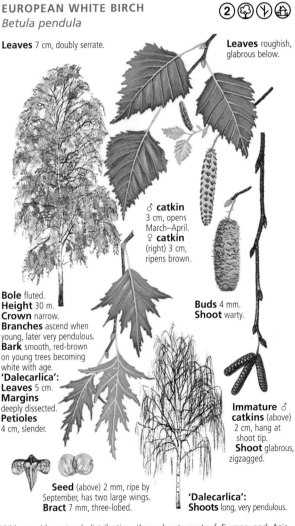

Leaves 7 cm, doubly serrate.

Leaves roughish, glabrous below.

♂ catkin 3 cm, opens March–April.
♀ catkin (right) 3 cm, ripens brown.

Bole fluted.
Height 30 m.
Crown narrow.
Branches ascend when young, later very pendulous.
Bark smooth, red-brown on young trees becoming white with age.
'Dalecarlica':
Leaves 5 cm.
Margins deeply dissected.
Petioles 4 cm, slender.

Buds 4 mm.
Shoot warty.

Immature ♂ catkins (above) 2 cm, hang at shoot tip.
Shoot glabrous, zigzagged.

Seed (above) 2 mm, ripe by September, has two large wings.
Bract 7 mm, three-lobed.

'Dalecarlica':
Shoots long, very pendulous.

With a wide natural distribution throughout most of Europe and Asia Minor, European white birch is recognizable by its distinctive bark and hairless twigs. It thrives on light, dry and sandy soils, dislikes shade and is plentiful on heaths and moorlands. 'Dalecarlica' (Swedish birch), from southern Sweden, is one of its graceful cultivars.

RIVER BIRCH
Betula nigra

④ 🐿️ 🌱 🌳 🍂

Bud 6 mm, covered with pale hairs in summer, glabrous, shiny brown in winter.

♀ **catkin** 4 cm, erect, cylindric. 1 cm hairy peduncle.

Shoot densely hairy at first, becoming shiny red-brown by first winter, later dull and darker.

Bract with narrow, erect, ciliate lobes.
Fruit a winged nutlet.

Leaves 8 cm, ovate, midrib hairy below.
Base cuneate.
Petiole hairy, flattened.

Leaves lustrous above.
Apex acute.
Margins coarsely double serrate.

Bark peels in papery flakes; black, pale pink-brown in fissures.

This species is native to lowland sites in the southern and eastern United States and is the only birch that grows in the extreme Southeast. It grows to 25 m with an irregular crown, usually dividing into two or three stems, and can tolerate prolonged flooding.

GRAY BIRCH
Betula populifolia

③ 🐿️ 🌱 🌳 🍂

Leaves 8 cm, drawn out at apex.
Petiole 3 cm, with black glands.

Height 12 m.
Crown open, narrow, irregular cone.
Bole often divided.
Shoot slender, glandular.

♀ **catkin** 2 cm, hairy, cylindric, pendent or spreading.

Margins coarsely doubly serrate, except at base.

Bud 6 mm, ovoid, acute.
Bark thin, tight, gray-white.

Gray birch is very similar to Paper birch but can be identified by the long, tail-like apex of its leaf and its tight, rather than peeling bark. It is restricted to the Northeast and springs up rapidly in barren soils, such as abandoned farmland.

PAPER BIRCH
Betula papyrifera

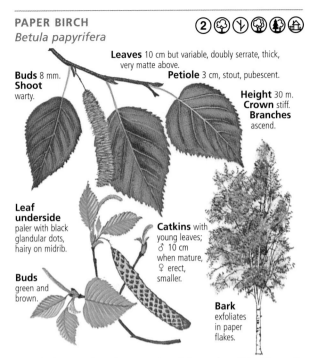

Leaves 10 cm but variable, doubly serrate, thick, very matte above.

Buds 8 mm.
Shoot warty.

Petiole 3 cm, stout, pubescent.

Height 30 m.
Crown stiff.
Branches ascend.

Leaf underside paler with black glandular dots, hairy on midrib.

Buds green and brown.

Catkins with young leaves; ♂ 10 cm when mature, ♀ erect, smaller.

Bark exfoliates in paper flakes.

Paper birch grows throughout Canada and the northern United States. Its creamy or pinkish-white bark was once used by Native Americans to cover their canoes. Szechuan birch (*B. platyphylla* var. *szechuanica*) has a chalky white bark and leathery, 12 cm leaves, glaucous below.

YELLOW BIRCH
Betula alleghaniensis

Leaves 11 cm, elliptic, deep green.
Margins irregularly doubly serrate.

Leaves 12–15 pairs of veins, hairy below.
Petiole 2 cm, grooved.

Bark bronze, yellowish or gray, peeling, aromatic, ignitable even when wet.

Apex acute.
Shoot dull gray-brown, initially pubescent.

♀ **catkin** 4 cm, erect, subsessile, with spreading scales.

Yellow birch is named after its vivid autumn colors and grows to 30 m in its native eastern United States. It has an open or ovoid domed crown, and is notable for the long hairs on leaves and shoots.

EUROPEAN ALDER / BLACK ALDER
Alnus glutinosa

③ 🌳 🍂 ⊛

Height 25 m.
Crown broad, conic, often on two or three stems, purplish.

Flowers open on ♂ and ♀ catkins, before leaves in late March. ♂ flowers yellow, ♀ flowers 6 mm, erect, red.

♂ catkins 5 cm when fully open.

Catkins exposed over winter, purple.

Bark fissured, gray, in small plates.

Leaves 10 cm, persist until very end of autumn.
Petiole 3.5 cm, speckled.
Buds 7 mm, flat, on 3 mm stalks, narrowed at base, with 2-3 scales.

Shoot purple by autumn.

♀ catkins 1.5 cm, ovoid, set in clusters 1-4.

Leaves glabrous, paler below.
Vein axils tufted.

Seed small-winged nutlet.
Leaf margins slightly waved.
Teeth irregular, shallow.
Veins impressed.

♀ catkin woody by time it ripens and releases seeds in October, very persistent as empty "cone."

Alders grow in damp locations and have buoyant seeds that are distributed by water. The deep roots help to conserve river banks and improve the soil with their nitrogen-fixing nodules. The tree survives on drier sites but does not regenerate there. 'Laciniata' and 'Imperalis' are forms with deeply lobed leaves.

RED ALDER
Alnus rubra

♀ **strobilus** 3 cm, ovoid or oblong, in clusters of up to six on orange peduncles to 15 cm, persist after opening.
Fruits round with narrow wings.

Leaves red-haired below.
Apex acute.

♀ **catkins** red, scaly, exposed over winter.

Leaves 15 cm, ovate to elliptic.
Petiole grooved.
Bud 1 cm, dark red, stalked, scurfy.
Leaf base rounded or cuneate.
Shoot at first green with long hairs, becoming bright, shiny red, angled.

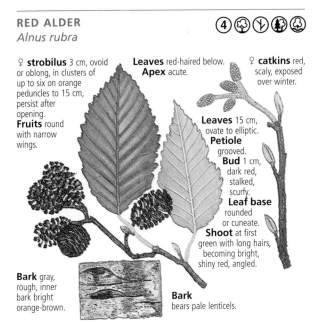

Bark gray, rough, inner bark bright orange-brown.

Bark bears pale lenticels.

With a wide range on the West Coast of the United States, Red alder forms a domed tree to 25 m, which is a prodigious colonizer of bare ground, preceding longer-lived conifers. White alder (*A. rhombifolia*) grows farther inland and has singly, not doubly, serrated leaves.

FILBERT
Corylus maxima

Apex acuminate.

Leaves 13 cm, cordate, broad obovate or rounded.
Margins coarsely double-serrate.
Petiole 1 cm, stout, pubescent, glandular.

Leaves very hairy on undersides.

Fruit subtended by incised leafy involucre or bract.

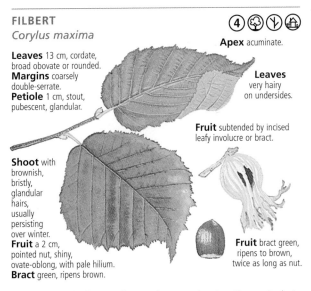

Shoot with brownish, bristly, glandular hairs, usually persisting over winter.
Fruit a 2 cm, pointed nut, shiny, ovate-oblong, with pale hilium.
Bract green, ripens brown.

Fruit bract green, ripens to brown, twice as long as nut.

Filbert, a large shrub or small tree native to southeastern Europe, is planted in North America for its sweet, oily nuts. Similar native species include the shrubby but occasionally tree-like Beaked hazel (*C. cornuta*), which has finely toothed leaves and an involucre constricted beyond the nut.

EUROPEAN HAZEL
Corylus Avellana

♂ **catkins** 5 cm, open February.
♀ **catkins** 5 mm.

Shoot covered in long stiff hairs with swollen tips.
Leaf 10 cm, hairy above and below doubly serrate.

Nuts 2 cm, ripen brown in clusters of 1–4.

Height 10 m.
Crown shrubby.
Nuts in papery, toothed bracts.

European hazel, usually growing as a shrub, is native to almost all of Europe. It is recognized by its nuts, densely haired twigs and leaves and its plump, male catkins. Its female catkins are small and have red styles. 'Contorta,' with twisted stems, is a useful ornamental.

EASTERN HOP HORNBEAM
Ostrya virginiana

Leaves 15 cm, oblong-lanceolate, yellow-green, paler below; underside very hairy at first, later tufts in axils.
Margins doubly serrate, teeth incurved.
Veins 11–15 pairs.

Shoot light green, hairy at first, orange and lustrous by first summer, dark brown when mature.
Bud 6 mm, ovoid, acute.

Bark thick, reddish-brown, broken into narrow adpressed plates, shaggy at ends.

♂ **catkins** exposed over winter.

Fruit a winged nutlet to 1 cm, in brown hop-like bladder, in 7 cm clusters.

Eastern hop hornbeam is a native of the eastern United States and forms a round-topped tree to 20 m. Ironwood (*O. Knowltonii*), or Western hop hornbeam, a rare tree from the Southwest, has smaller 5 cm leaves with five to eight pairs of veins. The seed, totally enclosed by the involucre, distinguishes *Ostrya* from *Carpinus*.

AMERICAN HORNBEAM
Carpinus caroliniana

③ 🐿 🌱 🌳 🌲

Leaves 10 cm, oval or ovate, long-pointed, dull green above, light, yellow-green below. **Base** rounded or cuneate, usually oblique. **Veins** slender, deeply impressed.
Petiole 1 cm, hairy, bright red when young.

Leaf glabrous above, hairy in vein axils below.

Shoot slender, initially with long, silky white hairs, becoming red-brown shiny, later dull gray, tinged red.

Margins doubly serrate. **Teeth** sharp, spreading, glandular.

Fruit in 8–11 pairs, a nutlet subtended by trident bract, hanging in 15 cm clusters on slender pubescent red-brown stems.
Bract leafy, green, ripening to brown.
Involucre 4 x 2.5 cm, coarsely toothed, often only on one margin.

Catkins 4 cm, appear with leaves in spring.

Nutlet 8 mm.

♂ **catkins** bud overwinter, open in spring. **Buds** 3 mm, ovoid, acute. **Scales** brown with white margins.

Height 15 m.
Crown usually bushy, dense and flat-topped.
Branches zigzag, slender, wiry, pendulous at tips.

Bole short, characteristically fluted.

Bark smooth, broad horizontal patches.

American hornbeam, native to eastern United States from the Great Lakes as far south as Honduras, is sometimes called Bluebeech on account of the similarity of its bark to beech. It is a small tree, often a shrub, and assumes rich autumnal colors. European hornbeam (*C. Betulus*) is more tree-like in habit, reaching 25 m, and is often planted as an ornamental in North America. It is best distinguished by its winter buds, which are slender, spindle-shaped and 6 mm or more in length.

The members of this large, mainly temperate family have simple and alternate leaves and fruit in the form of nuts. These are either fully enclosed by an involucre (or cupule) of fused bracts as in *Fagus* and *Castanea*, or merely supported by it as in *Quercus*. Male and female flowers are carried in separate catkins on the same tree.

EUROPEAN BEECH
Fagus sylvatica

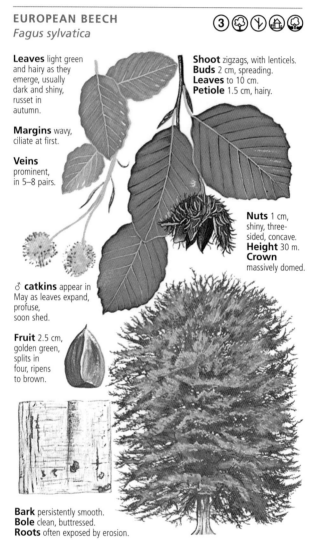

Leaves light green and hairy as they emerge, usually dark and shiny, russet in autumn.

Margins wavy, ciliate at first.

Veins prominent, in 5–8 pairs.

Shoot zigzags, with lenticels.
Buds 2 cm, spreading.
Leaves to 10 cm.
Petiole 1.5 cm, hairy.

Nuts 1 cm, shiny, three-sided, concave.
Height 30 m.
Crown massively domed.

♂ **catkins** appear in May as leaves expand, profuse, soon shed.

Fruit 2.5 cm, golden green, splits in four, ripens to brown.

Bark persistently smooth.
Bole clean, buttressed.
Roots often exposed by erosion.

This majestic tree is instantly recognizable by its smooth bark. Although its natural range includes most of continental Europe and southern Britain, it has been widely planted elsewhere for its timber, and thrives on chalk and limestone. Oriental beech (*F. orientalis*), from the Balkans and Asia Minor, has leafy cupules and broader, larger leaves which have seven to 10 pairs of veins.

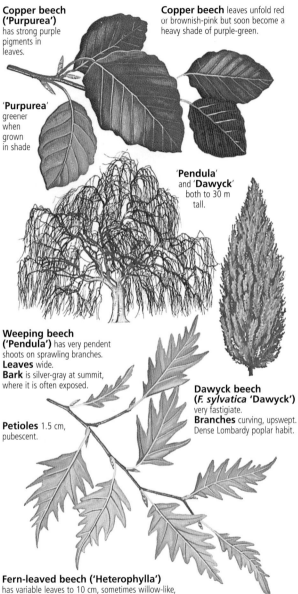

Copper beech ('Purpurea') has strong purple pigments in leaves.

Copper beech leaves unfold red or brownish-pink but soon become a heavy shade of purple-green.

'Purpurea' greener when grown in shade

'Pendula' and 'Dawyck' both to 30 m tall.

Weeping beech ('Pendula') has very pendent shoots on sprawling branches.
Leaves wide.
Bark is silver-gray at summit, where it is often exposed.

Petioles 1.5 cm, pubescent.

Dawyck beech (*F. sylvatica* 'Dawyck') very fastigiate.
Branches curving, upswept. Dense Lombardy poplar habit.

Fern-leaved beech ('Heterophylla') has variable leaves to 10 cm, sometimes willow-like, very deeply cut, hairy below.

Beech is noted for the variety of its cultivars. Copper beech, the most common, may have deep purple ('Purpurea') or red-leaved clones. Weeping and Dawyck beeches have distinctive habits, 'Heterophylla' has remarkable leaves. Others include 'Zlatia,' with new foliage golden until July, and 'Rotundifolia' with small, almost round leaves and variegated forms.

AMERICAN BEECH
Fagus grandifolia

③ 🌳 🍂 🌲 🏠

Buds 2.5 cm, slender, spindle-shaped, pale brown, set singly at sharp angle, made of many imbricate scales, finely hairy at apex.

Shoot green initially, becoming reddish-brown by winter, later ash-gray; has long hairs at first, soon lost.

Bark smooth, gray.

Height 30 m, often surrounded by suckers.
Crown rounded, compact, with spreading, slightly drooping branches.

Shoot slender, often zigzagged, spotted with oblong orange lenticels.

Petiole 1.3 cm, hairy.

Leaves 15 cm, oblong-obovate or elliptic, acuminate, with 11–15 pairs of veins.
Base cuneate.

Nuts 2 cm, triangular, in pairs, shiny brown.

♂ **catkins** a bunch of pendent stamens.
Cupule woody, four-valved, hairy, with recurved prickles.

Margins coarsely serrate.
Teeth spreading or incurved.
Cupule on stout, hairy peduncle.

American beech, native to the eastern North America from New Brunswick and the Great Lakes to the Gulf, is the only beech which produces suckers, and a thicket is often formed around the tree. The leaves are usually glabrous except along the midrib and on the underside veins, but downy forms are occasionally found. In the southern part of its range, *F. g.* var. *caroliniana* is usually encountered, differing in its firmer, less coarsely toothed leaves, which are a darker, lustrous green above.

Oaks *Quercus*

This large and important group of noble trees comprises over 400 separate species as well as many hybrids and is found throughout the temperate areas of Europe, Asia and North America. All oaks are noted for their acorns, which may ripen over either one or two years and provide the best means of identification. Another is the arrangement of leaves and buds, which cluster at the end of shoots and separate *Quercus* from most other genera. Oaks have separate male and female flowers appearing on the same tree; the females are erect but inconspicuous while the males appear in long, pendulous catkins at the same time as the new leaves open. The genus contains both deciduous and evergreen species.

SESSILE OAK
Quercus petraea

Height 40 m.
Crown tall.

Branches straight, spreading, radiating.
Bole long.

Buds 6 mm, ovoid, with many finely pubescent scales, set in clusters at shoot tips, open in May.
Shoot shiny, straighter than that of English oak.

Bark thick, vertically fissured.
Leaves 12 cm, hard or leathery, widest at middle, very flat, not so prone to caterpillar attacks as English oak.

Leaf base cuneate, without auricles.
Acorns in clusters of 2–6, sessile or on very short peduncles.
Leaf underside has brownish pubescence on veins.
Lobes shallow, in 5–9 pairs.

Petiole to 3 cm.

With a long bole that extends well into the crown, this oak can be further distinguished from English oak by its almost stalkless, slightly smaller acorns and the wedge-shaped bases of its leaves. It grows well on light, acid, stony soil. The similar Downy oak (*Q. pubescens*) has densely hairy leaves and shoots.

ENGLISH OAK
Quercus robur

Foliage set in bunches.

Height 35 m.
Crown wide.

Branches large and heavy, very irregular, bear sprouts.

Crown irregularly domed.
Bole short, very stout.
Bark fissures into tiers of rectangular plates.

Lobes in 4 or 5 pairs, deeply cut.

Leaves have small auricles at bases.
Leaf stalk 1 cm.

Leaves to 12 cm, widest above middle.

Acorns 2.5 cm, usually in pairs on long, thin peduncle to 10 cm.

Cypress oak (*Q. robur* 'Fastigiata') has upswept crown, narrow when young; grows in central Europe.

English oak is very common throughout Europe and is also grown in the United States. It thrives on heavy clay but can adapt to the lighter, stonier soil favored by *Q. petraea*. Unlike Sessile oak, its leaves are glabrous below and have auricles at their bases. Its acorns are carried on long stalks and give the tree its alternative name of Pedunculate oak. Many predators, such as the larvae of the Purple hairstreak butterfly (Quercusia quercus), attack its young foliage but do no permanent damage since further flushes of growth occur in September.

WHITE OAK
Quercus alba

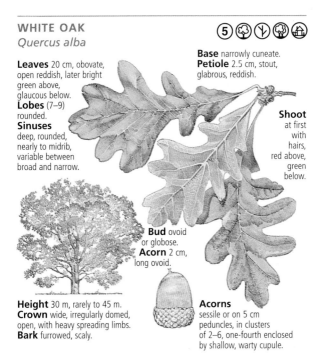

Leaves 20 cm, obovate, open reddish, later bright green above, glaucous below.
Lobes (7–9) rounded.
Sinuses deep, rounded, nearly to midrib, variable between broad and narrow.

Base narrowly cuneate.
Petiole 2.5 cm, stout, glabrous, reddish.

Shoot at first with hairs, red above, green below.

Bud ovoid or globose.
Acorn 2 cm, long ovoid.

Height 30 m, rarely to 45 m.
Crown wide, irregularly domed, open, with heavy spreading limbs.
Bark furrowed, scaly.

Acorns sessile or on 5 cm peduncles, in clusters of 2–6, one-fourth enclosed by shallow, warty cupule.

This is the most common of the white oaks, which is a group recognized by their rounded lobes. This important lumber tree is found throughout the eastern United States and is recognizable by its leaves, the largest of any oak, and the shallow cupule of its acorn.

OREGON WHITE OAK
Quercus Garryana

Leaves 15 x 5–12 cm, thick, leathery, hairy below.
Lobes (5–9) may be slightly toothed.

Sinuses very deep.

Acorn 3 cm, ovoid, sessile or short-stalked.
Cupule up to one-third encloses acorn, very thin, loose, scaly, hairy outside, inside glabrous, pale.

Apex toothed or blunt.
Base cuneate or rounded.

Margin down-turned.

Petiole 2.5 cm, stout, hairy

Bud 1.3 cm, acute, hairy.

This species resembles White oak but is found along the western coastal strip from mid-California northward, being the only oak in Washington and British Columbia. It grows to 20 m with a broad crown, and the sweet acorns are edible.

CALIFORNIA WHITE OAK
Quercus lobata

⑨ 🌿 🍂 🌳

Height 30 m.
Crown open, wide, spreading, dividing low.
Branches drooping at tips.
Acorn 3.5 cm,
long conic.

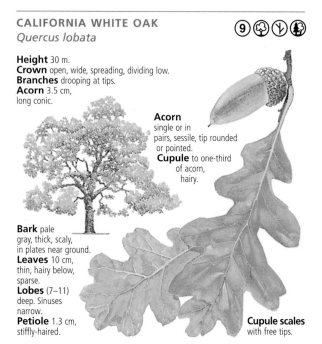

Acorn
single or in
pairs, sessile, tip rounded
or pointed.
Cupule to one-third
of acorn,
hairy.

Bark pale
gray, thick, scaly,
in plates near ground.
Leaves 10 cm,
thin, hairy below,
sparse.
Lobes (7–11)
deep. Sinuses
narrow.
Petiole 1.3 cm,
stiffly-haired.

Cupule scales
with free tips.

The largest of the western oaks, this species, also known as Valley oak, occasionally grows as high as 45 m and can be recognized by its unusual long-conic acorn. The buds are orange-brown and hairy, and the acorn kernel is sweet.

POST OAK
Quercus stellata

⑤ 🌿 🍂 🌳

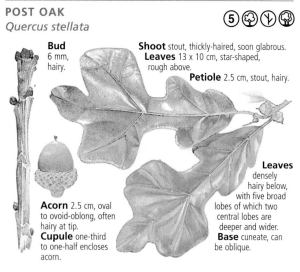

Bud
6 mm,
hairy.

Shoot stout, thickly-haired, soon glabrous.
Leaves 13 x 10 cm, star-shaped,
rough above.
Petiole 2.5 cm, stout, hairy.

Leaves
densely
hairy below,
with five broad
lobes of which two
central lobes are
deeper and wider.
Base cuneate, can
be oblique.

Acorn 2.5 cm, oval
to ovoid-oblong, often
hairy at tip.
Cupule one-third
to one-half encloses
acorn.

Post oak rarely grows beyond 25 m, with a rounded crown, and is distinguished from other white oaks by the rough upper surface of its leaves. It is found throughout southern and eastern United States and is an important lumber tree, producing a tough wood.

CHESTNUT OAK
Quercus prinus

④ 🌰 🍂 🌳

Shoot stout, with pale red- or orange-brown hairs at first, later glabrous, ash-gray.
Acorn 3.5 cm, shiny, on short, stout, hairy 1 cm stalk.

Leaves obovate or elliptic.
Acorns single or in pairs.

Leaves 22 cm.

Height 30 m.

Bole divided.

Cupule shallow, thin.
Scales fused, warty, hairy.
Margins with large crenate teeth.
Apex acuminate.

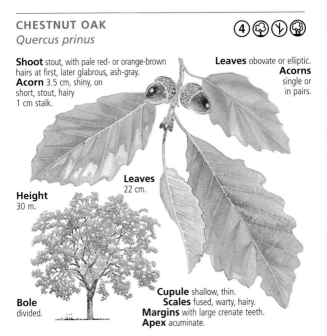

Chestnut oak, from New England, is distinctive in its foliage, which resembles that of chestnut without the spiny tips to the lobes. Swamp chestnut oak (*Q. Michauxii*), from the Southeast, has obovate leaves, silvery white below, and cuneate scales on the thick cupule.

CHINKAPIN OAK
Quercus Muehlenbergii

⑤ 🌰 🍂 🌳

Shoot slender, very hairy at first, red-brown, later glabrous, gray.
Bud 4 mm, acute, ovoid.
Acorn 2 cm, ovoid, chestnut brown or nearly black, sessile or short-stalked.
Cupule up to one-half enclosing acorn.
Base cuneate.

Leaves 18 cm, obovate or oblong-lanceolate, shiny yellow-green above, whitish, hairy below.
Petiole 4 cm, slender.

Apex acuminate.
Margins regularly serrate.

Scales free at tips.

Teeth incurved, ending in glandular tipped point.

Cupule thin.

Growing in the East to 20 m, or rarely 50 m, this species is named after the resemblance of its foliage to Chinkapin chestnut. Swamp white oak (*Q. bicolor*) has broad obovate-oblong leaves and a 3 cm acorn on a 10 cm peduncle.

BUR OAK
Quercus macrocarpa

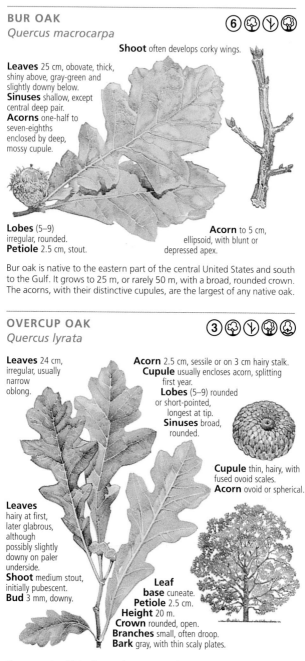

Shoot often develops corky wings.

Leaves 25 cm, obovate, thick, shiny above, gray-green and slightly downy below.
Sinuses shallow, except central deep pair.
Acorns one-half to seven-eighths enclosed by deep, mossy cupule.

Lobes (5–9) irregular, rounded.
Petiole 2.5 cm, stout.

Acorn to 5 cm, ellipsoid, with blunt or depressed apex.

Bur oak is native to the eastern part of the central United States and south to the Gulf. It grows to 25 m, or rarely 50 m, with a broad, rounded crown. The acorns, with their distinctive cupules, are the largest of any native oak.

OVERCUP OAK
Quercus lyrata

Leaves 24 cm, irregular, usually narrow oblong.

Acorn 2.5 cm, sessile or on 3 cm hairy stalk.
Cupule usually encloses acorn, splitting first year.
Lobes (5–9) rounded or short-pointed, longest at tip.
Sinuses broad, rounded.

Cupule thin, hairy, with fused ovoid scales.
Acorn ovoid or spherical.

Leaves hairy at first, later glabrous, although possibly slightly downy on paler underside.
Shoot medium stout, initially pubescent.
Bud 3 mm, downy.

Leaf base cuneate.
Petiole 2.5 cm.
Height 20 m.
Crown rounded, open.
Branches small, often droop.
Bark gray, with thin scaly plates.

Overcup oak, which often makes no more than a comparatively small oak to 20 m, is native to the southeastern United States and is easily identified by its cupule, which usually completely encloses the acorn. Like other white oaks, the acorns are produced on the current year's shoots and ripen in the first year.

TURKEY OAK
Quercus cerris

Stipules long,
2.5 cm, round all buds.
Shoot pubescent.

Bark fissures
shallow; deeper
and plating
on old trees.

Acorn
large, 2.5 cm,
in sessile, "mossy"
cup whose 4 mm
filaments are parted,
pointing upward on
upper half of cup.

Leaves 13 cm,
very variable, rough, glossy above;
gray, downy below.
Lobes angular, usually in 5–9 pairs.

This hardy native of southern and southwest Europe naturalizes easily and
grows vigorously into a mature and massively domed tree which can reach
40 m. It is more upright than *Q. robur*; unlike all other oaks, it has stipules
arranged around all its buds.

LUCOMBE OAK
Quercus hispanica 'Lucombeana'

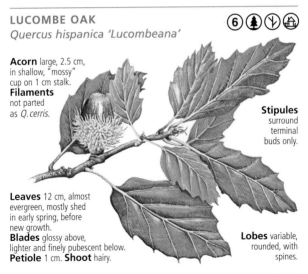

Acorn large, 2.5 cm,
in shallow, "mossy"
cup on 1 cm stalk.
Filaments
not parted
as *Q. cerris*.

Stipules
surround
terminal
buds only.

Leaves 12 cm, almost
evergreen, mostly shed
in early spring, before
new growth.
Blades glossy above,
lighter and finely pubescent below.
Petiole 1 cm. **Shoot** hairy.

Lobes variable,
rounded, with
spines.

Lucombe oak is a form of the natural but variable hybrid of Turkey oak and
Cork oak. It inherited the habit, leaf shape, stipulate buds and acorns of
the former species and the bark and semi-evergreen nature of the latter.
This tree was first raised by William Lucombe, an Exeter nurseryman, in
about 1765.

ALGERIAN OAK
Quercus canariensis

⑨ Ⓡ 🌲 🌱 🏛

Leaf 15 cm.
Teeth shallow, up to 13 pairs, smaller nearer tip.

Leaf matte and paler below.
Leaf stalk 1 cm, wooly at first.

Acorns 2 cm, in shallow cups on short stalks; ripen in first year.

Shoot glabrous, wooly initially.
Buds 7 mm, conic.

Height 30 m.
Crown broad conic when young, domed when mature, semi-evergreen.
Branches ascend sharply.
Bark deeply fissured.

One of the largest trees to retain a proportion of green leaves throughout the winter, this species is native to north Africa, Spain and Portugal. Caucasian oak (*Q. macranthera*) is similar but its wholly deciduous leaves have more rounded lobes and it carries dark red, shiny buds on pubescent shoots.

HUNGARIAN OAK
Quercus Frainetto

⑥ Ⓡ 🌳 🌱 🏛

Buds large, to 1 cm, with many downy scales.
Shoot downy becoming glabrous; ridged when tree young.

Lobes large, in 7–11 pairs, with lobulate margins.
Sinuses the most deeply cut of any oak.
Leaves large, to 25 cm, with basal auricles.
Blade sub-glossy above, hairy below.
Petiole 1 cm, pubescent.

Height 30 m.
Crown strongly domed.
Branches radiate.
Bole stout.
Bark dark, fissured.

Native to southeastern Europe and planted as an ornamental in park lands in North America, this vigorous species, also known as Italian oak, is unmistakable in its boldly lobed foliage. Its acorns, similar to those of Algerian oak, ripen in one year, a characteristic of all the white oaks, and are carried at the end of the current year's shoot in a sessile cup with downy scales.

RED OAK
Quercus rubra

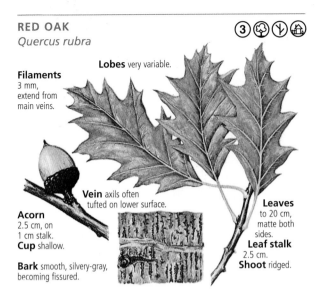

Lobes very variable.

Filaments 3 mm, extend from main veins.

Vein axils often tufted on lower surface.

Acorn 2.5 cm, on 1 cm stalk.
Cup shallow.

Bark smooth, silvery-gray, becoming fissured.

Leaves to 20 cm, matte both sides.
Leaf stalk 2.5 cm.
Shoot ridged.

Glorious in the autumnal hues which give Red oak its name, this sturdy species from the eastern United States typifies a large group of New World oaks, which have filamented leaves and smoothish barks. Red oak has heavy branches and grows vigorously to produce a broadly domed crown reaching 35 m.

SHUMARD OAK
Quercus Shumardii

Leaves simple, alternate, deciduous, obovate with 5–7 deeply incised lobes following the major lateral pinnate veins.

Lobes terminate in one or more acuminate bristle tips.
Leaves leathery, dark green, smooth on top and up to 12 x 20 cm with slender petioles to 5 cm.
Leaves turn red to reddish-purple in autumn.
Twigs smooth, grayish, pointed terminal buds about 6 mm long that appear waxy.

Fruit acorn, borne on short stalks, often in pairs.
Acorn 2–3 cm long, black striations, sits in a shallow, thick cap, matures the second year.

Bark gray-brown, smooth when young, becoming narrowly fissured and almost black at maturity.

Shumard oak is a large tree valued for its lumber that grows to 30 m and is found in the eastern and southern United States on moist soils. It is widely used in landscaping for its shade and fall coloration value. Texas red oak (*Q. Texana*) has a similar appearance, though a somewhat smaller tree, and is more tolerant of drought and rocky soil conditions.

SCARLET OAK
Quercus coccinea

5 🌳 🍂 🏠

Shoot olive, later gray, with prominent lenticels.

Buds pointed, ovoid, with ciliately margined scales.

Leaves to 14 cm, very glossy on undersides.

Petiole to 6 cm.

Lobes in three pairs, bristle-tipped.

Autumn leaves begin to turn on one or two branches only, some persist until January.

Scarlet oak has a more restricted range in the eastern United States than Red oak and assumes much richer autumnal colors, turning deep scarlet. For the rest of the year, it is identifiable by its smaller, glossy, more deeply lobed leaves and smaller acorns. Its bud scales have pubescent margins, and the tree grows to 25 m.

BLACK OAK
Quercus velutina

5 🌳 🍂 🌲 🌲

Leaves shiny above.

Leaves 23 cm.

Bud 12 mm, angled, hairy.
Shoot stout, densely hairy at first.
Leaves hard, leathery.
Petiole stout.
Leaves have 5–7 lobes ending in bristly tips.

Acorn 2 cm.
Cup dull, scaly.

Leaves coppery-brown below, with reddish, axillary tufts.

Acorn one-third to one-half enclosed by involucre.

Widely distributed in the eastern United States, Black oak grows to 45 m with a narrow, open crown. The tree is distinguishable by the deep orange color of its inner bark showing in the fissures, its unusually tough leaves and its initially hairy shoots.

PIN OAK
Quercus palustris

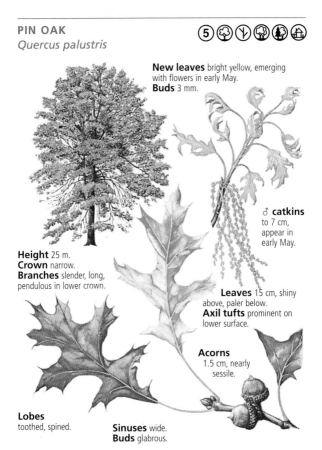

New leaves bright yellow, emerging with flowers in early May.
Buds 3 mm.

♂ **catkins** to 7 cm, appear in early May.

Height 25 m.
Crown narrow.
Branches slender, long, pendulous in lower crown.

Leaves 15 cm, shiny above, paler below.
Axil tufts prominent on lower surface.

Acorns 1.5 cm, nearly sessile.

Lobes toothed, spined.

Sinuses wide.
Buds glabrous.

Small pin-like branches, which sometimes grow on its bole, help to identify this bottomland tree. Its prominent axillary tufts and its shallow acorn cups are also distinctive. Pin oak's narrowly lobed leaves turn red in autumn but not as richly as some of its cousins. Northern pin oak (*Q. ellipsoidalis*) has sessile acorns to 2.5 cm.

SOUTHERN RED OAK
Quercus falcata

(6) (🌰) (🌱) (🌳)

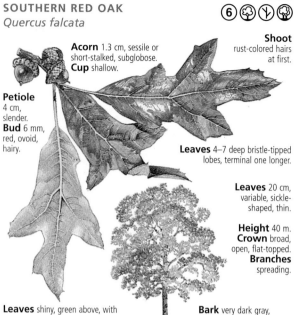

Acorn 1.3 cm, sessile or short-stalked, subglobose. **Cup** shallow.

Shoot rust-colored hairs at first.

Petiole 4 cm, slender. **Bud** 6 mm, red, ovoid, hairy.

Leaves 4–7 deep bristle-tipped lobes, terminal one longer.

Leaves 20 cm, variable, sickle-shaped, thin.

Height 40 m. **Crown** broad, open, flat-topped. **Branches** spreading.

Leaves shiny, green above, with russet or gray pubescence below.

Bark very dark gray, fissured with scaly ridges.

This variable species is native to the southeastern United States. The foliage illustrated above is typical, but sometimes leaves with three shallow lobes at the apex are found. Its var. *pagodifolia* has stout hairy petioles and leaves with six–11 lobes.

CALIFORNIA BLACK OAK
Quercus Kelloggii

(9) (🌳) (🌱) (🌳) (🌲)

Lobes have several teeth.

Teeth bristly.

Bud 6 mm, ovoid, acute, ciliate. **Acorn** 4 cm, oblong to obovate hairy at acute apex. **Petiole** 5 cm, slender.

Leaves 20 cm, with 7 (rarely 5) deep lobes, shiny green above, silvery-white below.
Acorn solitary or in small cluster on short stalk, up to half enclosed by thin, scaly involucre.

Shoot at first hairy.

Although similar to some eastern United States oaks, such as Black oak, this species is the only red oak in the western United States and is easily identifiable in its native Oregon and California. It grows to 40 m with a broad, rounded crown and dark brown bark, becoming fissured with age and divided into oblong, scaly plates.

LIVE OAK
Quercus virginiana

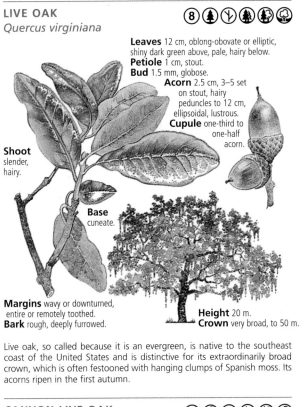

Leaves 12 cm, oblong-obovate or elliptic, shiny dark green above, pale, hairy below.
Petiole 1 cm, stout.
Bud 1.5 mm, globose.
Acorn 2.5 cm, 3–5 set on stout, hairy peduncles to 12 cm, ellipsoidal, lustrous.
Cupule one-third to one-half acorn.

Shoot slender, hairy.

Base cuneate.

Margins wavy or downturned, entire or remotely toothed.
Bark rough, deeply furrowed.

Height 20 m.
Crown very broad, to 50 m.

Live oak, so called because it is an evergreen, is native to the southeast coast of the United States and is distinctive for its extraordinarily broad crown, which is often festooned with hanging clumps of Spanish moss. Its acorns ripen in the first autumn.

CANYON LIVE OAK
Quercus chrysolepis

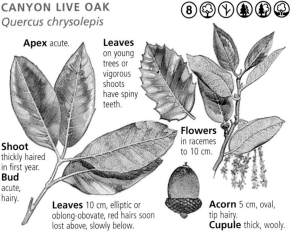

Apex acute.

Leaves on young trees or vigorous shoots have spiny teeth.

Shoot thickly haired in first year.
Bud acute, hairy.

Leaves 10 cm, elliptic or oblong-obovate, red hairs soon lost above, slowly below.

Flowers in racemes to 10 cm.

Acorn 5 cm, oval, tip hairy.
Cupule thick, wooly.

This southwestern United States oak reaches 25 m. Spined and entire leaves may be found on the same branch and persist three to four years. Interior live oak (*Q. Wislizenii*), from California and with smaller acorns, has an acorn more than half enclosed in the cupule. It keeps its leaves for two years while California live oak (*Q. agrifolia*) is one-third enclosed and loses its leaves yearly.

WILLOW OAK
Quercus phellos

⑦ 🌳 🍂 🌲 🏠

Leaf 12 cm.
Petiole 4 mm.

Acorn
1 cm, nearly
sessile.

Leaves
entire.

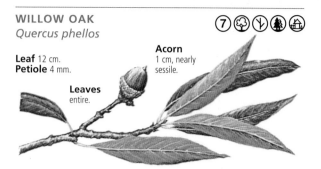

From the southeastern United States, Willow oak has foliage which opens yellow and becomes golden in autumn. Schoch oak (*Q. x Schochiana*) is its hybrid with Pin oak and has leaves with one or two lobes. Shingle oak (*Q. imbricaria*) has wider, entire leaves.

SHINGLE OAK
Quercus imbricaria

⑤ 🌳 🍂 🌳 🌿

Leaves 15 cm, elliptic or
oblong-obovate, shiny above,
pale, hairy below.

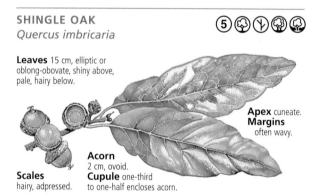

Apex cuneate.
Margins
often wavy.

Acorn
2 cm, ovoid.
Scales
hairy, adpressed.
Cupule one-third
to one-half encloses acorn.

Shingle oak rarely grows much above 20 m tall. It has a slender, rounded crown and a scaly, gray-brown bark with irregular shallow fissures. Shingle oak is a native of the northeastern United States.

LAUREL OAK
Quercus laurifolia

Acorn 2 cm, ovoid or hemispherical, sessile or short-stalked, usually single.
Cupule shallow, to one-fourth of acorn.
Scales pubescent.

Leaves 10 cm, elliptic, very lustrous above, duller below, tapered at base and apex.

Leaves hairy at first, lobed irregularly.
Leaves flat or wavy.

Shoot slender, glabrous, with reddish tinge.
Bud 7 mm, acute.

Believed to be a natural hybrid between Willow oak and Water oak (*Q. nigra*) this tree grows to 20 m, or rarely 30 m, with a dense, rounded crown. It is often planted as a shade tree along the Gulf and Atlantic coasts of the American Southeast.

CORK OAK
Quercus Suber

Leaves 7 cm, hard, glossy above, gray felted below.
Margins crinkled.
Lobes very shallow, tipped with short, blunt spines.
Petiole 1 cm.

Shoot short-haired.
Buds 2 mm, ovoid.

Bark very thick with wide fissures and corky ridges.

Height 20 m.
Crown open, domed.
Branches heavy, twisted.
Bole red-brown where bark removed.

The leaves of this Mediterranean tree resemble those of the Holm and Turkey oaks. Its useful bark, harvested commercially about every ten years, is similar to that of Lucombe oak and Chinese cork oak (*Q. variabilis*) whose wholly deciduous leaves have filamented teeth and are silvery-gray below.

HOLM OAK/HOLLY OAK
Quercus Ilex

Young leaves
yellow, hairy.

♂ **flowers** open in June.

Leaves
10 cm,
variable.

Acorns 2 cm, pointed.

Bark thin, in small plates,
often curling.

Leaves glossy, densely
pubescent below.
Spined leaves carried by young
trees and sucker shoots.

A broadly domed species reaching up to 30 m, Holm oak becomes brighter for a brief period in June when its new, yellowish leaves open. Kermes oak (*Q. coccifera*) is another native of the Mediterranean and hosts the Kermes insect from which scarlet grain dye is prepared. Young trees have Holly-like leaves giving it the common name Holly oak.

BLACKJACK OAK
Quercus marilandica

Bud 1 cm, rusty-haired.

Acorn 2 cm, ovoid-oblong, yellow-brown,
often found in pairs, on short peduncle.
Cupule covers one-third to two-thirds
acorn, thick, red-brown, hairy inside.
Scales loosely overlapping,
ciliate, hairy.

Shoot stout,
initially
thickly haired,
becoming
ash-gray.

Bud angled,
conical.
Petiole
2 cm, stout,
yellow.
Leaves 18 cm,
obovate, as broad
as long, with 3 (rarely 5)
shallow lobes ending in
a bristly tip at broad apex.

Leaves shiny yellow-green above, scurfy, hairy below.
Margins entire or toothed.
Base rounded or cuneate.

Remarkable for the shape of its leaves, this native of central and south-eastern United States grows to 15 m with an irregular crown and rough, blackish bark furrowed into square plates.

TANBARK OAK
Lithocarpus densiflorus

Flowers unisexual,
♂ are usually borne in
erect catkins,
♀ occur at the base
of the male catkin similar
to the chestnut.
Fruit very dark nut,
partly enclosed in
a spineless, shallow
cup resembling an acorn;
fruit takes two years
to mature.

Leaves
evergreen,
alternate,
leathery, serrate
and oblong to 15 x 5 cm
wide, much resembling a chestnut
leaf; young leaves and shoots are covered
with a rusty-orange tomentum which
disappears as the leaves mature.

Tanbark oak is the only member of this largely Asiatic genus of about 100 to 200 species that is native to North America, specifically California and Oregon. As the name implies, the bark is an important source of tannins for the leather industry.

ROBL'E BEECH
Nothofagus obliqua

Leaves 8 cm,
ovate-oblong,
deep green; pale,
glaucous below.
Veins (7–11 pairs)
impressed, extend
to tips of teeth.
Base cuneate,
slightly oblique.
Petiole
5 mm, red.

Margins irregularly serrate.
Teeth sharp.
Bud 5 mm, ovoid, spreading.

Height 30 m.
Crown ovoid,
open, spreading.

Shoot
slender,
hairy, dark
red above
and paler
below.

Leaves
sometimes develop lobes.
Fruit 8 cm, set singly,
four-ribbed, bears small scales.

**Lower
branches**
pendulous.
Bark fissured.

The southern beeches are a genus of about 40 species native to the Southern Hemisphere and planted in North America usually in gardens. They have smaller leaves and fruits than true beeches, and most are evergreen, although Roblé beech is not. The Roblé beech is native to Chile and Argentina.

AMERICAN CHESTNUT
Castanea dentata

④ ® ⊛ ⓨ ⊛

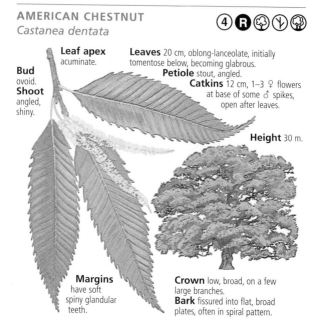

Leaf apex acuminate.

Bud ovoid.
Shoot angled, shiny.

Leaves 20 cm, oblong-lanceolate, initially tomentose below, becoming glabrous.
Petiole stout, angled.
Catkins 12 cm, 1–3 ♀ flowers at base of some ♂ spikes, open after leaves.

Height 30 m.

Margins have soft spiny glandular teeth.

Crown low, broad, on a few large branches.
Bark fissured into flat, broad plates, often in spiral pattern.

This once important species, native from New England down to the Appalachians, has now been almost totally exterminated by Chestnut blight, a fungal disease. Chinese chestnut (*C. mollissima*), on which the fungus was introduced, is resistant, and is grown for its nuts. It has hairy buds and leaves with rounded bases.

GOLDEN CHINKAPIN
Castanopsis chrysophylla

⑧ ⊛ ⓨ ⊛

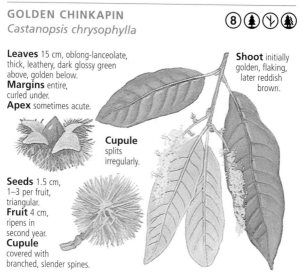

Leaves 15 cm, oblong-lanceolate, thick, leathery, dark glossy green above, golden below.
Margins entire, curled under.
Apex sometimes acute.

Shoot initially golden, flaking, later reddish brown.

Cupule splits irregularly.

Seeds 1.5 cm, 1–3 per fruit, triangular.
Fruit 4 cm, ripens in second year.
Cupule covered with branched, slender spines.

Very similar to American chestnut but with entire evergreen leaves, this species is native to the Pacific Coast of the United States, where it grows to 30 m. Tanbark oak (*Lithocarpus densiflorus*) is similar in flower and range but has toothed leaves and an acorn fruit enclosed in a cup.

This family of trees and shrubs has a worldwide distribution and comprises about 15 genera, of which *Ulmus* and *Celtis* are most commonly encountered in North America. The family is characterized by simple, usually oblique, leaves that are carried alternately and often have rough surfaces and buds with overlapping scales. Its flowers are usually perfect, have many stamens and appear with or before the leaves. The fruits are broad samaras in *Ulmus*, berries in *Celtis* and nutlets in *Zelkova*.

AMERICAN ELM
Ulmus americana

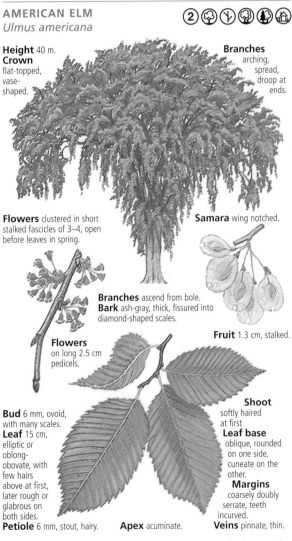

Height 40 m.
Crown flat-topped, vase-shaped.

Branches arching, spread, droop at ends.

Flowers clustered in short stalked fascicles of 3–4, open before leaves in spring.

Samara wing notched.

Branches ascend from bole.
Bark ash-gray, thick, fissured into diamond-shaped scales.

Flowers on long 2.5 cm pedicels.

Fruit 1.3 cm, stalked.

Bud 6 mm, ovoid, with many scales.
Leaf 15 cm, elliptic or oblong-obovate, with few hairs above at first, later rough or glabrous on both sides.
Petiole 6 mm, stout, hairy.

Apex acuminate.

Shoot softly haired at first
Leaf base oblique, rounded on one side, cuneate on the other.
Margins coarsely doubly serrate, teeth incurved.
Veins pinnate, thin.

American elm, a native of the East from southern Canada down to the Gulf, is recognizable by its crown and notched seed wing. It was once familiar in streets and gardens as a shade tree, but has been sadly depleted by Dutch elm disease.

135

ROCK ELM
Ulmus Thomasii

④ 🌳 🌲 🌳

Buds 6 mm, ovoid.
Scales ciliate, downy, chestnut-brown, marked with white at apex.
Shoot slender, hairy in first year, often develops thick, corky 1.5 cm wings after three to four years.

Apex acuminate.
Fruit 2.5 cm, very hairy, ciliate.
Apex shallowly notched.

Fruit in threes, twos or fours.

Bark thick, irregularly deeply fissured, scaly, dark gray and red-brown.

Leaves 13 cm, obovate or oval, hairy below.
Margins doubly serrate.
Base rounded, oblique.

Rock elm is native around and to the south of the Great Lakes, where it forms a tree to 30 m with a somewhat vase-shaped crown on a long straight bole. The very hairy buds and the flowers in racemes distinguish it from other elms. It produces a very tough and heavy timber, which is red-tinged.

SLIPPERY ELM
Ulmus rubra

③ 🌳 🌲 🌳

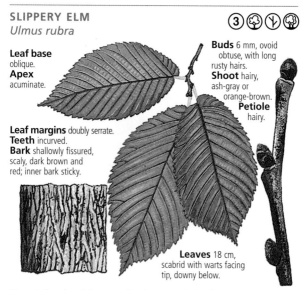

Leaf base oblique.
Apex acuminate.

Buds 6 mm, ovoid obtuse, with long rusty hairs.
Shoot hairy, ash-gray or orange-brown.
Petiole hairy.

Leaf margins doubly serrate.
Teeth incurved.
Bark shallowly fissured, scaly, dark brown and red; inner bark sticky.

Leaves 18 cm, scabrid with warts facing tip, downy below.

Named after the sticky aromatic substance which is found in its inner bark, Slippery elm is found throughout the eastern United States and forms a tree to 30 m. It can be distinguished from other elms by its leaves, which feel smooth if stroked toward the leaf apex.

ENGLISH ELM
Ulmus procera

Height 40 m.
Crown narrow, billowing, broadest at top, most dense of all elms.

Shoot slender, zigzags.
Buds 3 mm, slightly hairy.

Branches heavy, large, ascending.

Bole straight, grows through to top of crown, massive, burred.

Bark finely cracked into small plates, dark brown.

Leaves short-tipped.
Veins in 10–12 pairs.

Flower bisexual, opens April, before leaves.

Leaves to 10 cm, thick, rounded, obliquely based.
Petiole 5 mm, downy.

Teeth double, sharp.
Leaves rough above, densely hairy below, remain green until November.

Fruit 1.2 cm, notched at apex.
Seeds not set centrally.

The most common English tree until recently, this elm has been widely planted in the United States since the 18th century. Its origins, however, remain an enigma; it was either a very early introduction or may have arisen as a hybrid. Fertile seeds are rarely set, and reproduction is nearly always by root suckering. Fluttering elm (*U. laevis*) has very long peduncles.

WYCH ELM
Ulmus glabra

Leaves large, 16 cm, variable.

Leaf tips acuminate.

Shoot stout, densely haired.

Buds large, 6 mm, hairy.

Seeds central.

Bases oblique.
Petiole 5 mm, usually hidden by leaf base.

Fruit 1.5 cm, notched at apex.

Fruit pale green in April when appearing before leaves, shed in July when ripe.

Height 40 m.
Crown broad, domed.
Branches arch.
Bole short, stout, heavily buttressed, burred.

Bark broadly ridged and cracked; silvery-gray, smooth, shiny on young trees.
Suckers rare.

Although sometimes shrubby on exposed sites, Wych elm is renowned for its majestic, spreading crown, which is especially attractive in autumn. Its botanical name derives from the smoothness of its young bark and not from the leaves, which are very rough above. Most Wych elm seeds are fertile, and it very rarely produces suckers. The fruit, appearing well before the foliage, is often produced so abundantly that the tree appears to be fully clothed. It is native to most of Europe and western Asia and is the only elm unquestionably indigenous to Britain.

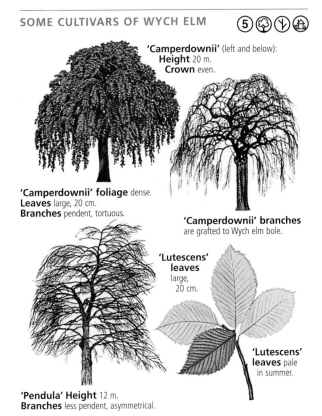

'Camperdownii' (left and below):
Height 20 m.
Crown even.

'Camperdownii' foliage dense.
Leaves large, 20 cm.
Branches pendent, tortuous.

'Camperdownii' branches
are grafted to Wych elm bole.

**'Lutescens'
leaves**
large,
20 cm.

**'Lutescens'
leaves** pale
in summer.

'Pendula' Height 12 m.
Branches less pendent, asymmetrical.

These compact, relatively small forms make ideal garden trees. Camperdown elm is the most common and has a more symmetrical crown than 'Pendula,' whose branches form "herringbone" patterns. 'Lutescens' reaches 12 m.

SIBERIAN ELM ④ 🌳 🌱 🏠 🌲
Ulmus pumila

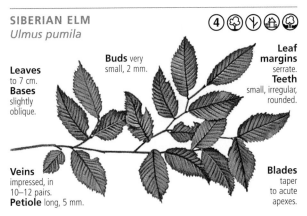

Leaves
to 7 cm.
Bases
slightly
oblique.

Buds very
small, 2 mm.

**Leaf
margins**
serrate.
Teeth
small, irregular,
rounded.

Veins
impressed, in
10–12 pairs.
Petiole long, 5 mm.

Blades
taper
to acute
apexes.

Almost evergreen and apparently very resistant to Dutch elm disease, Siberian elm grows fairly quickly into a small, flat-domed, leafy tree. Winged elm (*U. alata*), from the Southeast, has corky, winged glabrous shoots and hairy fruits.

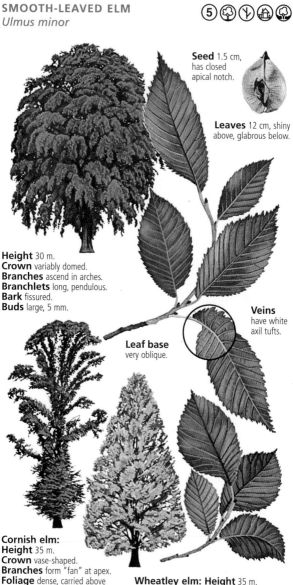

SMOOTH-LEAVED ELM
Ulmus minor

⑤ 🌳 🌱 🏠 🌳

Seed 1.5 cm, has closed apical notch.

Leaves 12 cm, shiny above, glabrous below.

Height 30 m.
Crown variably domed.
Branches ascend in arches.
Branchlets long, pendulous.
Bark fissured.
Buds large, 5 mm.

Veins have white axil tufts.

Leaf base very oblique.

Cornish elm:
Height 35 m.
Crown vase-shaped.
Branches form "fan" at apex.
Foliage dense, carried above branches.

Wheatley elm: Height 35 m.
Crown evenly conic. **Branches** set at c. 45°. **Leaves** (above) longer, rounder than Cornish elm.

Native to most of Europe, this hedgerow tree was probably introduced to southern Britain as a boundary marker in the first century B.C. and regional varieties — sometimes classified as species — have developed since then. Those most often seen are Wheatley (or Jersey) elm (*U. c.* var. *sarniensis*), planted in avenues, and Cornish elm (*U. c.* var. *cornubiensis*) which occurs "wild" in southwest England and southern Ireland. Its leaves are cupped and smaller than those of Wheatley elm.

CHINESE ELM
Ulmus parvifolia

⑤ 🌵 🌵 🌵

Leaves 5 cm, oval, elliptic or obovate-lanceolate, lustrous above, glabrous except along midrib.
Petiole 8 mm, hairy.

Height 25 m.
Crown rounded dome, very dense.

Branches pendulous with age.

Margins singly serrate with forward crenate teeth.
Base rounded, slightly oblique.

Bark smooth, later flaking, cracked; gray or red-brown with large, orange lenticels.

Apex acute.

Shoot very slender, hairy.
Bud 2 mm, ovoid.

Often semi-evergreen, this introduced ornamental produces its small, greenish flowers in autumn at the base of the leaves, and is further distinguished by the herringbone pattern of its shoots. Red elm (*U. serotina*) differs in its corky, winged shoots, its oblique, doubly serrate leaves and its flowers in racemes.

JAPANESE ZELKOVA
Zelkova serrata

⑦ Ⓡ 🌲 🌱 ⌂

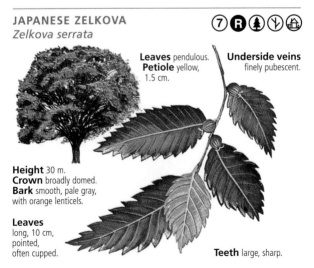

Leaves pendulous.
Petiole yellow, 1.5 cm.

Underside veins finely pubescent.

Height 30 m.
Crown broadly domed.
Bark smooth, pale gray, with orange lenticels.

Leaves long, 10 cm, pointed, often cupped.

Teeth large, sharp.

Much prized in its native Japan for the quality of its timber, this zelkova is planted across the United States and is resistant to Dutch elm disease. Its larger leaves have pointed teeth, longer petioles and assume autumn shades of yellow, pink and bronze. Its fine, zigzagged shoots carry 1 mm buds. The zelkovas can be easily distinguished by their asymmetrical, fleshy drupes.

HACKBERRY
Celtis occidentalis

Leaf
9 cm,
ovate,
with 3 veins
at base.
Base obliquely
rounded.
Veins pubescent.
Petiole 2 cm, silky.

Fruit 8 mm, an ovoid to
obovoid drupe, in leaf axils.
Fruit persists on
shoots after leaf-fall.
Pedicel 2 cm.

Shoot
slender with long, white hairs.
Bud 6 mm, adpressed.
Margins singly serrate
toward apex, entire
at base.

Bark silvery-gray, flaky, with warts and
longitudinal-winged ridges.
Leaf apex often at angle to midrib.

Apex
acuminate.

Hackberry, which can grow to 40 m, is one of a group of trees from the eastern United States similar to elms but differing in their fruit. Sugarberry (*C. laevigata*) has oblong-lanceolate leaves to 12 cm and orange-red fruits on shorter pedicels.

Mulberry Family *Moraceae*

The Mulberry family contains about 1800 species of trees, shrubs and herbs distributed world-wide. Many of the trees have a very sticky, milky sap, which is not poisonous as in the Euphorbiaceae. The family provides fruits, such as figs, a food source for the silkworm caterpillar, rubber, timber and medicines. The bast fibers of Mulberry trees have been used since ancient times for making rope, textiles and baskets.

WHITE MULBERRY
Morus alba

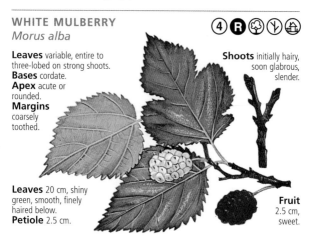

Leaves variable, entire to
three-lobed on strong shoots.
Bases cordate.
Apex acute or
rounded.
Margins
coarsely
toothed.

Shoots initially hairy,
soon glabrous,
slender.

Leaves 20 cm, shiny
green, smooth, finely
haired below.
Petiole 2.5 cm.

Fruit
2.5 cm,
sweet.

White mulberry is a small tree of Chinese origin reaching up to 16 m. Its fruit, which ripens from green to white, pinkish or violet purple, is insipid, although sweet. Black mulberry (*M. nigra*) has deeply cordate leaves, while those of Red mulberry (*M. rubra*) are truncate.

RED MULBERRY
Morus rubra

Leaves alternate, simple, broadly ovate, acuminate and truncate at the base, to 20 mm long.
Margins serrate, may be mitten-shaped to three-lobed on vigorous shoots, dark green, scabrous above, pale green, pubescent below.

Flowers unisexual, borne on separate trees. Both sexes occur as hairy, green catkins about 3 cm long and appear at the time of leafout.
Fruit multiple of druplets, purple to dark red, about 3 cm and edible.

Twigs slender, reddish-brown, appear zigzag and smooth at maturity.
Terminal buds absent and lateral buds are about 6 mm, ovoid and have distinctive overlapping reddish-brown scales.

Stems smooth, light gray bark when young, becoming reddish-brown, narrowly fissured with long and narrow papery scales at maturity.

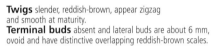

Red mulberry is a medium-sized tree, to 20 m, with a broad, dense and rounded crown. The wood has been used for furniture and inlay due to its rich brown color upon aging and resistance to decay. The tree is used only occasionally as an ornamental. It occurs on rich soils in mixed hardwood forests throughout the eastern United States and is a favorite tiebreaker on field exams for budding foresters. Broken leaves and petioles, as well as twigs, exude a characteristic milky sap.

FIG
Ficus carica

⑦ 🌣 🜄 🏠

Leaves 20 cm, usually deeply lobed but occasionally unlobed, cordate.

Leaves shiny, white hairs on veins below.
Bark smooth, patterned gray.

Fruit 5–8 cm.
Seeds enclosed in tasty flesh.

Shoot stout, glabrous, ridged.
Sap milky.
Bud conic, acute, laterally squat.

Fruit pear-shaped, ripens from green to purple-black.

Fig, a native of southern Europe and southwestern Asia, is hardy only in warm climates. It forms a spreading tree to 8 m, with a fruit developing from a modified shoot tip. Weeping fig (*F. benjamina*) has elliptic, leathery leaves and dark red fruits. Fiddle-leaf fig (*F. lyrata*) has 50 cm glossy leaves with sinuate margins and white-spotted green fruit.

OSAGE ORANGE
Maclura pomifera

⑤ 🌣 🜄 🌣

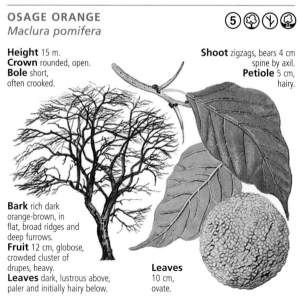

Height 15 m.
Crown rounded, open.
Bole short, often crooked.

Shoot zigzags, bears 4 cm spine by axil.
Petiole 5 cm, hairy.

Bark rich dark orange-brown, in flat, broad ridges and deep furrows.
Fruit 12 cm, globose, crowded cluster of drupes, heavy.
Leaves dark, lustrous above, paler and initially hairy below.

Leaves 10 cm, ovate.

The striking fruit of this widely planted windbreak is full of an acrid, milky juice and small brown nutlets. It is totally unpalatable. The tree is often dioecious, although the flowers are inconspicuous, in either racemes (♂) or globose heads (♀).

Protea Family *Protaceae*

The Protea family is native to the drier regions of the Southern Hemisphere, mainly the Cape region of South Africa. Among the more notable features of this family are its showy flowers, one species of which produces one of the largest single flowers known among the flowering plants. The family is an important source for tropical timber and provides the confectioners trade with Macadamia nuts.

SILK OAK TREE
Grevillea robusta

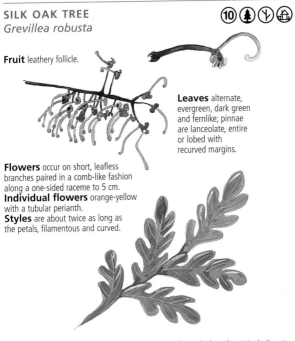

Fruit leathery follicle.

Leaves alternate, evergreen, dark green and fernlike; pinnae are lanceolate, entire or lobed with recurved margins.

Flowers occur on short, leafless branches paired in a comb-like fashion along a one-sided raceme to 5 cm.
Individual flowers orange-yellow with a tubular perianth.
Styles are about twice as long as the petals, filamentous and curved.

This native of Australia is widely planted in subtropical and tropical climates as a street and shade tree. Its evergreen, fern-like foliage is distinctive and often used in the nursery and florist trade. In its native range, it is a large tree, to 50 m, and a valuable source of timber.

Katsura Family *Cercidiphyllaceae*

The Katsura family has but a single genus and two species. They are deciduous, dioecious trees that can grow to 30 m. The fruit is a follicle.

KATSURA
Cercidiphyllum japonicum

Leaves 8 cm, cordate, sometimes nearly circular, open bright pink, soon turning to fresh green; autumn color varies, may be gold, scarlet, purple.

Shoot very slender, reddish above, green below, sub-shiny, glabrous, thickened below buds.
Margins serrate.

Apex variable.
Petiole 4 cm, red.

Leaf veins palmate on spur shoots, pinnate on long shoots, in fives or sevens.

Teeth shallow, rounded.

Bud 6 mm, shiny dark brown, set in opposite pairs.
Spur shoots short, slow-growing.
Shoot straight, downcurved in outer crown.

Katsura is native to central China and Japan and is noted for its colorful foliage. It grows to 25 m with a columnar crown, often on a divided stem with dull gray fissured bark.

146

Buckwheat Family *Polygonaceae*

The Buckwheat family contains about 40 genera and 800 species of mostly herbs, vines and shrubs native to Northern Temperate regions of the world. Several species are cultivated for their seeds, from which a type of flour is made.

SEAGRAPE
Coccoloba Uvifera

Height 6 m.
Shoot orange.
Crown rounded, compact.

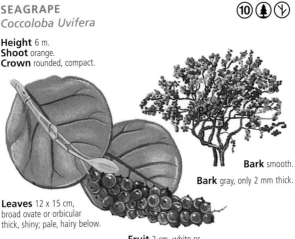

Bark smooth.

Bark gray, only 2 mm thick.

Leaves 12 x 15 cm, broad ovate or orbicular thick, shiny; pale, hairy below.

Fruit 2 cm, white or purple, in 25 cm racemes.

Seagrape is a small, open evergreen restricted to coastal sites in southern Florida. Its white flowers are followed by purple fruits.

Papaya Family *Caricaceae*

The Papaya family contains two genera native to the tropics. The trees and vines are succulent to semi-woody with milky sap. The fruit, a fleshy berry, is edible and quite delicious.

PAPAYA
Carica Papaya

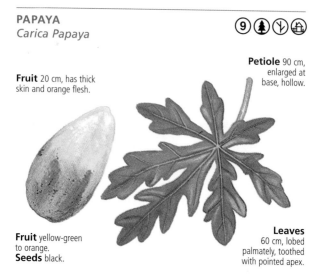

Fruit 20 cm, has thick skin and orange flesh.

Petiole 90 cm, enlarged at base, hollow.

Fruit yellow-green to orange.
Seeds black.

Leaves 60 cm, lobed palmately, toothed with pointed apex.

Papaya is a subtropical tree native from Florida southward, which grows up to 10 m. It is cultivated for its fruits, which are frequently borne on the single stem of female or hermaphrodite trees.

Magnolia Family *Magnoliaceae*

The Magnolia family contains about 12 genera largely native to the temperate regions of the Northern Hemisphere. They typically produce showy flowers, and several species are widely used as ornamentals. Some species are also used for timber.

SAUCER MAGNOLIA
Magnolia x Soulangiana

Fruit comprises spirally set carpels, each splitting to release one or two seeds.

Leaves
15 cm (larger in some forms), downy below, tapered at both base and apex, russet in autumn.

Height 10 m.
Crown low.

Bole short.
Bark smooth, gray.
Flowers before or with new leaves.

Flowers to 20 cm, appear before leaves
Petals (6–9) each 10 cm.

This classic Magnolia, first raised in France, is a hybrid of two wild Chinese species, *M. heptapeta* and *M. quinquepeta*. Also from China, Sprenger magnolia (*M. Sprengeri*) has broader leaves and Sargent magnolia (*M. Sargentiana*) obliquely cuneate ones.

SOUTHERN MAGNOLIA
Magnolia grandiflora

⑦ 🌲 🌿 🏠

Fruit 10 cm, on stout, 1.5 cm stalk, hairy.

Petiole 2.5 cm, stout, hairy.

Flowers 25 cm, from May to August.

Leaves 20 cm, thick, leathery, shiny, laurel-like, rufously pubescent below.

This evergreen from the southern United States can be grown in less warm climates but may require the shelter of a wall to survive and flower. The Chinese Delavay magnolia (*M. Delavayi*), also evergreen, has larger, very wide, matte, sea-green leaves.

JAPANESE MAGNOLIA
Magnolia Kobus

⑦ Ⓡ 🌳 🌿 🏠

Bare branches regularly clothed in white flowers on older trees; younger trees shy to flower.

Shoot shiny greenish-brown.

Leaves 15 cm, crinkled, shiny below.
Veins impressed.
Petiole 1.5 cm.

Height 15 m.
Crown of young trees broad and conic, becoming domed.
Branches level.

Flowers 12 cm.

Flowers carried profusely, appear in April, before leaves.

This small species, also known as Star magnolia, may reach 20 m and has slender, curved leaf buds and gray, downy flower buds. Its shoots are fragrant when crushed. *M. Kobus* var. *borealis* is hardier and has pointed leaves. Those of Willow magnolia (*M. salicifolia*), also from Japan, are slender while its crown is an elegant, narrow dome.

CUCUMBER TREE
Magnolia acuminata

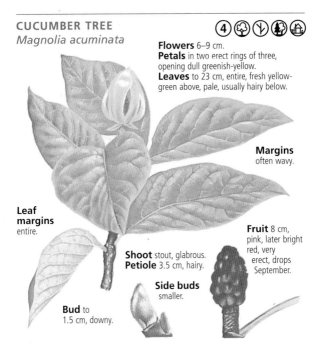

Flowers 6–9 cm.
Petals in two erect rings of three, opening dull greenish-yellow.
Leaves to 23 cm, entire, fresh yellow-green above, pale, usually hairy below.

Margins often wavy.

Leaf margins entire.

Fruit 8 cm, pink, later bright red, very erect, drops September.

Shoot stout, glabrous.
Petiole 3.5 cm, hairy.

Side buds smaller.

Bud to 1.5 cm, downy.

From the eastern United States and named after the resemblance of its young seed clusters to cucumbers, this stately tree grows to about 25 m. Wilson magnolia (*M. Wilsonii*), from China, hardly reaches a third of this and produces hanging, pure white flowers.

SWEET BAY
Magnolia virginiana

Fruit 5 cm, containing 6 mm flattened seeds.
Leaves bluntly tipped with prominent midribs.

Flowers to 7.5 cm, fragrant, June–July on leafy spur shoots.

Leaves to 15 cm, shiny above.

Petioles 2 cm, slender.
Shoot has lenticels.

Leaf underside glaucous, pubescent, minutely warty.

Sweet bay is native to the coastal swamps and rivers of the eastern United States and evergreen in the southern part of this range. In the late 17th century, it was the first magnolia grown in Europe where its small flowers sometimes persist until December.

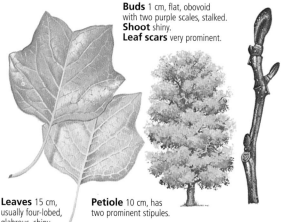

Buds 1 cm, flat, obovoid with two purple scales, stalked.
Shoot shiny.
Leaf scars very prominent.

Leaves 15 cm, usually four-lobed, glabrous, shiny, glaucous below.

Petiole 10 cm, has two prominent stipules.

Height 35 m.
Crown dense, becomes broader, more open with age.

Branches regular.

Native to the eastern United States, this species, also called Yellow poplar, produces yellow-green tulip-shaped flowers in June, followed by erect, cone-shaped fruits. Chinese tulip tree (*L. chinense*) has thinner leaves which are deeply lobed and minutely warted below. Tulip tree is an important North American timber tree.

Laurel Family *Lauraceae*

The Laurel family is a large family of mostly tropical and subtropical shrubs and trees, which are often aromatic. Several genera are important sources of flavoring, food and pharmaceuticals.

AVOCADO
Persea americana

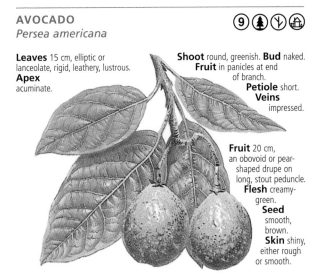

Leaves 15 cm, elliptic or lanceolate, rigid, leathery, lustrous. **Apex** acuminate.

Shoot round, greenish. **Bud** naked. **Fruit** in panicles at end of branch. **Petiole** short. **Veins** impressed.

Fruit 20 cm, an obovoid or pear-shaped drupe on long, stout peduncle. **Flesh** creamy-green. **Seed** smooth, brown. **Skin** shiny, either rough or smooth.

Growing to 20 m with a rounded, spreading crown, Avocado is widely planted in warm climates beyond its native Central America for its well-known fruit. It bears small greenish flowers.

CAMPHOR TREE
Cinnamomum Camphora

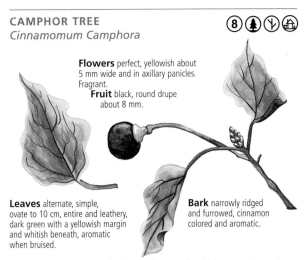

Flowers perfect, yellowish about 5 mm wide and in axillary panicles. Fragrant. **Fruit** black, round drupe about 8 mm.

Leaves alternate, simple, ovate to 10 cm, entire and leathery, dark green with a yellowish margin and whitish beneath, aromatic when bruised.

Bark narrowly ridged and furrowed, cinnamon colored and aromatic.

Camphor tree, a native of China and Japan, is widely grown in southern United States as an ornamental. It is a large evergreen tree, to 30 m, with an attractive, wide spreading, globose crown. In temperate climates, leaves are shed at about the time of new leaf emergence. Camphor oil is distilled from the wood of this species.

CALIFORNIA LAUREL
Umbellularia californica

Leaves 15 cm, oblong-lanceolate or elliptic, dark, lustrous above, dull paler below.
Bud naked.

Fruit to 5 cm, in umbels of 2-3, a subglobose berry, green ripening to purple.
Flesh thin.
Seed brown, smooth.

Leaves flat, glabrous, evergreen, turning yellow when shed in second year.
Margins entire, down-turned.
Midrib whitish.
Apex either acute or rounded.
Leaf base cuneate.
Petiole 6 mm, slender.

Height 25 m.
Crown a dense, rounded dome, often on several stems.
Shoot hairy at first, yellow, later brown, glabrous.

Bark dark red-brown, thin, smooth.

This is the only species in this genus. It is named after its pale yellow flowers, which appear in early spring in small umbels; it is also known as Headache tree because of the unpleasant effect of too much sniffing of its aromatic foliage.

SASSAFRAS
Sassafras albidum

Shoot shiny, brittle, rather glaucous bright green, marked with elevated leaf scars.
Bud 1 cm.

Leaves quite variable; same tree may carry entire ovate leaves, or leaves with two or three lobes.

Leaves 15 cm, three main veins.

Fruit 1 cm, an ovoid dark blue drupe, in short racemes, on 5 cm pedicel, thickened, red.

Calyx persistent.

Leaves thin, light green above, glaucous below.
Petiole 3 cm.

This freely suckering tree grows to 25 m with an open, flat-topped crown and closely furrowed, dark brown bark. It is a native of the eastern United States, and the aromatic twigs, bark and roots have long been used to produce a fragrant oil or tea.

Witch-Hazel Family *Hamamelidaceae*

The Witch-hazel family has members indigenous to North America, Asia, Africa and Australia. Several species are cultivated as ornamentals and as sources of timber.

SWEET GUM
Liquidambar styraciflua

⑥ 🌱 🍃 🌳 🏠

Crown broad dome, ovoid-conic when young, turns orange, red or purple in autumn.
Height 30 m.

Leaves 15 cm, five-lobed (rarely seven), glabrous except axillary tufts.

Buds 5 mm, shiny.

Bark gray or brown, fissured in squares, furrowed when old.
Leaf margins with incurved teeth.

Shoot wooly at first, round with corky wings.

Sweet gum is native to the eastern United States and as far south as Guatemala. The four species in this genus have globose flowers and globose, pendulous fruits, which are aggregates of beaked capsules. Leaves are similar to maples but alternate.

PERSIAN IRONWOOD
Parrotia persica

⑤ Ⓡ 🌱 🍃 🏠

Flowers before leaves.   **Shoot** green-brown, has star-shaped, stiff hairs.

Buds downy, brown or black-purple.

Flowers have colored stamens.

Bark similar to that of London plane, peels to expose brown or yellow.

Bark smooth, pink-brown or gray-green, exfoliating in large flakes.

Leaf margins waved, glossy.

Persian ironwood, native to the lush forests around the Caspian Sea, can grow to 15 m, but is usually a sprawling shrubby tree. It is attractive in autumn when it assumes gold and crimson tints. It is distinguishable by its unusual bark.

155

COMMON WITCH-HAZEL
Hamamelis virginiana

Leaves simple, alternate, deciduous, and obovate to 7 cm x 15 cm with coarse sinuate detentions toward the acuminate apex.

Flowers are fragrant.

Flowers perfect with four twisted strap-like yellow petals about 15 mm long, appear during October-December.

Leaves are dark green above and paler beneath with hairs on the principal veins.

Petioles are short and the blade is wedge-shaped and unequal at the base.

Twigs slender, zigzagged, tawny and glabrous when mature.
Buds naked, stalked, including the terminal bud, yellowish-brown, tend to be adpressed and hairy.

Fruit a 2-beaked, woody capsule splitting along two sutures and maturing one year after flowering.

Bark smooth, even on older trees, thin and grayish brown.
Inner bark purplish.

Common witch-hazel is a large shrub to small tree, to 10 m, and native to eastern North America along riverbanks. It typically occupies the understory of mesic hardwood forest types. Several Asiatic species and their cultivars are used in landscaping. The astringent witch-hazel lotion is extracted from the bark and used in treating minor skin ailments. Pioneers believed that forked, young branches had a mythical power to "divine" water and precious metals.

Rose Family *Rosaceae*

The Rose family is a large assemblage of trees, shrubs and herbs, with alternate leaves. The family is characterized by the flowers, which have the sepals, petals and stamens attached to the receptacle margin. The ovary may have one or several carpels, and may be either superior, above the petals and stamens, or inferior, below them. Four subfamilies are distinguished by fruit.

Two subfamilies, centered on *Rosa*, the Rose, and *Spirea*, contain only shrubs. *Prunoideae* is defined by having a fruit which is a drupe, a fleshy outer covering around a single bony seed. *Prunus* is the only tree genus, divided into sections based on the flower arrangements.

The subfamily *Pomoidae* has a fruit which is a pome, which has two to five carpels containing the seeds within a fleshy covering, and includes many tree genera.

DOWNY SERVICEBERRY
Amelanchier arborea

Flowers
massed, star-like, with five pure white obovate petals, 2 cm, in conical upright racemes.

Height 8 m.
Crown low rounded dome, often on several stems, red in autumn.

Leaves 7 cm, elliptic to oblong-obovate.
Margins finely toothed, dull green, rounded or cuneate at base, new leaves copper.

Fruit 6 mm, ripens from green to red to purple.

Amelanchier is a genus of small trees from North America and Asia. Downy serviceberry is a small tree or shrub native to eastern North America. It is most noticeable when the massed, white flowers bloom. The sweet black fruits are edible when they ripen in July.

SINGLE-SEED HAWTHORN
Crataegus monogyna

Leaves 10 cm, deeply lobed, with few teeth.
Thorns to 2.5 cm.

Veins pinnate.
Flowers in corymbs of up to 16, appear with leaves in May.

Fruit 1 cm, one-seeded, has persistent calyx, profusely set, ripening September.

Height 15 m. **Crown** dense.
Bole short, fluted.

Shoot purplish, stout.
Buds 2 mm, glabrous, set in pairs at bases of spines.

Hawthorn's other common names, May and Quickthorn, derive from its flowering season and the speed with which it can form hedges. It has pink-flower cultivars such as 'Pendula Rosea.' Midland hawthorn (*C. oxycantha*) is less spiny and has shallowly lobed leaves, two-seeded haws and veins all pointing forward.

COCKSPUR THORN
Crataegus crus-galli

Leaves 8 cm, serrate, glabrous.

Fruit 1.5 cm, two-seeded, sometimes persists in winter.

Shoots and spines purple-brown.
Spines to 8 cm.

Native to eastern United States, Cockspur thorn forms a low, rounded tree to 7 m and assumes rich orange tints in autumn. Frosted thorn (*C. pruinosa*) has elliptic, lobulate, coarsely serrated leaves to 4 cm; its 2 cm fruit is green with a glaucous bloom and has five seeds. Black hawthorn (*C. Douglasii*) has broad obovate, serrate leaves to 10 cm and many shiny black 1.3 cm fruits.

Mountain Ashes *Sorbus*

This genus produces large corymbs of flowers developing into red, white, pink or russet heads of berries. While the leaves of mountain ashes, or rowans, are pinnate, those of the European whitebeams are simple with white undersides.

MOUNTAIN ASH
Sorbus americana

Shoot hairy at first.
Fruit in dense broad heads.

Leaves 20 cm.
Bud 2 cm, glabrous or nearly so, sticky.

Fruit 10 cm, a subglobose pome, ripens to scarlet.
Leaflets (7–17) 10 cm, lanceolate.
Rachis grooved.

Native throughout northeastern North America from Newfoundland to the Appalachians, Mountain ash forms a tree to 10 m with thin, smooth or slightly scaly pale gray bark. It can grow on mountains and its leaves turn clear yellow in autumn. This tree is also known as American mountain ash.

EUROPEAN MOUNTAIN ASH
Sorbus aucuparia

Height 15 m.
Crown irregular, ovoid or columnar conic.

Pedicel densely hairy.

Flowers 1 cm, in flat 15 cm corymbs.

Bark shiny, smooth.

Leaves 20 cm.
Leaflets (11–19) 5 cm, lanceolate.
Apex round-pointed.

Shoot initially hairy, dull gray-purple.
Bud 1.7 cm, ovoid, purple with dense gray hairs.
Leaflets serrate.

This native of Eurasia and North Africa has become naturalized in North America and is also widely grown as an ornamental. It can be distinguished from the native Mountain ash by its hairy buds and smaller leaflets with rounder apexes.

159

Apples and Pears

These trees comprise a group of mainly northern temperate genera whose fleshy fruit has major economic importance. The multi-seeded fruit is derived from two to five fused carpels. The outer fleshy part of the the fruit is derived from the enlargement of a portion of the receptacle and caylx surrounding the inferior ovary. The flesh of pears is gritty due to the presence of stone cells, whereas apple flesh is smooth and evenly textured.

CRAB APPLE
Malus sylvestris

②®✿⌇⌂

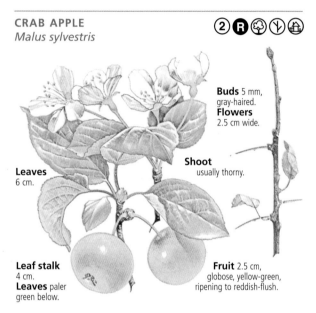

Buds 5 mm, gray-haired.
Flowers 2.5 cm wide.

Shoot usually thorny.

Leaves 6 cm.

Leaf stalk 4 cm.
Leaves paler green below.

Fruit 2.5 cm, globose, yellow-green, ripening to reddish-flush.

A native of Britain, western Europe and western Asia, Crab apple has white flowers faintly flushed pink and yields a fruit which, while hard and sour, makes excellent jelly. Crab apple is a parent of Orchard apple (*M. domestica*), which has much pinker flowers and sweeter, softer and larger fruit.

SIBERIAN CRAB APPLE
Malus baccata

②🌲🌳🏛

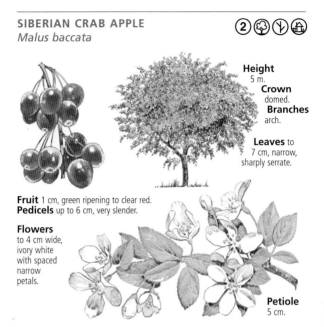

Height
5 m.
Crown
domed.
Branches
arch.

Leaves to
7 cm, narrow,
sharply serrate.

Fruit 1 cm, green ripening to clear red.
Pedicels up to 6 cm, very slender.

Flowers
to 4 cm wide,
ivory white
with spaced
narrow
petals.

Petiole
5 cm.

With a wide natural distribution from Siberia through northern China to the Himalayas, this tree has fruit which persists through winter when the pointed buds also assist identification. Southern crab apple (*M. angustifolia*) has 5 cm leaves and 2.5 cm fruits. It is found from Virginia to eastern Texas.

PURPLE CRAB APPLE
Malus x purpurea

②🌲🌳🏛

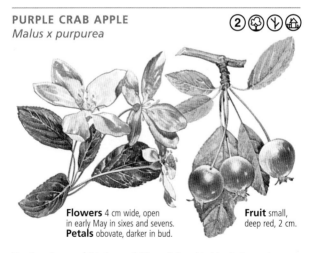

Flowers 4 cm wide, open
in early May in sixes and sevens.
Petals obovate, darker in bud.

Fruit small,
deep red, 2 cm.

The 8 cm leaves of this tree unfold purplish-red in May but soon become green and glossier above with their main veins purplish below. The form is sparsely branched and reaches 6 m; its cultivars are bigger and more vigorous and include 'Aldenhamensis,' 'Eleyi,' 'Lemoinei' and 'Profusion.'

JAPANESE CRAB APPLE
Malus floribunda

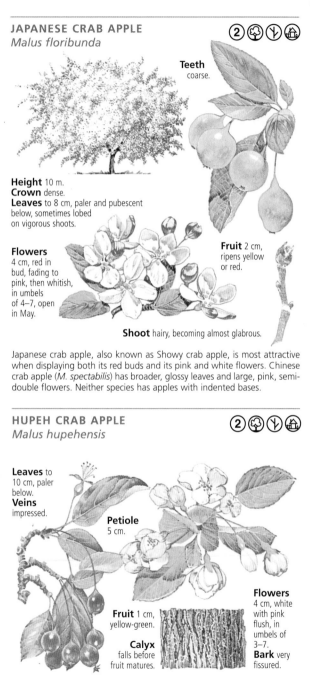

Teeth coarse.

Height 10 m.
Crown dense.
Leaves to 8 cm, paler and pubescent below, sometimes lobed on vigorous shoots.

Flowers 4 cm, red in bud, fading to pink, then whitish, in umbels of 4–7, open in May.

Fruit 2 cm, ripens yellow or red.

Shoot hairy, becoming almost glabrous.

Japanese crab apple, also known as Showy crab apple, is most attractive when displaying both its red buds and its pink and white flowers. Chinese crab apple (*M. spectabilis*) has broader, glossy leaves and large, pink, semi-double flowers. Neither species has apples with indented bases.

HUPEH CRAB APPLE
Malus hupehensis

Leaves to 10 cm, paler below.
Veins impressed.

Petiole 5 cm.

Fruit 1 cm, yellow-green.
Calyx falls before fruit matures.

Flowers 4 cm, white with pink flush, in umbels of 3–7.
Bark very fissured.

Hupeh crab apple has shiny, slightly downy, purple shoots and thorny spur shoots. The leaves can be made into a "red tea." It is very attractive in flower and vigorous, growing to 15 m. Sikkim crab apple (*M. sikkimensis*) has thornier spur shoots and wooly leaves.

TSCHONOSKI CRAB APPLE
Malus Tschonoskii

② ⊕ ⊕ ⊕

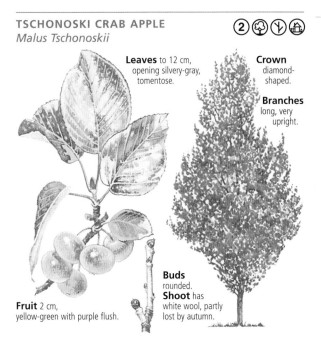

Leaves to 12 cm, opening silvery-gray, tomentose.

Crown diamond-shaped.

Branches long, very upright.

Buds rounded.
Shoot has white wool, partly lost by autumn.

Fruit 2 cm, yellow-green with purple flush.

A native of Japan, this makes a good street tree because of its vigorous growth and upright habit. It has brilliant autumn colors. Yunnan crab apple (*M. yunnanensis*) has yellow-green leaves and 1–2 cm yellow or bright red fruit, speckled white.

WILD PEAR
Pyrus communis

③ ⊕ ⊕ ⊕ ⊕

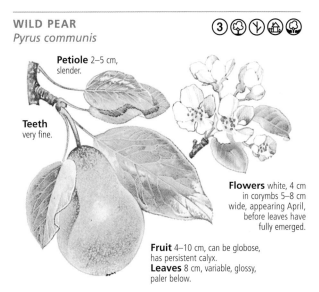

Petiole 2–5 cm, slender.

Teeth very fine.

Flowers white, 4 cm in corymbs 5–8 cm wide, appearing April, before leaves have fully emerged.

Fruit 4–10 cm, can be globose, has persistent calyx.
Leaves 8 cm, variable, glossy, paler below.

Wild pear is native to most of western Europe, but most trees encountered have probably hybridized with selected orchard forms. The crown is narrowly conic at first, becoming tall and domed. 'Beech Hill' is spire-like.

BRADFORD PEAR
Pyrus Calleryana 'Bradford'

⑥ 🌲 🍂 🏠

Leaves alternate, simple deciduous, ovate to about 7 cm, acuminate at the apex and truncated at the base.
Margins entire to finely serrate.
Leaves dark green, glabrous, turning to russet or purplish-red in the fall.

Twigs stout, reddish-brown with ovoid and elongated terminal buds to 1 cm, and wooly scales.
Bark smooth, tending to be blocky and glossy brown at maturity.
Twigs and **branches** lack thorns.

Flowers borne in axillary clusters at or before leaf emergence.
Flowers perfect with five white petals to 20 mm across.
Fruit a small, brown globose pome to 15 mm in diameter.

This small tree, native to China, has become the darling of landscapers. It is seen along city streets and in yards in virtually every town and city in eastern North America. Its globose to pyramidal crown, with dense branching habit, makes it an attractive specimen tree. Its magnificent shower of white flower clusters, in early March, is the harbinger of warmer weather. Unfortunatley, it is a short-lived tree, usually 10–15 years, and its branches are brittle and break easily.

WILLOW-LEAFED PEAR
Pyrus salicifolia

③ 🌲 🍂 🏠

Leaves 9 x 2 cm, entire, downy at first but soon glossy above.
Height 8 m

Flowers 2 cm, opening April, in dense corymbs.
Petiole 1.5 cm, slender.

Crown domed.
Branches slender, pendulous, may have thorns.
Fruit 2–3 cm, lenticels.

A native of the Caucasus, a region between the Black and Caspian Seas, this is usually seen as the 'Pendula' clone, which, as a young tree, has a distinctly weeping habit. Snow pear (*P. nivalis*), from southern Europe, has broader, less glossy leaves and rounded fruit. It reaches 20 m.

Cherries and Plums *Prunus*

The trees in this genus, which includes Blackthorn, Peach, Apricot and Almond, have fleshy single-seeded fruit, which develops from a single ovary. Most species have up to four glands at the junction of their petioles and leaf bases; those without have shoots which are partially green for two or more years. Prominent horizontal bands of lenticels are obvious on the bark in the cherries.

SWEET CHERRY
Prunus avium

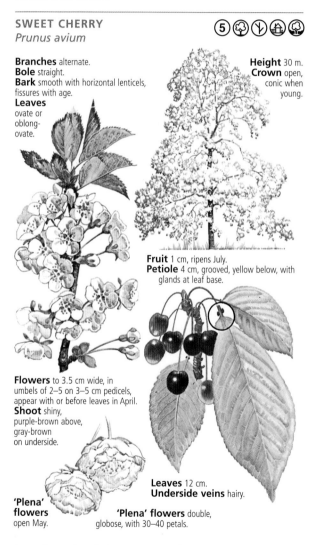

Branches alternate.
Bole straight.
Bark smooth with horizontal lenticels, fissures with age.
Leaves ovate or oblong-ovate.

Height 30 m.
Crown open, conic when young.

Fruit 1 cm, ripens July.
Petiole 4 cm, grooved, yellow below, with glands at leaf base.

Flowers to 3.5 cm wide, in umbels of 2–5 on 3–5 cm pedicels, appear with or before leaves in April.
Shoot shiny, purple-brown above, gray-brown on underside.

Leaves 12 cm.
Underside veins hairy.

'Plena' flowers open May.
'Plena' flowers double, globose, with 30–40 petals.

Sweet cherry, also called Gean or Mazzard, is native to Europe and western Asia and is striking in flower. Its leaves are bronze and, in autumn, they turn yellow and red. It is cultivated in areas too cold for apples and is the predominant parent of most domestic fruiting cherries. 'Plena' does not set fruit, but its larger flowers persist for up to three weeks. Sour cherry (*P. Cerasus*) has a shrubbier, suckering habit, glabrous leaves and tart fruit.

SARGENT CHERRY
Prunus Sargentii

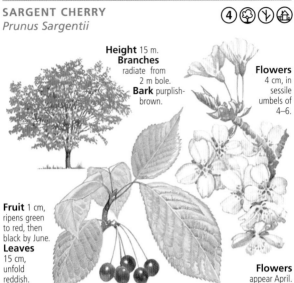

Height 15 m.
Branches radiate from 2 m bole.
Bark purplish-brown.

Flowers 4 cm, in sessile umbels of 4–6.

Fruit 1 cm, ripens green to red, then black by June.
Leaves 15 cm, unfold reddish.

Flowers appear April.

Notable for the brilliant reds and scarlets of its early autumn foliage, Sargent cherry is a large tree that reaches 25 m when growing wild in the mountains of Japan. In cultivation, it is much smaller. It is identifiable by its dark, lustrous bark.

AUTUMN CHERRY
Prunus subhirtella 'Autumnalis'

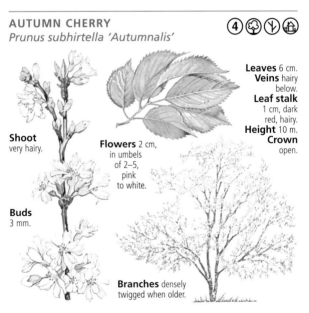

Leaves 6 cm.
Veins hairy below.
Leaf stalk 1 cm, dark red, hairy.
Height 10 m.
Crown open.

Shoot very hairy.

Flowers 2 cm, in umbels of 2–5, pink to white.

Buds 3 mm.

Branches densely twigged when older.

This tree has the asset of flowering intermittently in winter in warm climates and its semi-double flowers are carried from October to early spring. It is a cultivar of Japanese Higan cherry, which is far less common and only carries flowers in April.

JAPANESE CHERRIES

Individually identifiable by their various flowers and habits, Japanese cherries comprise about forty small trees which have usually been grafted to a Wild cherry rootstock. Of mixed parentage, they are usually discussed as non-specific cultivars of *Prunus* rather than classified as varieties of *Prunus serrulata*, the species from which most have probably been developed. Collectively, they are sometimes referred to as the "Sato Zakura" (domestic cherries).

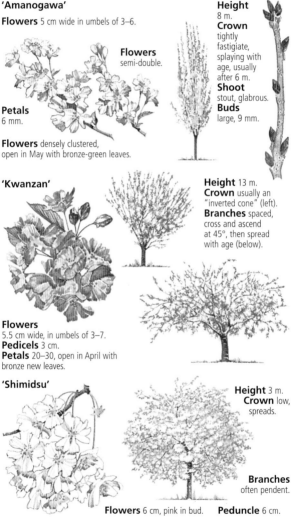

'Amanogawa'

Flowers 5 cm wide in umbels of 3–6.

Flowers semi-double.

Petals 6 mm.

Flowers densely clustered, open in May with bronze-green leaves.

Height 8 m.
Crown tightly fastigiate, splaying with age, usually after 6 m.
Shoot stout, glabrous.
Buds large, 9 mm.

'Kwanzan'

Flowers 5.5 cm wide, in umbels of 3–7.
Pedicels 3 cm.
Petals 20–30, open in April with bronze new leaves.

Height 13 m.
Crown usually an "inverted cone" (left).
Branches spaced, cross and ascend at 45°, then spread with age (below).

'Shimidsu'

Flowers 6 cm, pink in bud.   **Peduncle** 6 cm.

Height 3 m.
Crown low, spreads.

Branches often pendent.

All Sato Zakura have large leaves up to 20 cm long, which turn gold or pink in autumn and shoots as shown. The 'Amanogawa' habit instantly identifies it, as do the ascending and crossing branches of the very common 'Kwanzan'; no other cherry is as sprawling in old age. The flowers of 'Shimidsu' are notable for their long peduncles.

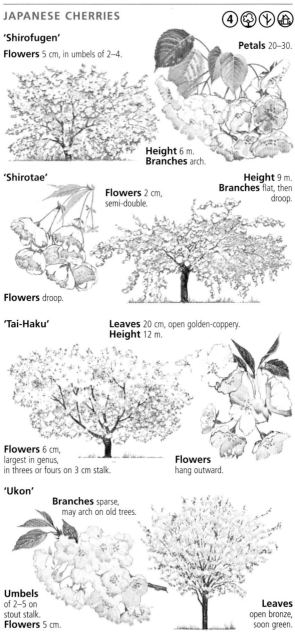

'Shirofugen'

Flowers 5 cm, in umbels of 2–4.

Petals 20–30.

Height 6 m.
Branches arch.

'Shirotae'

Height 9 m.
Branches flat, then droop.

Flowers 2 cm, semi-double.

Flowers droop.

'Tai-Haku'

Leaves 20 cm, open golden-coppery.
Height 12 m.

Flowers 6 cm, largest in genus, in threes or fours on 3 cm stalk.

Flowers hang outward.

'Ukon'

Branches sparse, may arch on old trees.

Umbels of 2–5 on stout stalk.
Flowers 5 cm.

Leaves open bronze, soon green.

'Shirofugen,' like 'Shimidsu,' flowers very late, in mid-May, but has a vigorous, spreading habit, slightly larger leaves and flowers opening with a pink tinge. The semi-double flowers of 'Shirotae' open a month earlier. 'Ukon' is one of several Japanese cherries with yellow or greenish flowers. 'Tai-Haku' has the largest flowers of any *Prunus* species and is probably closest to the Wild cherry ancestor of the Sato Zakura.

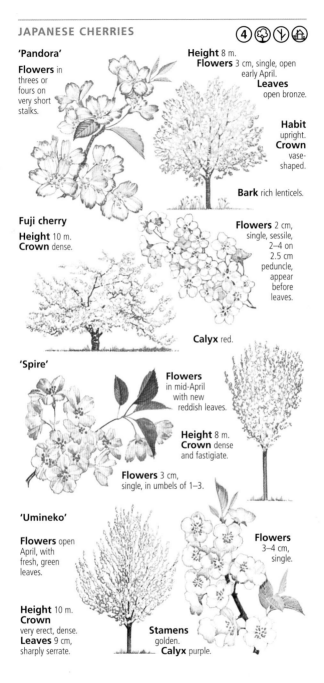

'Pandora'

Flowers in threes or fours on very short stalks.

Height 8 m.
Flowers 3 cm, single, open early April.
Leaves open bronze.

Habit upright.
Crown vase-shaped.

Bark rich lenticels.

Fuji cherry

Height 10 m.
Crown dense.

Flowers 2 cm, single, sessile, 2–4 on 2.5 cm peduncle, appear before leaves.

Calyx red.

'Spire'

Flowers in mid-April with new reddish leaves.

Height 8 m.
Crown dense and fastigiate.

Flowers 3 cm, single, in umbels of 1–3.

'Umineko'

Flowers open April, with fresh, green leaves.

Flowers 3–4 cm, single.

Height 10 m.
Crown very erect, dense.
Leaves 9 cm, sharply serrate.

Stamens golden.
Calyx purple.

All these cherries have petals set singly and produce small black fruit. Fuji cherry (*P. incisa*) was crossed with Sargent cherry to give *P. x Hillieri*, whose 'Spire' clone is an ideal street tree, and with Oshima cherry (*P. speciosa*) to produce *P.* 'Umineko.' 'Pandora' is another non-specific *Prunus* cultivar.

TIBETAN CHERRY
Prunus serrula

Flowers white, 2 cm, in umbels of 2–4, on 4 cm stalks, appear in May.
Leaves 12 cm, finely toothed.

Bark glossy, with long bands of lenticels on vigorous trees, flaky.

Fruit 5 mm, on 4 cm pedicels.
Leaves hairy below.
Petiole 1 cm.

Primarily planted for the magnificence of its bark, Tibetan cherry is also noted for its finely serrate willow-like leaves. These are unique among true cherries. *P. x schmittii* has a similar but less spectacular bark, an upright habit and pink flowers.

YOSHINO CHERRY
Prunus x yedoensis

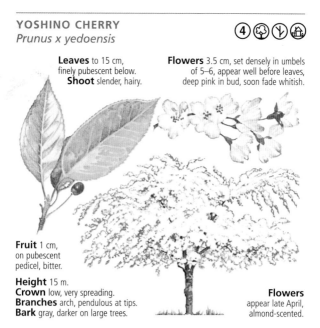

Leaves to 15 cm, finely pubescent below.
Shoot slender, hairy.

Flowers 3.5 cm, set densely in umbels of 5–6, appear well before leaves, deep pink in bud, soon fade whitish.

Fruit 1 cm, on pubescent pedicel, bitter.

Height 15 m.
Crown low, very spreading.
Branches arch, pendulous at tips.
Bark gray, darker on large trees.

Flowers appear late April, almond-scented.

Yoshino is unknown in the wild but is believed to be a hybrid of Higan cherry and Oshima cherry (*P. speciosa*). It is unusual among Japanese flowering cherries in having densely pubescent leaves, flower stalks and shoots. Its ripe fruit is black.

BIRD CHERRY
Prunus Padus

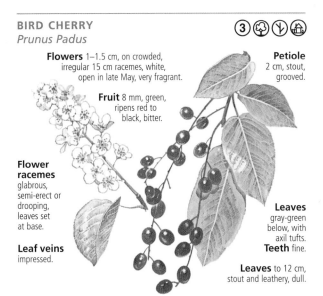

Flowers 1–1.5 cm, on crowded, irregular 15 cm racemes, white, open in late May, very fragrant.

Petiole 2 cm, stout, grooved.

Fruit 8 mm, green, ripens red to black, bitter.

Flower racemes glabrous, semi-erect or drooping, leaves set at base.

Leaves gray-green below, with axil tufts.
Teeth fine.

Leaf veins impressed.

Leaves to 12 cm, stout and leathery, dull.

Bird cherry has a wide distribution across northern Eurasia to Japan, and is easily recognized when in flower by its semi-erect racemes. Its smooth, dark, bitter-smelling bark was once used to prepare medicinal infusions. This tree has glabrous shoots and pointed, conic 5 mm buds.

BLACK CHERRY
Prunus serotina

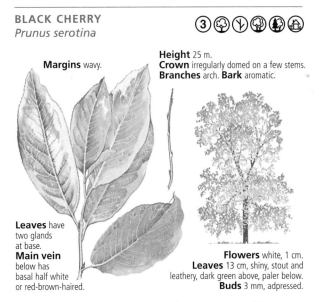

Margins wavy.

Height 25 m.
Crown irregularly domed on a few stems.
Branches arch. **Bark** aromatic.

Leaves have two glands at base.
Main vein below has basal half white or red-brown-haired.

Flowers white, 1 cm.
Leaves 13 cm, shiny, stout and leathery, dark green above, paler below.
Buds 3 mm, adpressed.

Black cherry, one of the largest trees in the genus, grows wild in eastern North America. Its fruits hold persistent calyxes, something missing from the fruit of Choke cherry (*P. virginiana*), which has thin leaves with spreading teeth. In the United States, Pin, or Fire cherry (*P. pensylvanica*) has lanceolate to narrowly ovate leaves with finely serrate margins. The fruit is a light red drupe.

CHERRY LAUREL
Prunus Laurocerasus

④ 🌲 🍃 🏠

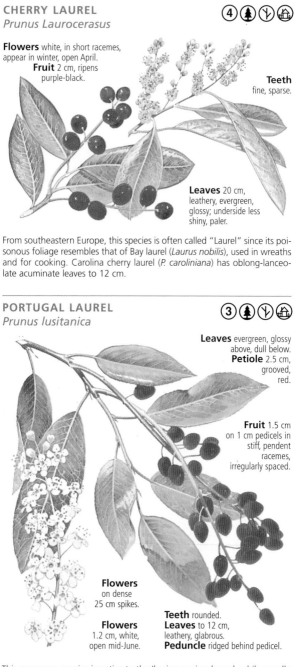

Flowers white, in short racemes, appear in winter, open April.

Fruit 2 cm, ripens purple-black.

Teeth fine, sparse.

Leaves 20 cm, leathery, evergreen, glossy; underside less shiny, paler.

From southeastern Europe, this species is often called "Laurel" since its poisonous foliage resembles that of Bay laurel (*Laurus nobilis*), used in wreaths and for cooking. Carolina cherry laurel (*P. caroliniana*) has oblong-lanceolate acuminate leaves to 12 cm.

PORTUGAL LAUREL
Prunus lusitanica

③ 🌲 🍃 🏠

Leaves evergreen, glossy above, dull below.
Petiole 2.5 cm, grooved, red.

Fruit 1.5 cm on 1 cm pedicels in stiff, pendent racemes, irregularly spaced.

Flowers on dense 25 cm spikes.

Flowers 1.2 cm, white, open mid-June.

Teeth rounded.
Leaves to 12 cm, leathery, glabrous.
Peduncle ridged behind pedicel.

This evergreen species is native to the Iberian peninsula and, while usually a shrubby tree of about 8 m, this tree may sometimes reach 16 m. Hollyleaf cherry (*P. ilicifolia*), from California, has ovate leaves to 5 cm with spiny teeth and almost sessile flowers.

CHERRY PLUM · PURPLE LEAF PLUM
Prunus cerasifera · P. cerasifera 'Pissardii'   ④ 🌳 🌱 🏠

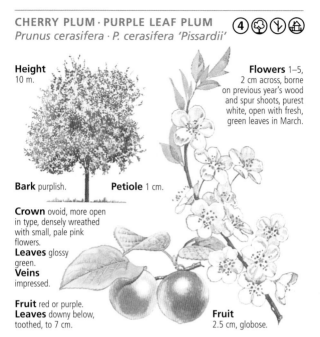

Height
10 m.

Flowers 1–5,
2 cm across, borne
on previous year's wood
and spur shoots, purest
white, open with fresh,
green leaves in March.

Bark purplish.   **Petiole** 1 cm.

Crown ovoid, more open
in type, densely wreathed
with small, pale pink
flowers.
Leaves glossy
green.
Veins
impressed.

Fruit red or purple.
Leaves downy below,
toothed, to 7 cm.

Fruit
2.5 cm, globose.

This attractive tree has an early flowering season, sometimes even in January or as late as April. The normal green and purple leaf forms are about equally common. Willow-leaf plum (*P. salicina*), a native of China, is distinguishable by having its flowers in clusters of three and obovate-oblong leaves to 10 cm.

BLACKTHORN/SLOE
Prunus spinosa   ⑤ 🌳 🌱

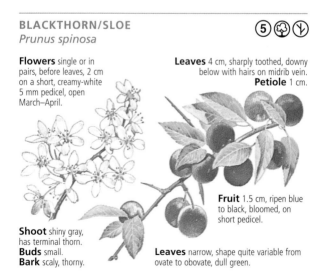

Flowers single or in
pairs, before leaves, 2 cm
on a short, creamy-white
5 mm pedicel, open
March–April.

Leaves 4 cm, sharply toothed, downy
below with hairs on midrib vein.
Petiole 1 cm.

Fruit 1.5 cm, ripen blue
to black, bloomed, on
short pedicel.

Shoot shiny gray,
has terminal thorn.
Buds small.
Bark scaly, thorny.

Leaves narrow, shape quite variable from
ovate to obovate, dull green.

Blackthorn, or Sloe, native to Europe, is a suckering shrub or small tree to 6 m. In early spring, it is a mass of small, creamy-white flowers which obliterate the black of the bark and branches. The fruit ripens in October, and is used to flavor gin.

PLUM
Prunus domestica

⑤ 🌳 🍃 🌲 🏠 🌳

Shoot hairy when young, later slightly downy.
Fruit black-purple or red.

Petiole 2.5 cm.

Fruit 8 cm, fleshy, sweet, ovoid or ellipsoid, grooved.
Stone flat with angled sides, free from flesh.

Leaves to 10 cm, obovate or elliptic.
Margins with shallow, rounded teeth.

Flowers on last year's wood, single or in pairs, greenish-white, 2 cm.

Leaves dull above, pubescent on the veins and midrib below.

Plum, a small suckering tree to 10 m, is now thought to be a hybrid between Cherry plum and Blackthorn. Many named varieties are cultivated. American plum (*P. americana*) has flowers in umbels of two to five and oblong-obovate leaves to 10 cm with an acuminate apex and doubly serrate margins.

APRICOT
Prunus Armeniaca

④ 🌳 🍃 🏠

Leaves 10 cm, rounded or ovate.
Base cuneate.
Margins finely toothed.

Buds 2 mm, single or in pairs.

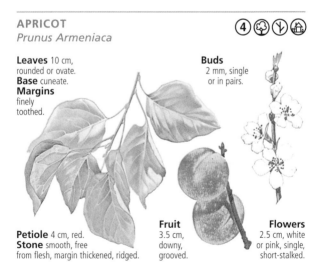

Petiole 4 cm, red.
Stone smooth, free from flesh, margin thickened, ridged.

Fruit 3.5 cm, downy, grooved.

Flowers 2.5 cm, white or pink, single, short-stalked.

Apricot makes a small rounded tree to 10 m, and is mostly cultivated for its delicious orange-red fruit. It does not come from Armenia but from northern China. Desert apricot (*P. Fremontii*), from the southwest United States, has 2 cm rounded or ovate leaves.

ALMOND
Prunus dulcis

⑦ 🌳 🌿 🏛

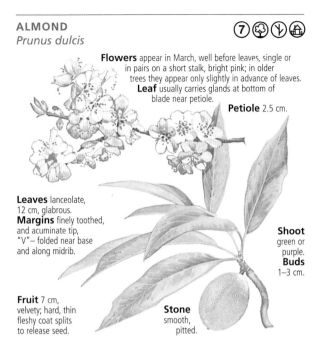

Flowers appear in March, well before leaves, single or in pairs on a short stalk, bright pink; in older trees they appear only slightly in advance of leaves.

Leaf usually carries glands at bottom of blade near petiole.

Petiole 2.5 cm.

Leaves lanceolate, 12 cm, glabrous.
Margins finely toothed, and acuminate tip, "V" – folded near base and along midrib.

Shoot green or purple.
Buds 1–3 cm.

Fruit 7 cm, velvety; hard, thin fleshy coat splits to release seed.

Stone smooth, pitted.

Almond grows wild, with spiny branches, in its native Mediterranean countries. Its early flowering season has endeared it to gardeners, although it is a short-lived tree with a spreading crown to 10 m. Its nuts are used in confectionery.

PEACH
Prunus Persica

⑤ 🌳 🌿 🏛

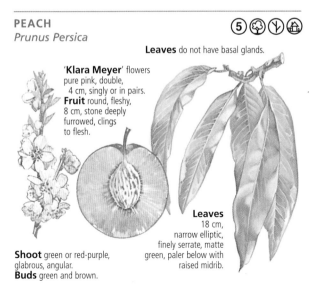

Leaves do not have basal glands.

'Klara Meyer' flowers pure pink, double, 4 cm, singly or in pairs.
Fruit round, fleshy, 8 cm, stone deeply furrowed, clings to flesh.

Leaves 18 cm, narrow elliptic, finely serrate, matte green, paler below with raised midrib.

Shoot green or red-purple, glabrous, angular.
Buds green and brown.

Peach, which only grows to 8 m, is renowned for its juicy fruit, but is also notable for its single, pale rose flowers when in blossom. Long ago, it was introduced from China. Nectarine differs only in having a glabrous fruit.

Legume or Pea Family *Leguminoseae*

The Legume, or Pea family, comprising several thousand species of trees, shrubs and herbs occurring all over the world, is characterized by pod-like fruits which have a line of seeds along the upper of the two seams. In most familiar species, which belong to the sub-family *Faboideae*, the flowers consist of 10 stamens and five petals — a "standard" petal covering the top, two wing petals and two "keel" petals.

The second sub-family, the *Caesalpinioideae* has different flower forms, often with the front two petals enclosing all the others in bud. The *Mimosoideae* has tiny flowers clustered in heads or on racemes. All genera except *Bauhinia* and *Cercis* have pinnate or bipinnate leaves.

JUDAS TREE
Cercis siliquastrum

⑥ 🌸 🌱 🏛

Height 15 m.
Crown one-sided.
Bark purplish, pinkish or gray, ridged at first, later becoming fissured.

Flowers to 2 cm, in fascicles, on old or new shoots, branches, or even directly on bole.

Leaves to 10 cm, either yellowish or dark green above and paler and glaucous beneath.
Leaves round with cordate base.
Petiole 5 cm.

Apex rounded or notched.

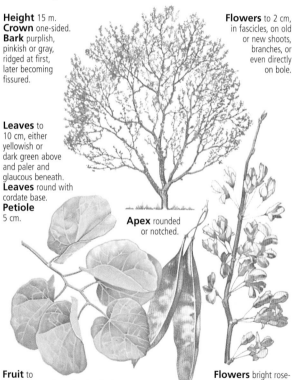

Fruit to 13 cm, thin, red-purple, ripening brown, flat, with 8–12 seeds, hairy at base.

Flowers bright rose-purple; standard petal small, below wing petals.

Judas tree, not, as commonly supposed, the tree upon which Judas Iscariot hung himself, but named after its native Judea, is unusual in the Legume family for its orbicular leaves, similar to Katsura but distinguishable by the paired buds. Eastern redbud (*C. canadensis*) differs in the shallowly cordate leaves, shiny above, with an abrupt acuminate apex and 1.2 cm flowers.

EASTERN REDBUD
Cercis canadensis

⑤ 🌿 🍂 🌳 🏠

Twigs slender, zigzag and lack a terminal bud.

Leaves deciduous, alternate, simple, cordate, apex, to 10–15 cm long and about as wide. Generally, dark green, glabrous, with prominent palmately radiating veins (5).

Fruit a flat, thin, brown, pendant, legume 1 x 10 cm long, often persisting into the fall.

Flowers in clusters along twigs and even older branches; rosy-pink, pea-like flowers, to 1 cm, appear early spring, often two to three weeks before the leaves.

Petiole 30-50 mm long with a prominent *pulvinus* at the base of the blade.

Lateral buds are small, adpressed and often superposed.

Eastern Redbud is regarded as a harbinger of spring throughout most of eastern North America. It is a small tree, usually less than 10 m in height, but often sought after as an ornamental because of its spring flower show. More than a dozen showy cultivars have been introduced into the ornamental market.

ORCHID TREE /
HONG KONG ORCHID TREE
Bauhinia Blakeana

⑩ 🌲 🍂 🏠

Fruit believed to be a sterile hybrid, it does not set seed.

Flowers in long racemes from October–March, rich red to reddish-purple, about 15 cm across with five prominent stamens, very fragrant.

Leaves alternate, simple shaped like a hoof, 20 cm across, and divided into two lobes for about one-fourth of their length.

These are small trees to about 15 m tall and considered to be one of the outstanding flowering trees of the world. Originally discovered as a single tree by monks in China, it has been propagated by cuttings and introduced into the United States in mid-1900. The tree is considered to be an evergreen, although there is often a short deciduous period in subtropical areas. It derives its name because its flowers resemble orchids in their shape. The genus is widely cultivated in tropical and subtropical climates and is comprised of over 200 species. Anacacho orchid tree (B. congesta) occurs in southern Texas and northeastern Mexico.

BLACK LOCUST
Robinia pseudoacacia

③ 🌳 🔶 🌲 🏠

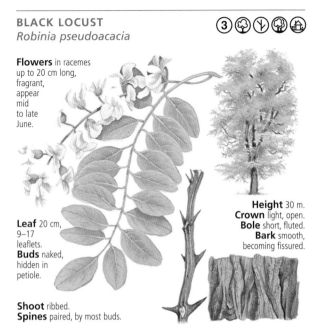

Flowers in racemes up to 20 cm long, fragrant, appear mid to late June.

Height 30 m.
Crown light, open.
Bole short, fluted.
Bark smooth, becoming fissured.

Leaf 20 cm, 9–17 leaflets.
Buds naked, hidden in petiole.

Shoot ribbed.
Spines paired, by most buds.

Black locust, also called False acacia, is native to the eastern United States. 'Frisia' has golden leaves. Clammy locust (*R. viscosa*) has glands on the shoot which secrete a sticky exudation.

HONEY LOCUST
Gleditsia triacanthos

⑤ 🌳 🔶 🌲 🏠

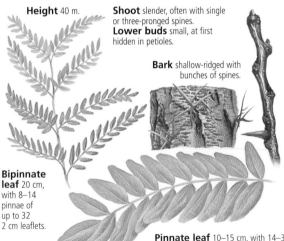

Height 40 m.

Shoot slender, often with single or three-pronged spines.
Lower buds small, at first hidden in petioles.

Bark shallow-ridged with bunches of spines.

Bipinnate leaf 20 cm, with 8–14 pinnae of up to 32 2 cm leaflets.

Pinnate leaf 10–15 cm, with 14–36 leaflets each 2–4 cm, remotely serrate.

Honey locust has a twisted pod to 20 cm long and thorns on the stem, although 'Inermis' is often preferred in towns as it lacks thorns. Water locust (*G. aquatica*) has oval 5 cm pods. Texas honey locust (*G. x texana*), with 12 cm pods, is their hybrid.

PAGODA TREE
Sophora japonica

④ ⊛ ⊽ ⌂

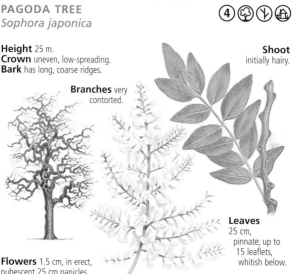

Height 25 m.
Crown uneven, low-spreading.
Bark has long, coarse ridges.

Shoot initially hairy.

Branches very contorted.

Leaves 25 cm, pinnate, up to 15 leaflets, whitish below.

Flowers 1.5 cm, in erect, pubescent 25 cm panicles, appearing August–September.

Pagoda tree is a native of China and Korea and differs from Robinia in its pointed, hairy leaflets and its lack of spines. It produces white, pea-shaped flowers and pods of up to 8 cm. Texas sophora (*S. affinis*) has white flowers, tinged pink, in a raceme and pods constricted around each seed.

SILVER WATTLE
Acacia dealbata

⑨ ⊛ ⊽ ⌂

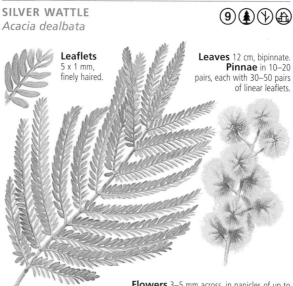

Leaflets 5 x 1 mm, finely haired.

Leaves 12 cm, bipinnate.
Pinnae in 10–20 pairs, each with 30–50 pairs of linear leaflets.

Flowers 3–5 mm across, in panicles of up to 30 globular heads, appearing January.

This short-lived, Australian tree is common only in the warmest areas of California, where it is widely planted as a street tree. It rarely exceeds 15 m.

MIMOSA / SILK TREE
Albizia Julibrissin

Shoots lacking terminal buds, lateral buds small, rounded, brownish with 2–3 scales.
Twigs slender, angled, grayish at maturity with abundant lenticels, glabrous.
Bark smooth, gray-brown.

Fruit thin, glabrous, brownish legume 12–18 cm, 25 mm wide, maturing September–October, often persisting until spring.

Flowers short-peduncled heads crowded toward ends of branches, fragrant.
Stamens numerous, to 3 cm, pinkish, tubed at base surrounding ovary. Flowering from May–August.

Leaves alternate, deciduous, bipinnately compound to 30 cm, with up to 25 pinnae and 40 or more 0.5–1 cm oblong, falcate, dark green leaflets, sometimes pubescent below, emerge May prior to flowering.

A small tree to 10 m with a broad, often flat-topped, open crown and fern-like leaves. Flowers vary in color from white and pink to red presenting a visual powder puff effect. This species is native to southern Asia, China and Japan. Introduced in the mid-18th century, its brightly colored flowers and profuse flowering habit earned the Mimosa a favored place in landscapes in the southern United States.

GOLDEN-SHOWER TREE
Cassia fistula

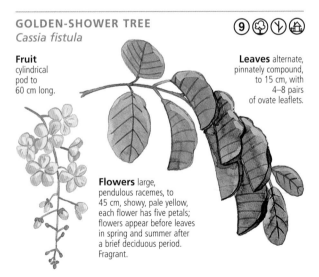

Fruit cylindrical pod to 60 cm long.

Leaves alternate, pinnately compound, to 15 cm, with 4–8 pairs of ovate leaflets.

Flowers large, pendulous racemes, to 45 cm, showy, pale yellow, each flower has five petals; flowers appear before leaves in spring and summer after a brief deciduous period. Fragrant.

Introduced from India, Golden-shower tree is one of the more common trees in subtropical and tropical America. Although rarely exceeding 10 m in height, its broad crown and profusion of blooms make this an exceptional ornamental. Classed as deciduous, it can retain some foliage throughout the year under favorable conditions. The seedpods have medicinal properties, particularly as a laxative.

MESQUITE
Prosopis glandulosa

⑥ 🌳 🍂 🌿

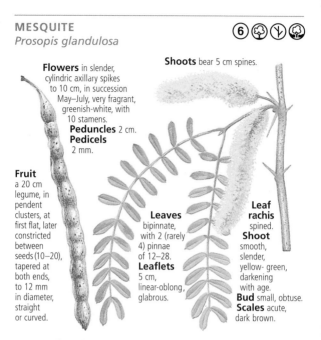

Flowers in slender, cylindric axillary spikes to 10 cm, in succession May–July, very fragrant, greenish-white, with 10 stamens.
Peduncles 2 cm.
Pedicels 2 mm.

Shoots bear 5 cm spines.

Fruit a 20 cm legume, in pendent clusters, at first flat, later constricted between seeds (10–20), tapered at both ends, to 12 mm in diameter, straight or curved.

Leaves bipinnate, with 2 (rarely 4) pinnae of 12–28.
Leaflets 5 cm, linear-oblong, glabrous.

Leaf rachis spined.
Shoot smooth, slender, yellow-green, darkening with age.
Bud small, obtuse.
Scales acute, dark brown.

Mesquite, from the southwestern United States, is a shrubby tree to 8 m, or rarely 15 m, often on several stems, with an open, irregular crown and thick, fissured dark red-brown bark. Screwbean mesquite (*P. pubescens*) differs in its thick, spirally-twisted pod, which only reaches 5 cm, and the leaflets with 10–16 hairy segments.

ROYAL POINCIANA
Delonix regia

⑩ 🌳 🍂 🏠

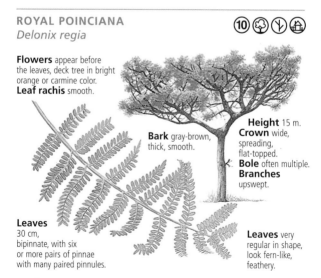

Flowers appear before the leaves, deck tree in bright orange or carmine color.
Leaf rachis smooth.

Bark gray-brown, thick, smooth.

Height 15 m.
Crown wide, spreading, flat-topped.
Bole often multiple.
Branches upswept.

Leaves 30 cm, bipinnate, with six or more pairs of pinnae with many paired pinnules.

Leaves very regular in shape, look fern-like, feathery.

Royal poinciana is a native of Madagascar but is now widely planted as an ornamental in tropical and subtropical regions, being valued for its dense racemes of showy flowers, with five petals with wavy margins. The fruit is a red-brown legume.

PRIDE-OF-BARBADOS /
DWARF POINCIANA
Caesalpinia pulcherrima

Twigs pronounced spines.

Leaves alternate bipinnately compound and resemble those of the Royal poinciana (*Delonix regia*). Deciduous in areas having prolonged dry seasons.

Fruit a flat, brown legume to 10 cm.

Flowers produced in panicles with five, showy, red petals with yellow margins and 10 exserted stamens having brightly colored red filaments about 5 cm long. Flowering often occurs during intervals from spring–fall.

Pride-of-Barbados is widely planted throughout the tropics and subtropics and highly valued as an ornamental because of its spectacular blooms. A native of the West Indies, it can attain a height of 5 to 8 m, although, in ornamental plantings, it is often shrubby and less than 3 m tall.

KENTUCKY COFFEE TREE
Gymnocladus dioicus

④🌳🌲🌳🌲

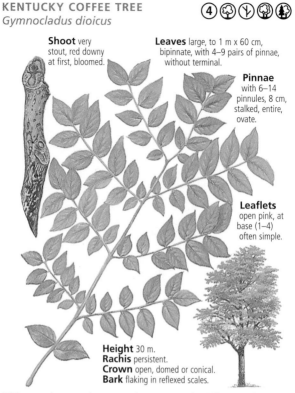

Shoot very stout, red downy at first, bloomed.

Leaves large, to 1 m x 60 cm, bipinnate, with 4–9 pairs of pinnae, without terminal.

Pinnae with 6–14 pinnules, 8 cm, stalked, entire, ovate.

Leaflets open pink, at base (1–4) often simple.

Height 30 m.
Rachis persistent.
Crown open, domed or conical.
Bark flaking in reflexed scales.

With stout shoots and enormous leaves, Kentucky coffee tree, from central eastern United States, is unmistakable. Separate trees bear male and female flowers, the latter in 30 cm panicles, and the 2 cm black seeds, in pods to 30 cm, were once used to make coffee.

YELLOWWOOD
Cladrastis lutea

⑤Ⓡ🌲🌳

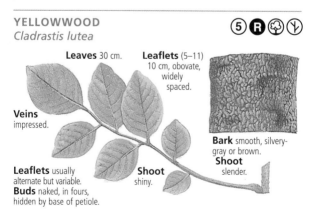

Leaves 30 cm.

Leaflets (5–11) 10 cm, obovate, widely spaced.

Veins impressed.

Leaflets usually alternate but variable.
Buds naked, in fours, hidden by base of petiole.

Shoot shiny.

Bark smooth, silvery-gray or brown.
Shoot slender.

This rare native of the middle eastern United States forms a tree to 15 m with a rounded crown and very bright green foliage. The white flowers are in terminal panicles to 40 cm, and the fruit is a flat, acuminate 8 cm pod. *Cladrastis*, meaning brittle, refers to the shoots. Some dendrologists refer to this species as *C. kentukea*.

GOLDEN CHAIN TREE
Laburnum x Watereri 'Vossii'

Bark smooth, with columns of buff-brown lenticels.

Leaflets to 6–8 cm, entire, elliptic or oval with cuneate base, matte above, glaucous and glabrous below, often cupped.

Height 8 m.
Crown spreading on arching, ascending branches.

Leaves compound, comprising three leaflets.

Flowers yellow, 2 cm, with five petals, two upper petals having brown markings.

Shoot gray-green at first, with adpressed hairs.

Buds gray-brown, ovoid with silky white hairs.

Fruit pods 4–6 cm, sparsely haired, 1–3 from each raceme.
Seeds toxic.
Flowers borne in dense racemes, 25–30 cm long, in late May–June.

One of the showiest of small garden trees, this hybrid of Laburnum (*L. anagyroides*) and Scotch laburnum (*L. alpinum*) combines the longer flowers of the former species with the dense racemes of the latter; both differ from the hybrid in having silky hairs on their leaf undersides. Hop tree (*Ptelea trifoliata*), in the *Rutaceae*, has similarly compound leaves spotted with oil glands. Its seeds have flat wings like those of elms.

Quassia Family *Simaroubaceae*

The Quassia family consists of mainly tropical and subtropical trees and shrubs. Some species produce substances used in medicines. Tree-of-heaven was the inspiration for the book *A Tree Grows in Brooklyn* by Betty Smith.

TREE-OF-HEAVEN
Ailanthus altissima

Shoot stout with gray scars.

Bark smooth gray-brown, with shallow cracks.

Leaf 60 cm, pinnate.
Leaflets (13–31) ovate with 1–3 basal teeth, red-stalked, open red.

Fruit a samara.

Bud ovoid; terminal absent.
Seed wings thin, 4 cm.

Tree-of-heaven, with a domed crown to 25 m, comes from north China. It grows rapidly and tolerates pollution, thriving in city streets and parks. Suckering prodigiously, it can produce leaves up to a meter long when such shoots are cut back.

Box Family *Buxaceae*

The Box family is a group of seven genera of mostly evergreen shrubs or small trees. It is widely distributed in temperate and subtropical regions. Four genera are cultivated as ornamentals and quite useful in topiary formations.

BOXWOOD
Buxus sempervirens

⑧ 🌲 🎍 🏛

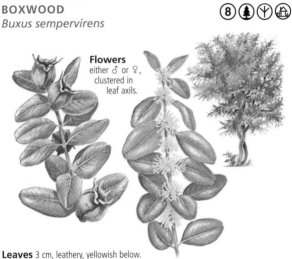

Flowers either ♂ or ♀, clustered in leaf axils.

Leaves 3 cm, leathery, yellowish below.
Fruit 1 cm, a capsule of three segments.

Native to some chalky areas of southern England, Boxwood is more common in Mediterranean countries. Its green shoots are square in section and covered in orange hairs while its flowers open in April. It is an ideal tree for hedging and topiary since its small, evergreen leaves are able to withstand repeated clipping. Its hard, heavy wood is much sought-after for engraving.

Members of the Mahogany family are mostly tropical in their distribution. There are 50 genera and about 1400 species. Eleven genera are cultivated, four of which produce valuable tropical hardwood lumber, while others provide insecticides and pharmaceuticals.

CHINABERRY
Melia azedarach

⑦ 🌳 🍂 🏛

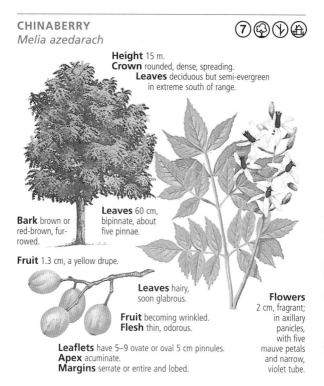

Height 15 m.
Crown rounded, dense, spreading.
Leaves deciduous but semi-evergreen in extreme south of range.

Bark brown or red-brown, furrowed.

Leaves 60 cm, bipinnate, about five pinnae.

Fruit 1.3 cm, a yellow drupe.

Leaves hairy, soon glabrous.

Fruit becoming wrinkled.
Flesh thin, odorous.

Leaflets have 5–9 ovate or oval 5 cm pinnules.
Apex acuminate.
Margins serrate or entire and lobed.

Flowers 2 cm, fragrant; in axillary panicles, with five mauve petals and narrow, violet tube.

The fruit of this fast-growing, short-lived tree is poisonous, but its hard bony seeds are used as beads. It is a native of Indo-China, now extensively planted in subtropical areas.

Spurge Family *Euphorbiaceae*

Euphorbiaceae, or the Spurge family, has over 7300 species worldwide. They range from spiny, cactus-like herbs to shrubs and small trees. Many members of the family have milky sap, which is poisonous and often an allergenic irritant. The sap of Manchineel tree of south Florida is extremely toxic and reportedly used as an arrow poison by indigenous peoples. Poinsettia is known for providing showy Christmas decorations.

POPCORN TREE / CHINESE TALLOW TREE
Sapium sebiferum

⑧ 🐿 🌱 🏠 🐿

Leaves alternate, simple, broadly rhombic and acuminate, 3–6 cm, on a long petiole having two glands at the junction with the blade. **Margins** entire.

Flowers monoecious, in slender, greenish-yellow spikes 5 cm long, usually clustered at the ends of branches. **Individual flowers** small, unisexual.

Leaves medium, green, resemble Trembling aspen, turn a variety of colors in the fall from yellow through orange-red to purplish-red.

Twigs and **Branches** slender, smooth, turning brown at maturity, dotted with small lenticels.
Twigs and **leaves** exude a milky sap when broken.
Bark at maturity is narrowly fissured, black and reticulate.

Fruit globose, whitish, waxy capsule, to 15 mm, splitting along three sutures and resembling a piece of popcorn when ripe.

Chinese tallow tree, a native of China, Japan and Korea, was introduced into the warm regions of the southern United States in the mid-1800s. A small tree, usually 10 m tall, with its fall coloration and prolific white, waxy fruit, which persists into the early winter, make it an attractive lawn tree. It is an aggressive invader of wetlands along the coastal plains of the southern United States and was declared a noxious weed in several southern states. The waxy coat on the seeds is extracted and provides a source of tallow in China. The milky sap and seeds are poisonous.

188

Cashew Family *Anacardiaceae*

The *Anacardiaceae* are represented by 60 genera extending from the tropics to temperate regions. It provides such familiar fruits and nuts as mangos, cashews and pistachios. The family also provides such noxious plants as Poison ivy, Poison oak and Poison sumac.

CASHEW
Anacardium occidentale

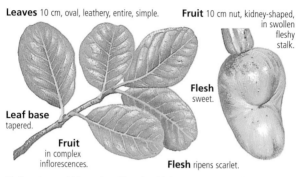

Leaves 10 cm, oval, leathery, entire, simple.

Fruit 10 cm nut, kidney-shaped, in swollen fleshy stalk.

Flesh sweet.

Leaf base tapered.

Fruit in complex inflorescences.

Flesh ripens scarlet.

Cashew tree, which reaches 12 m, is widely grown not only for its familiar nuts but also for the Cashew apple whose edible flesh develops from the flower stalk and is used to make a lubricant. It is native to South America.

AMERICAN SMOKE TREE / CHITTAMWOOD
Cotinus obovatus

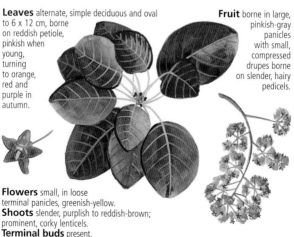

Leaves alternate, simple deciduous and oval to 6 x 12 cm, borne on reddish petiole, pinkish when young, turning to orange, red and purple in autumn.

Fruit borne in large, pinkish-gray panicles with small, compressed drupes borne on slender, hairy pedicels.

Flowers small, in loose terminal panicles, greenish-yellow.
Shoots slender, purplish to reddish-brown; prominent, corky lenticels.
Terminal buds present.
Habit a large shrub or small tree to 10 m.

Bark thin, scaly, gray to gray-brown.

American smoke tree is named for the large, fuzzy, purplish panicles bearing the flowers, which, from a distance, give the appearance of haze or smoke. The tree is a native of the southeastern United States and grows on rocky, often calcareous soils. It is used as an ornamental and is drought tolerant. A yellow dye can be extracted from the wood.

189

PISTACHIO
Pistacia vera

(7) (🌲) (🍂) (🏠)

Leaves palmately compound, with 3–11 leaflets, on long petiole.
Leaflets 6 cm, ovate.

Fruit 2.5 cm, an ovoid drupe, in erect panicles to 10 cm, reddish, develops from flowers on ♀ trees only.

Stone bony.
Seed green or yellow.

Leaflets sessile, at first downy, later leathery.
Apex acuminate.

Pistachio, a native of western Asia, grows to 10 m and is valued for the nut kernels, much used in confectionery. Pepper tree (*Schinus Molle*), a pendulous-branched tree to 15 m, has 15–25 toothed leaflets and pink, pepperlike fruits.

STAGHORN SUMAC
Rhus typhina

(5) (🌳) (🍂) (🏠)

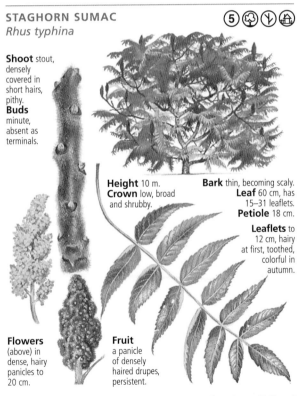

Shoot stout, densely covered in short hairs, pithy.
Buds minute, absent as terminals.

Height 10 m.
Crown low, broad and shrubby.

Bark thin, becoming scaly.
Leaf 60 cm, has 15–31 leaflets.
Petiole 18 cm.

Leaflets to 12 cm, hairy at first, toothed, colorful in autumn.

Flowers (above) in dense, hairy panicles to 20 cm.

Fruit a panicle of densely haired drupes, persistent.

The brilliance of its autumn foliage and the curiosity of its crimson "lollipop" fruits persisting well into winter have made this sumac, native to the woods of the northeastern United States, a popular garden tree. Its common name refers to its branching habit and hairy twigs.

Holly Family *Aquifoliaceae*

The Holly family contains two genera of mostly evergreen shrubs and trees. Many of the species are cultivated for their attractive foliage and red berries often used in Christmas decorations.

AMERICAN HOLLY
Ilex opaca

⑤ 🌲 🜁 🌲 🏠

Height 15 m, occasionally 30 m.
Crown narrow, dense, conical.
Leaves more spiny on lower branches.
Crown of wild trees more open.
Branches upswept at tips.

Shoot densely hairy at first, red-brown, later smooth, brown.

Leaves 10 cm, thick, leathery, glossy, dark green above, yellowish below with prominent veins, persist three years.

♂ **flowers** in cymes of 3–9.
♀ **flowers** single or in threes.

Fruit 6 mm, ovoid, in clusters.
Skin red, tough.
Flesh yellow, holds four ribbed, yellow seeds.

Bark light gray, thin, smooth but warty.
Bud small, green, sharply pointed.
Fruit ripens autumn, persistent.

A slow growing tree, this species is widely distributed in the southeast United States and as far north as Massachusetts. It is often cultivated and clipped in hedges. The berried branches of female trees are used for decoration. English holly (*I. Aquifolium*) has smaller, more glossy leaves and flowers on last year's shoots.

YAUPON
Ilex vomitoria

⑧ 🌲 🜁 🌲

Apex obtuse.
Bud obtuse, very dark.

Bark very thin, only 6 mm, light red-brown, developing small scales.

Margins serrate.
Petiole grooved.
Leaves 5 cm, shiny dark green above, pale, opaque below, elliptic to oblong.

Fruit 6 mm, in great abundance on previous year's shoots, short-stalked, soon falls.

Native to the Southeast, Yaupon does not grow beyond 8 m, but is noticeable because of the abundance of its flowers and berries. Dahoon (*I. Cassine*), from the same region, has usually entire 7 cm leaves and shoots initially with silky hairs.

Rue Family *Rutaceae*

The Rue family contains about 1600 tropical and temperate species. The family is primarily noted for its citrus fruit, although it provides essential oils and medicines.

LIME
Citrus aurantifolia

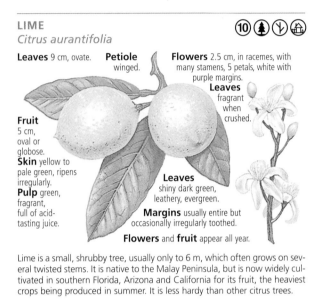

Leaves 9 cm, ovate. **Petiole** winged. **Flowers** 2.5 cm, in racemes, with many stamens, 5 petals, white with purple margins.

Leaves fragrant when crushed.

Fruit 5 cm, oval or globose. **Skin** yellow to pale green, ripens irregularly. **Pulp** green, fragrant, full of acid-tasting juice.

Leaves shiny dark green, leathery, evergreen.

Margins usually entire but occasionally irregularly toothed.

Flowers and **fruit** appear all year.

Lime is a small, shrubby tree, usually only to 6 m, which often grows on several twisted stems. It is native to the Malay Peninsula, but is now widely cultivated in southern Florida, Arizona and California for its fruit, the heaviest crops being produced in summer. It is less hardy than other citrus trees.

LEMON
Citrus Limon

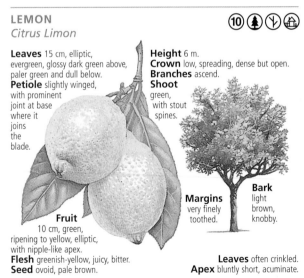

Leaves 15 cm, elliptic, evergreen, glossy dark green above, paler green and dull below. **Petiole** slightly winged, with prominent joint at base where it joins the blade.

Height 6 m. **Crown** low, spreading, dense but open. **Branches** ascend. **Shoot** green, with stout spines.

Fruit 10 cm, green, ripening to yellow, elliptic, with nipple-like apex. **Flesh** greenish-yellow, juicy, bitter. **Seed** ovoid, pale brown.

Margins very finely toothed.

Bark light brown, knobby.

Leaves often crinkled. **Apex** bluntly short, acuminate.

Lemon was introduced from the Far East. Although the fruit is a very familiar one, the tree is less widely distributed in the South than the lime, which is tolerant of a wider range of soils. The tree fruits throughout the year. The flowers, which are very fragrant, are white with a purple flush on the outside and have up to 40 stamens.

MANDARIN / TANGERINE
Citrus reticulata

⑨ 🌲 🌱 🏠

Shoots green, with fine thorns.

Leaves 10 cm, oval or lanceolate; glossy, dark green above, paler and dull below; entire.

Petiole 1 cm, not winged.

Fruit 8 cm, globose with broad dimpled ends.

Fruit divided into several fleshy segments inside loose, pithy skin.
Seeds attached to central edge of segments.

Although it can tolerate only the mildest of frosts, Mandarin, or Tangerine, is one of the hardiest of fruiting citrus species. It is further distinguished by its smaller leaves, its unarmed petiole and the loose skin of its fruit. It is a native of China and grows to 6 m with a spreading crown.

SWEET ORANGE
Citrus sinensis

⑨ 🌲 🌱 🏠

Shoot occasionally bears spines.
Leaves 15 cm, oblanceolate to ovate.
Petiole narrowly winged.

Flowers 3 cm, white, fragrant, single or in small lax clusters.

Height 10 m.
Crown rounded, dense.
Bole short.
Branches horizontal.

Fruit 10 cm, globose, orange-red or red, more rarely green or yellow, appear October–June.
Skin shiny, smooth.
Flesh red-orange.

Leaves dark, lustrous, yellow dots above, pale below.

This Chinese species is now widely grown commercially in the warmer regions, having been originally introduced by the European explorers. Its fruit, the familiar eating orange, often appears on the tree alongside the flower.

193

GRAPEFRUIT
Citrus x paradisi

(9)(🌲)(Y)(🏠)

Shoot glabrous, usually bears stout spines.
Leaves 15 cm, ovate, glabrous, soft, lustrous mid-green, paler below.
Petiole to 1.5 cm across, broadly winged.

Flowers 5 cm, white, in broad flat terminal or axillary clusters, Febuary–April.
Leaf margins undulate.

Height 15 m.

Crown dense, broad, conical or rounded, sometimes reaches ground level.
Branches pendulous at tips.
Bole short, often crooked.
Fruit always present, most ripening November–April.

Fruit 15 cm, globose, usually single, green, ripen yellow.
Skin very thick, smooth.
Flesh pale, juicy.

Grapefruit's large, juicy fruits have made it an important commercial tree. It can be grown in sites unsuitable for other citrus trees as its dense crown makes it resistant to wind.

KUMQUAT
Fortunella margarita

(9)(🌲)(Y)(🏠)

Leaves 6 cm, lanceolate or narrowly elliptic.
Base rounded.

Margins sometimes finely serrate.

Leaves lustrous dark green above, paler with yellow dots below.
Margins slightly crinkled.
Apex acute.

Fruit 3 cm, oblong or oval, pale orange, solitary or in small clusters.
Skin spotted with translucent glands.

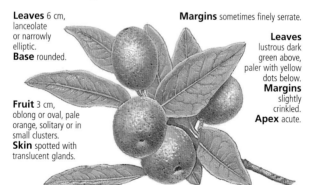

Discovered in eastern China in the middle of the last century by the botanist Robert Fortune, Kumquat forms a small tree, sometimes only to 5 m, with a spreading crown. The small fruits are eaten whole and have a distinctive bittersweet flavor.

KOREAN EVODIA
Evodia Danielii

(8) (R) (🌳) (Y) (🏛)

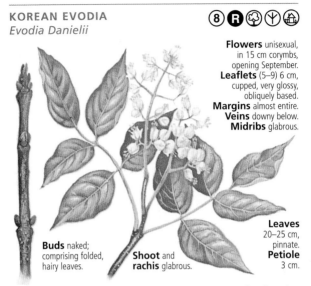

Flowers unisexual,
in 15 cm corymbs,
opening September.
Leaflets (5–9) 6 cm,
cupped, very glossy,
obliquely based.
Margins almost entire.
Veins downy below.
Midribs glabrous.

Leaves
20–25 cm,
pinnate.
Petiole
3 cm.

Buds naked;
comprising folded,
hairy leaves.

Shoot and
rachis glabrous.

This Korean and Chinese species is valuable for the lateness of its flowering. The Amur cork tree (*Phellodendron amurense*), noted for its thick and coarsely ridged corky bark, has larger leaves with 7–13 leaflets and smaller, grayish buds hidden in the leaf stalk. It is a native of northern China and Manchuria.

Spindle Family *Celastraceae*

Members of the Spindle, or Staff-tree family, are often cultivated for their showy foliage, flowers or fruit. The family is widely distributed around the world and contains about 800 species, some of which provide pharmaceuticals.

SPINDLE TREE
Euonymus europaea

(6) (🌸) (Y) (🏛) (🌳)

Flowers
1 cm,
four-petalled,
in cymes
of 3–8.

Shoot rounded, with four
longitudinal ridges.
Leaves 10 cm, opposite,
glabrous,
matte.
Height
6 m.

Fruit 15 mm, four-lobed,
deep pink, opening September
–October to reveal orange arils.

Crown
shrubby.

Native to most of Europe, Spindle is a small tree or shrub renowned for its showy fruit and the attractiveness of its purple-red autumn foliage. Its hard, non-splintering wood was once a useful material for making spindles and other domestic items such as skewers, pegs and knitting needles.

Planetree or Sycamore Family *Platanaceae*

The Planetree, or Sycamore, family has but a single genus native to the old and new world temperate regions. It is an important source of lumber and ornamental trees. While it has few botanical affiliations with the *Aceraceae*, the leaves of this family were once mistaken for those of maples. This is reflected in the specific epithets of two maples—*platanoides* and *pseudoplatanus*—and in that of *Platanus x acerifolia*. Planes always have alternate leaves.

ORIENTAL PLANE
Platanus orientalis

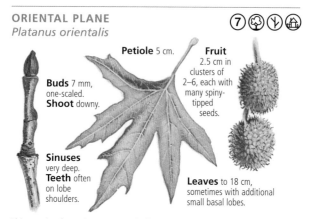

Petiole 5 cm.

Buds 7 mm, one-scaled. **Shoot** downy.

Fruit 2.5 cm in clusters of 2–6, each with many spiny-tipped seeds.

Sinuses very deep. **Teeth** often on lobe shoulders.

Leaves to 18 cm, sometimes with additional small basal lobes.

This species from the eastern Mediterranean region can grow 30 m high and is used as a shade tree in many southern European villages. Its shortish bole can achieve a girth as large as 13 m.

LONDON PLANE
Platanus x acerifolia

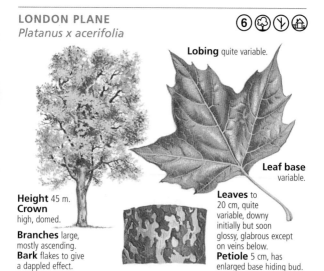

Lobing quite variable.

Leaf base variable.

Height 45 m. **Crown** high, domed.

Branches large, mostly ascending. **Bark** flakes to give a dappled effect.

Leaves to 20 cm, quite variable, downy initially but soon glossy, glabrous except on veins below. **Petiole** 5 cm, has enlarged base hiding bud.

A majestic habit, resistance to urban atmospheres and pollarding have contributed to this tree's popularity. Its success was confirmed last century when it became widely planted in London streets. It is a hybrid of *P. orientalis* and *P. occidentalis* and has been planted in the United States from coast to coast. Some dendrologists refer to London Plane as *P. x hispanica*.

AMERICAN SYCAMORE
Platanus occidentalis

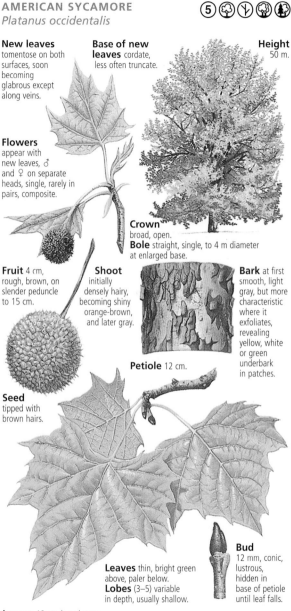

New leaves tomentose on both surfaces, soon becoming glabrous except along veins.

Base of new leaves cordate, less often truncate.

Height 50 m.

Flowers appear with new leaves, ♂ and ♀ on separate heads, single, rarely in pairs, composite.

Crown broad, open.
Bole straight, single, to 4 m diameter at enlarged base.

Fruit 4 cm, rough, brown, on slender peduncle to 15 cm.

Shoot initially densely hairy, becoming shiny orange-brown, and later gray.

Bark at first smooth, light gray, but more characteristic where it exfoliates, revealing yellow, white or green underbark in patches.

Petiole 12 cm.

Seed tipped with brown hairs.

Bud 12 mm, conic, lustrous, hidden in base of petiole until leaf falls.

Leaves thin, bright green above, paler below.
Lobes (3–5) variable in depth, usually shallow.

Leaves 18 cm, broad ovate.
Sinuses rounded.

American sycamore, the tallest native broadleaf tree, is found on moist sites throughout the eastern United States. The var. glabrata, found in Texas and Mexico, has less toothed leaves, which are more deeply lobed, often with acute sinuses. With more deeply lobed leaves and fruits in racemes of three to seven heads, California sycamore (*P. racemosa*) has dentately toothed leaves while Arizona sycamore (*P. Wrightii*) has entire lobing.

Maple Family *Aceraceae*

Maples are noted for the rich autumnal tints of their leaves which are usually palmately lobed and always set in opposite pairs. Small green or yellow flowers appear in corymbs, racemes or panicles and are normally bisexual. Distinctive samaras (fruit keys) consist of paired seeds (nutlets) set in flat, membranous wings to facilitate wind dispersal.

NORWAY MAPLE
Acer platanoides

Flowers open early April before leaves in erect corymbs of 20–30.
Petals 8 mm wide.
Buds 1 cm tall, red-purple.
Shoot stout, hairless, dark brown.

Height 25 m.
Crown broad-domed, densely leaved.
Bole short.
Bark gray-brown, finely ridged.

Leaf 12 x 15 cm, cordate. 2–6 coarse teeth per lobe, edges of central lobes parallel.
Blade underside paler.
Leaf stalk long, 15 cm, with milky sap distinguishing it from similar maples.

Samara nutlets flat.
Wings each 3–5 cm, almost horizontal.

'Schwedleri' opens pink-red, green by summer, then purple in autumn.

'Drummondii' has small leaves with white or cream variegation.

Native to northern and central Europe, the Norway maple is most attractive in spring when its flowers open and in autumn when its foliage turns deep yellow. This tree is suited to urban sites and a wide range of cultivars is available: 'Crimson King' has deep red-purplish leaves throughout summer.

PLANETREE / SYCAMORE MAPLE
Acer pseudoplatanus

⑤ 🌳 🌱 🏠

Shoot green-brown.
Buds ovoid, 1 cm, green, red margins.
Flowers 50–100, hanging in dense 12 cm panicles.

Samara wings each 3 cm, set at 90°.

Height 35 m.

Crown broad.
Branches billow.
Bark scaly, light gray-brown; silver, smooth on young trees.

Leaf to 18 x 26 cm on young trees, more often 15 x 20 cm, five lobes, (rarely 3–7).
Teeth coarse.
Blade underside glaucous.

Veins net-like.
Leaf stalk reddish.

1 **2**

1 **2** **3**

'Erectum' (1) has fastigiate branches. Leaves of **'Purpureum'** (2) are matte green with purple undersides.

'Brilliantissimum' leaf (1) opens shrimp-pink, turning through yellow to dark green. **'Leopoldii'** (2) can have leaves stained yellowish-pink. **'Worleei'** leaf (3) opens in gold and yellow, fading to green-yellow.

A wide tolerance of different sites and a facility to germinate, which can make it a rapacious weed, have enabled Sycamore maple to colonize most of Britain. It is found across the whole of North America, although it is less common than in Britain. Its resistance to salt spray makes it an ideal coastal tree. Sycamore maples are often grown for hard, close-grained timber and to act as windbreaks.

FIELD MAPLE / HEDGE MAPLE
Acer campestre

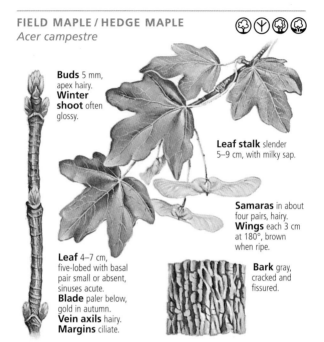

Buds 5 mm, apex hairy. **Winter shoot** often glossy.

Leaf stalk slender 5–9 cm, with milky sap.

Samaras in about four pairs, hairy. **Wings** each 3 cm at 180°, brown when ripe.

Leaf 4–7 cm, five-lobed with basal pair small or absent, sinuses acute. **Blade** paler below, gold in autumn. **Vein axils** hairy. **Margins** ciliate.

Bark gray, cracked and fissured.

Field maple, a common hedgerow tree throughout Europe and the only maple native to Britain, makes an excellent hedge or screen plant in the more temperate regions of the United States. The Miyabe maple (*A. Miyabei*), from Japan, has larger, paler leaves cut less than halfway to the leaf base.

ITALIAN MAPLE
Acer Opalus

Flowers appear in April before leaves, in pendulous corymbs. **Fruit** in bunches (8–16). **Wings** each 2.5 cm, acutely angled.

Winter twig glabrous with pale lenticels.

Leaf 12 cm, three- or five-lobed. **Teeth** coarse, irregular. **Veins** impressed. **Blade underside** glaucous, hairy. **Leaf stalk** 10 cm with watery sap.

Italian maple, also found in France and Spain, is a small tree reaching 15 m. Heldreich maple (*A. Heldreichii*) has deep, narrow leaf sinuses. Trautvetter's maple (*A. Trautvetteri*) has deep, wide leaf sinuses. Both these species have erect flower panicles.

OREGON MAPLE / BIGLEAF MAPLE
Acer macrophyllum ⑦ 🍁 🌳 🌲 🏠

Shoot stout, green.
Buds stout, conic with red-brown scales.

Leaf sinus deep, acute, rounded.

Leaf
paler below.
Leaf stalk
long, 15–35 cm,
red or green,
clasps stem
closely, almost
hiding bud.
Samaras
big, each wing
5 cm at 90°
or less.

Leaf blade very large, 20 x 35 cm,
five-lobed, thin-textured.
Teeth blunt.
Margins ciliate.

Flower panicles narrow, 25 cm.

This West Coast species, valued for its timber, grows quickly into a majestic tree of about 30 m with a tall, domed crown of ascending, arched branches. Oregon is the only maple with both milky sap and hanging panicles, and its large leaves and clasping leaf stalks will readily confirm this identification.

SUGAR MAPLE
Acer saccharum ③ 🍁 🌳 🌲 🌲 🏠

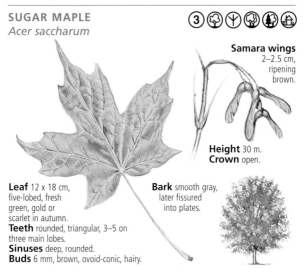

Samara wings 2–2.5 cm, ripening brown.

Height 30 m.
Crown open.

Leaf 12 x 18 cm,
five-lobed, fresh
green, gold or
scarlet in autumn.
Teeth rounded, triangular, 3–5 on
three main lobes.
Sinuses deep, rounded.
Buds 6 mm, brown, ovoid-conic, hairy.

Bark smooth gray,
later fissured
into plates.

In its native range stretching from eastern Canada to Texas, this is the tree tapped for maple syrup. Its leaf is not dissimilar to that of Norway maple, but has a watery sap. Black maple (*A. nigrum*) has darker, duller, yellow-veined leaves, which are cupped and three-lobed. Its bark is ridged.

SILVER MAPLE
Acer saccharinum

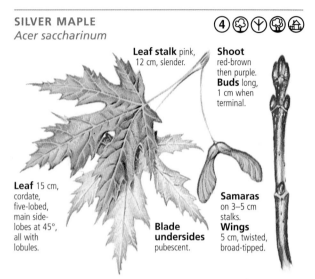

Leaf stalk pink, 12 cm, slender.

Shoot red-brown then purple. **Buds** long, 1 cm when terminal.

Leaf 15 cm, cordate, five-lobed, main side-lobes at 45°, all with lobules.

Blade undersides pubescent.

Samaras on 3–5 cm stalks. **Wings** 5 cm, twisted, broad-tipped.

Silver maple is native to eastern North America south of Quebec and grows to some 30 m with a tall, raggedly domed crown and a smooth, silvery bark. In early spring, its maroon flowers, opening before the leaves, enliven the tree; in autumn its foliage assumes spectacular hues of yellow, gold or red.

RED MAPLE
Acer rubrum

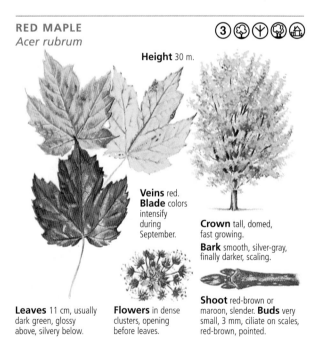

Height 30 m.

Veins red. **Blade** colors intensify during September.

Crown tall, domed, fast growing.

Bark smooth, silver-gray, finally darker, scaling.

Leaves 11 cm, usually dark green, glossy above, silvery below.

Flowers in dense clusters, opening before leaves.

Shoot red-brown or maroon, slender. **Buds** very small, 3 mm, ciliate on scales, red-brown, pointed.

This North American tree is aptly named since its flowers, fruits, shoots and autumn tints are all red or reddish; its leaf undersides and bark are silver. It is closely related to Silver maple, but has smaller, less deeply lobed leaves.

FULL-MOON MAPLE / JAPANESE MAPLE
Acer japonicum

⑥ 🌲 🌳 🏠

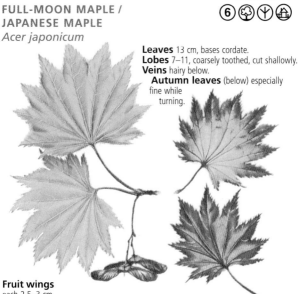

Leaves 13 cm, bases cordate.
Lobes 7–11, coarsely toothed, cut shallowly.
Veins hairy below.
Autumn leaves (below) especially fine while turning.

Fruit wings
each 2.5–3 cm.

Deriving its common name from its orbicular leaves, this tree is often represented by two clones: the larger 'Vitifolium' and the smaller, yellow-leaved 'Aureum,' which is often treated as *A. shivacalanum* 'Aureum.' Vine maple (*A. circinatum*), a small tree to 10 m from the Pacific Coast, has glabrous petioles.

DAVID MAPLE
Acer Davidii

④ Ⓡ 🌲 🌳 🏠

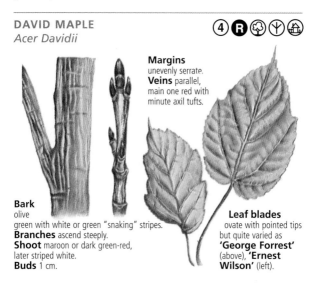

Margins unevenly serrate.
Veins parallel, main one red with minute axil tufts.

Bark olive green with white or green "snaking" stripes.
Branches ascend steeply.
Shoot maroon or dark green-red, later striped white.
Buds 1 cm.

Leaf blades ovate with pointed tips but quite varied as **'George Forrest'** (above), **'Ernest Wilson'** (left).

This is the most common of the snake-bark maples, which have distinctive barks with white or greenish stripes and flowers in long, dense racemes. It has a wide natural distribution in China and, as a species, is extremely variable. One form, 'Ernest Wilson,' has a lower, rounded habit and more yellow, narrow leaves folded at the base of their main vein.

KYUSHU MAPLE
Acer capillipes

(5) (R) (🌳) (🌿) (🏛)

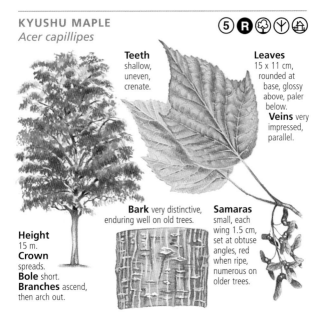

Teeth shallow, uneven, crenate.

Leaves 15 x 11 cm, rounded at base, glossy above, paler below.
Veins very impressed, parallel.

Height 15 m.
Crown spreads.
Bole short.
Branches ascend, then arch out.

Bark very distinctive, enduring well on old trees.

Samaras small, each wing 1.5 cm, set at obtuse angles, red when ripe, numerous on older trees.

This Japanese maple is the only snake-bark whose leaves have small forward-pointing side lobes, impressed veins and yellowish axil "pegs." Its autumn colors and red shoots and buds give it the alternative name of "Red snake-bark maple."

MOOSEWOOD MAPLE
Acer pensylvanicum

(5) (🌳) (🌿) (🏛)

Leaves to 20 cm, yellow in autumn, quite variable in size and shape but always cordate with rounded sinuses.

Leaf stalk stout and long, 12 cm, grooved.

Teeth sharp, uneven.
Sinuses shallow.
Veins have red hairs below.

Fruit 5 cm across, bunched, abundant.
Wings curved, widely set.

Moosewood, from eastern North America, is the only snake-bark not indigenous to eastern Asia. Honshu maple (*A. rufinerve*), from Japan, has smaller leaves with rufous, pubescent veins, buds bloomed white and small, round nutlets. Hers' maple (*A. Grosseri* var. *Hersii*) has matte leaves, larger fruit and no red coloring.

MONTPELIER MAPLE
Acer monspessulanum

⑤ Ⓡ 🌳 🌲 🏠

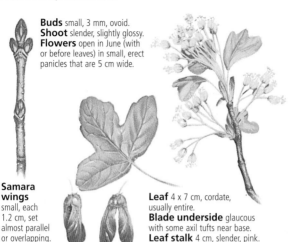

Buds small, 3 mm, ovoid.
Shoot slender, slightly glossy.
Flowers open in June (with or before leaves) in small, erect panicles that are 5 cm wide.

Samara wings small, each 1.2 cm, set almost parallel or overlapping.

Leaf 4 x 7 cm, cordate, usually entire.
Blade underside glaucous with some axil tufts near base.
Leaf stalk 4 cm, slender, pink.

This maple has a wide natural range from Mediterranean Spain and north Africa to Iran and is often used for hedging, very rarely reaching its maximum height of 15 m. Cretan maple (*A. sempervirens*) is almost evergreen and has small, stiff, variable leaves, which may be unlobed or have three rounded lobes.

AMUR MAPLE
Acer Ginnala

④ Ⓡ 🌳 🌲 🏠

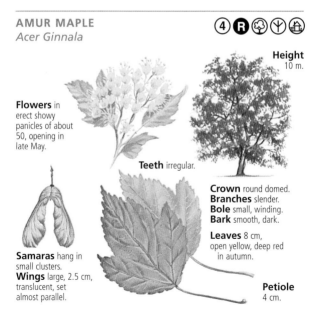

Height 10 m.

Flowers in erect showy panicles of about 50, opening in late May.

Teeth irregular.

Crown round domed.
Branches slender.
Bole small, winding.
Bark smooth, dark.

Leaves 8 cm, open yellow, deep red in autumn.

Samaras hang in small clusters.
Wings large, 2.5 cm, translucent, set almost parallel.

Petiole 4 cm.

Amur maple, from northeast Asia, is a small shrubby tree that shows its early autumn crimson for a brief period in September. Trident maple (*A. buergeranum*) has three-lobed leaves, the lobes pointing directly forward in the manner of Neptune's trident. These leaves have silvery undersides.

BOX ELDER
Acer negundo

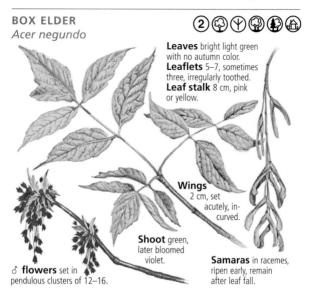

Leaves bright light green with no autumn color.
Leaflets 5–7, sometimes three, irregularly toothed.
Leaf stalk 8 cm, pink or yellow.

Wings 2 cm, set acutely, in-curved.

Shoot green, later bloomed violet.

♂ **flowers** set in pendulous clusters of 12–16.

Samaras in racemes, ripen early, remain after leaf fall.

Possibly overplanted, Box elder rarely produces a fine specimen; its cultivar 'Variegatum' produces both fruit and leaves that are variegated white. Henry maple (*A. Henryi*) is a Chinese species with red autumn foliage, pink-red leaf stalks and bright green, glossy shoots.

Pittosporum Family *Pittosporaceae*

Pittosporum, a member of the *Pittosporaceae*, is widely planted as an ornamental hedge in the warmer regions of the North Temperate landscapes. It is difficult to care for as it is plagued by several insect and fungal problems in humid conditions.

PITTOSPORUM
Pittosporum tenuifolium

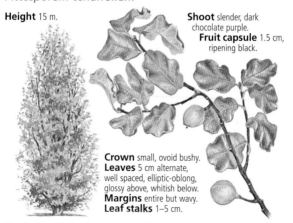

Height 15 m.

Shoot slender, dark chocolate purple.
Fruit capsule 1.5 cm, ripening black.

Crown small, ovoid bushy.
Leaves 5 cm alternate, well spaced, elliptic-oblong, glossy above, whitish below.
Margins entire but wavy.
Leaf stalks 1–5 cm.

The Pittosporum family comes mainly from Australasia, Southeast Asia and South Africa although one species is native to Madeira. Pittosporum itself, noticeable for its fragrant flowers, is native to both islands of New Zealand.

Horse Chestnut Family *Hippocastanaceae*

This small family named after the resemblance of its fruit to that of *Castanea*, is dominated by the *Aesculus* genus. Opposite, palmately compound leaves, showy and erect flower panicles and large seeds are identifying features.

HORSE CHESTNUT
Aesculus Hippocastanum

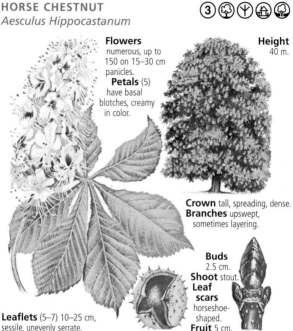

Flowers numerous, up to 150 on 15–30 cm panicles.
Petals (5) have basal blotches, creamy in color.

Height 40 m.

Crown tall, spreading, dense.
Branches upswept, sometimes layering.

Buds 2.5 cm.
Shoot stout.
Leaf scars horseshoe-shaped.
Fruit 5 cm.

Leaflets (5–7) 10–25 cm, sessile, unevenly serrate.

Children often collect and carve the fruit of this species. Japanese horse chestnut (*A. turbinata*) also has sticky buds and sessile leaflets, but the latter are evenly toothed and can be up to 40 cm long.

RED HORSE CHESTNUT
Aesculus x carnea

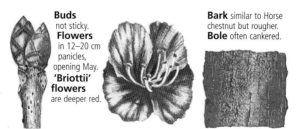

Buds not sticky.
Flowers in 12–20 cm panicles, opening May.
'Briottii' flowers are deeper red.

Bark similar to Horse chestnut but rougher.
Bole often cankered.

This hybrid is smaller than its Horse chestnut parent while its buds resemble those of its other parent, American red buckeye (*A. Pavia*), which has deeper red inflorescences.

CALIFORNIA BUCKEYE
Aesculus californica

Leaves palmately compound with 5 leaflets to 15 x 5 cm.

Flowers white or pale rose; fragrant; in dense upright panicles to 25 cm in June–July.
Stamens long.

Leaflet oblong-lanceolate, distinctly stalked.
Margins with fine, rounded teeth.

Fruit 10 cm, pale brown, smooth, obovoid, splits into three in late summer.
Seed single, shiny orange-brown.

Apex acuminate.
Base rounded.
Shoot smooth, pale green-brown.
Bud small, acute, thickly clear-resinous.

The only buckeye native to the western United States, this species forms a shrubby tree to 10 m with a broad, rounded crown, and bears a poisonous seed. Indian buckeye (*A. indica*) has seven lanceolate leaflets to 25 cm, glaucous below and pink and yellow blotched flowers.

YELLOW BUCKEYE
Aesculus octandra

Crown narrow with fine autumn yellows and orange-reds.
Branches small, pendulous, twisting.
Bole straight.
Bark gray or red-brown, smooth, becoming scaly.

Height 20 m.

Leaves have 5–7 leaflets with impressed veins.
Flowers 4 cm, dense, sometimes pink, on 10–15 cm panicles.
Petals (4) forward-pointing.

Leaflet margins finely serrate.

Leaflet 15 cm, glabrous, sometimes downy below, on 1.5 cm stalk.
Fruit 6 cm, smooth, two-seeded.

Buckeyes, whose name arose when their hila (pale, basal seed scars) were likened to the eyes of deer, are native to the eastern United States. They have non-sticky buds. Ohio buckeye (*A. glabra*) has a prickly fruit and keeled bud scales. The leaflets are smaller and have an unpleasant odor when crushed.

Linden Family *Tiliaceae*

Lindens have large, toothed, heart-shaped leaves, flowers that hang in cymes and large, distinctive bracts attached for half their length to the flower stalk. The fruit is dry and nutty.

LARGE-LEAVED LINDEN
Tilia platyphyllos

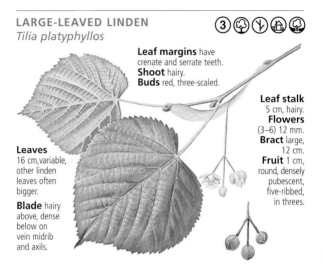

Leaf margins have crenate and serrate teeth.
Shoot hairy.
Buds red, three-scaled.

Leaf stalk 5 cm, hairy.
Flowers (3–6) 12 mm.
Bract large, 12 cm.
Fruit 1 cm, round, densely pubescent, five-ribbed, in threes.

Leaves 16 cm, variable, other linden leaves often bigger.

Blade hairy above, dense below on vein midrib and axils.

Large-leaved linden is native to most of Europe and has a narrow crown with branches that ascend steeply. Its bark is gray and fissured; shoots at the foot of the bole are rare. Lindens have fragrant flowers and may be planted for bee pasturage, as the honey produced from the nectar is pleasantly flavored.

SMALL-LEAVED LINDEN
Tilia cordata

Foliage dense, slightly pendent.
Leaves 6 cm.
Margins finely serrate.
Blades roundish, cordate, acuminate, shiny above, glaucous below.
Axil tufts prominent, orange-brown.

Height 30 m.

Crown narrow, very twiggy in winter.
Bole can be burred.

Winter shoot glossy brown with light lenticels.
Buds have two visible scales.

This species of linden is recognizable by the size of its roundish leaves and its flowers, which spread irregularly and do not hang. Mongolian linden (*T. mongolica*) is often planted where a smaller tree is required. Its leaves have large, coarse, triangular teeth which almost become lobes.

EUROPEAN LINDEN
Tilia x europaea

Leaf stalk
5 cm, hairless.
Buds green
or reddish.
Flowers in
cymes of 4–10,
fragrant.

Height 40 m.

Leaves 10 cm,
obliquely cordate.
Blades glabrous
below except for axil
tufts, often disfigured by
honeydew left by aphids.

Branches
ascend and billow.
Shoots sprout readily
on bole and in crown.
Bark ridged, heavily burred
where sprouts removed.

Often the largest broadleaf in an area, European linden is a natural hybrid of the Large- and Small-leaved species and its apparent ubiquity as a park and street tree has been attributed to 17th century Dutch horticulturists who found it easier to propagate than its parents. It is often pollarded.

CAUCASIAN LINDEN
Tilia x euchlora

Shoot usually green but can be
pink or red on outer foliage.
Buds red or yellow.

Flowers in cymes of 3–7.
Bract long, 8 cm.
Fruit hairy, five-ribbed, tapered.

Height
20 m.

Leaves
10 cm but can
be larger on basal
sprouts.
Blade obliquely
cordate, glossy green
with paler underside
and brown axil tufts.
Leaf stalk 5 cm.

Crown narrow, domed.
Branches ascend gently then
become very irregular and
decurrent, thicken with age and
sometimes touch the ground.
Bole smooth.

Caucasian linden has uncertain origins and may be a cross between the Small-leaved linden and the rare *T. dasystyla*, also from the Caucasus. Its agreeable foliage and immunity to aphids make it more suitable for streets than European linden although its lower branches eventually become far too decurrent for such sites.

AMERICAN LINDEN / AMERICAN BASSWOOD
Tilia americana

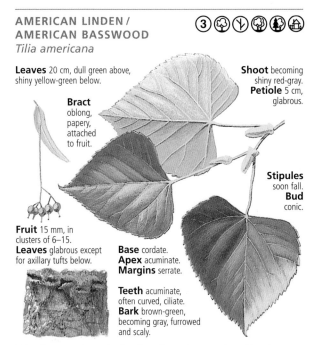

Leaves 20 cm, dull green above, shiny yellow-green below.

Shoot becoming shiny red-gray.
Petiole 5 cm, glabrous.

Bract oblong, papery, attached to fruit.

Stipules soon fall.
Bud conic.

Fruit 15 mm, in clusters of 6–15.
Leaves glabrous except for axillary tufts below.

Base cordate.
Apex acuminate.
Margins serrate.

Teeth acuminate, often curved, ciliate.
Bark brown-green, becoming gray, furrowed and scaly.

This tall tree, native to the East from Kentucky to southern Canada, grows to 40 m. It can be distinguished from other lindens by its bark and the flowers, which grow in cymes of 6–15 and are longer than the bracts.

WHITE BASSWOOD
Tilia heterophylla

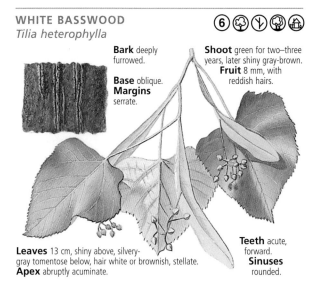

Bark deeply furrowed.

Shoot green for two–three years, later shiny gray-brown.
Fruit 8 mm, with reddish hairs.

Base oblique.
Margins serrate.

Leaves 13 cm, shiny above, silvery-gray tomentose below, hair white or brownish, stellate.
Apex abruptly acuminate.

Teeth acute, forward.
Sinuses rounded.

Native to inland sites in the southeastern United States, White basswood makes a tree to 25 m, distinguishable from American linden by its smaller leaves and hairy fruit. The name derives from the fibrous inner bark, or bast, once used for making ropes and brooms.

SILVER LINDEN
Tilia tomentosa

③ Ⓡ 🌳 🌱 🏠

Leaf blades 12 x 10 cm, rounded, obliquely cordate, silvery, densely pubescent below.
Buds 6–8 mm.
Shoot remains pubescent.

Leaf stalk to 5 cm, less than half blade length.

Height 30 m.

Bract 9 x 2 cm.
Flower buds (7–10) open late July.

Crown broadly domed.
Branches ascend steeply.
Bark smoothish gray with cross ridges.

Silver linden displays an attractive habit, especially when its pubescent leaves are ruffled by wind. It is a native of the Balkans. Oliver linden (*T. Oliveri*), from China, has larger, evenly cordate leaves and glabrous petioles and shoots.

PENDENT SILVER LINDEN
Tilia petiolaris

③ 🌳 🌱 🏠

Height 30 m.

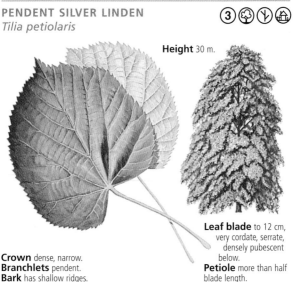

Crown dense, narrow.
Branchlets pendent.
Bark has shallow ridges.

Leaf blade to 12 cm, very cordate, serrate, densely pubescent below.
Petiole more than half blade length.

Usually grafted onto *T. x europaea* and producing an unsightly change in bark texture at a height of some 2 m, this tree hybridizes with *T. americana* to produce Von Moltke linden (*T. x Moltkei*), whose larger leaves are lightly pubescent below.

Soapberry Family *Sapindaceae*

Twenty-two of the 150 genera of the *Sapindaceae* family are cultivated for their ornamental or for their edible fruit value. Litchi produces a valuable fruit.

GOLDEN RAIN TREE
Koelreuteria paniculata

⑤ 🌳 🍂 🏠

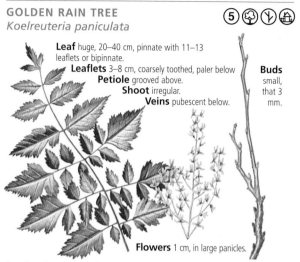

Leaf huge, 20–40 cm, pinnate with 11–13 leaflets or bipinnate.
Leaflets 3–8 cm, coarsely toothed, paler below
Petiole grooved above.
Shoot irregular.
Veins pubescent below.

Buds small, that 3 mm.

Flowers 1 cm, in large panicles.

A native of Japan and China, this tree was introduced into America in 1763. It reaches a maximum height of 15 m, has a widespreading crown and is distinguished by its decurrent leaflets, showy flowers and bladder-like fruit.

Tea Family *Theaceae*

Members of the Tea family are commonly cultivated for their showy flowers. One genus (*Camellia*) of this mainly tropical and subtropical family is the source of commercial tea.

CAMELLIA
Camellia japonica

⑦ 🌲 🍂 🏠

Flowers 10 cm, with five spreading petals.

Leaves 10 x 5 cm, oval or ovate, shiny green above, spotted below.

Height 12 m.
Bark smooth, gray.
Crown rounded or conical, often shrubby on many stems.

Leaves leathery.

Flowers solitary, sessile.

Margins shallowly toothed.

Commonly a garden shrub, Camellia is capable of making a small, broad tree. The fruit is a brown, woody capsule, and many of the 15,000 cultivars have flowers in colors other than the natural red. The Sasanqua camellia (*C. Sasanqua*) has hairy leaves and shoots.

JAPANESE STEWARTIA
Stewartia Pseudocamellia

Buds 5 mm, shiny.

Flowers 6 cm across, cup-shaped, on 1 cm pedicel.

Veins impressed.

Leaves 9 cm, dull above, shiny and silky-haired below.

Shoot glabrous, slender.

Bark brown with purple-gray scales, orange where flaking has occurred.

Japanese stewartia, a small, slender tree to 15 m, is noted for its attractive flowers, which remain in bloom over several weeks from July, and the brilliant colors of its autumn leaves. Mountain stewartia (*S. ovata*) has leaves with rounded bases and 10 cm flowers. The fruit is a five-celled, pointed capsule.

LOBLOLLY-BAY
Gordonia lasianthus

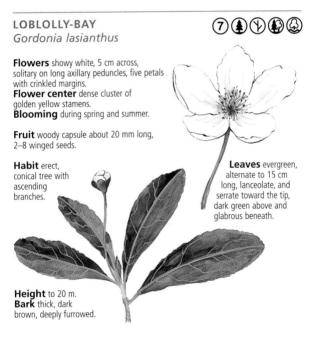

Flowers showy white, 5 cm across, solitary on long axillary peduncles, five petals with crinkled margins.
Flower center dense cluster of golden yellow stamens.
Blooming during spring and summer.

Fruit woody capsule about 20 mm long, 2–8 winged seeds.

Habit erect, conical tree with ascending branches.

Leaves evergreen, alternate to 15 cm long, lanceolate, and serrate toward the tip, dark green above and glabrous beneath.

Height to 20 m.
Bark thick, dark brown, deeply furrowed.

This native of the southeastern United States is commonly found in swamps and bays in coastal flatwoods. Its showy, white flowers attract the eye as one travels through the coastal piney woods. It is closely related to the Camellia, a showy, flowering shrub and a favorite of Southern gardeners.

Tupelo Family *Nyssaceae*

The Tupelo family contains three genera native to North America and Asia. Tupelo trees are important sources of timber, mainly for railroad ties. The other genera are mainly used as ornamentals.

TUPELO
Nyssa sylvatica

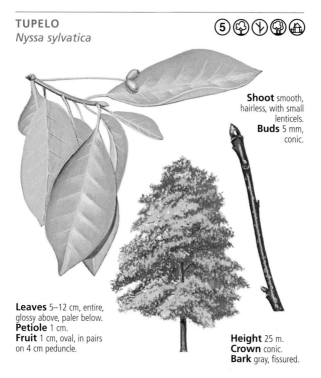

Shoot smooth, hairless, with small lenticels.
Buds 5 mm, conic.

Leaves 5–12 cm, entire, glossy above, paler below.
Petiole 1 cm.
Fruit 1 cm, oval, in pairs on 4 cm peduncle.

Height 25 m.
Crown conic.
Bark gray, fissured.

The genus *Nyssa* comprises four species: three from the eastern United States and one from China. Tupelo, or Sour gum, is the most common. Water tupelo (*N. aquatica*) has larger 2.5 cm fruits and oblong-obovate leaves, often toothed, to 18 cm.

Myrtle Family *Myrtaceae*

With over 3,000 species, the *Myrtaceae* is mainly a family of Southern Hemisphere, tropical and Asiatic trees and shrubs. Several genera, notably *Eucalyptus*, are important timber and fiber producers. Other genera are noted for their essential oil and spice production, including cloves and allspice.

CIDER GUM
Eucalyptus Gunnii

Adult leaves
10 cm, stalked alternate.

Juvenile leaves
sessile, opposite.

Fruit
in threes, 6 mm.

Height 35 m.
Crown conic, with wispy halo when growing fast.
Bark peels in orange strips to expose smooth gray surface below.

Cider gum — so called as a cider can be made from the sap — is the hardiest gum. It is a native of Tasmania and coppices readily if cut back. Before opening, the flowers are covered by a cap (operculum) of fused petals.

SNOW GUM
Eucalyptus niphophila

Flowers in clusters of 9–11, with mass of creamy white stamens and common stalk.
Buds set previous summer.

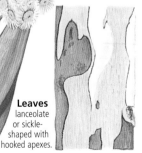

Bark bluish or bloomed snow-white, occasionally red-brown.

Leaves
lanceolate or sickle-shaped with hooked apexes.

Leaves 14 cm, thick, hard.
Petiole 2 cm, wrinkled.

A small tree reaching 10 m, Snow gum grows wild in southeastern Australia at elevations up to 2,000 m above sea level. Red flowering gum (*E. ficifolia*) grows to 15 m and is less hardy. Its flowers have red stamens with dark red anthers.

BLUE GUM
Eucalyptus globulus

Flower buds glaucous, ridged, wrinkled, 2.5 cm.

Leaves 30 cm, blue-green, glossy, alternate, on a short petiole.

Juvenile leaves opposite, sessile, glaucous blue.

Fruit
3 cm, semi-spherical, ridged, sessile, blue-white.

Flowers
4 cm, solitary or rarely in twos or threes, a cluster of creamy white stamens.

Leaves lanceolate or sickle-shaped, with odor of camphor.
Apex acuminate, often curved.

This subtropical evergreen from Australia grows to 40 m in California with a domed crown and is recognizable by its light brown bark, which peels in long ribbons to reveal the smooth blue-gray underbark. Red gum (*E. Camaldulensis*) has a white or gray bark and red flowers borne in clusters of five to 10.

CAJEPUT / PAPERBARK TREE
Melaleuca quinquenervia

Leaves evergreen, alternate, lanceolate to 10 cm, with prominent parallel veins (5).
Leaf margins entire.
Petiole short, aromatic.

Bark white, papery, exfoliates in long, thin strips.
Spongy bark often several cm thick.
Branches pendulous.

Flowers occur in cylindrical, dense spikes resembling a bottlebrush; usually 8 cm on branches that continue growth as a leafy shoot; flowers sessile on branch, white, with exserted stamens to 20 mm.

Fruit oblong capsule.

Paperbark tree, native to Australia and New Guinea, was introduced as an ornamental into southern Florida. It is an invasive species that can form dense thickets in sandy wetlands. Florida has declared this tree a noxious weed species. The flowers are also attractive to bees, but honey from this species is of such poor quality that it is difficult to sell.

Elaeagnus Family *Elaeagnaceae*

The *Elaeagnaceae*, or Elaeagnus family, comprises three genera of North Temperate trees and shrubs. They are mainly cultivated as ornamental shrubs. Their fruit is an important food source to migrating birds.

RUSSIAN OLIVE
Elaeagnus angustifolia

Flowers
1 cm, bell-shaped, short-stalked, solitary or in threes at leaf bases.
Leaves
9 cm, oblong or lanceolate.

Height to 10 m.
Crown rounded, spreading.

Bole often leans.

Bark fissured, peeling.

Leaves dull, scaly above, silvery-scaled, dotted below.

Shoot with silvery scales, sometimes spined.

Fruit 2 cm, with silvery scales.
Flesh mealy.

A popular ornamental often used as a windbreak, this species from western Asia is profusely covered with silvery scales. It can tolerate dry climates, but it sometimes will not grow beyond a shrub. The fruit, containing an ellipsoid stone, is edible.

Dogwood Family *Cornaceae*

The *Cornaceae*, or Dogwood family, is noted for its generally showy flowers and fruit. This is a North American and Asiatic family of about 10 genera commonly used as ornamentals. The wood of Flowering dogwood is used in shuttles, woodcuts and golf club heads.

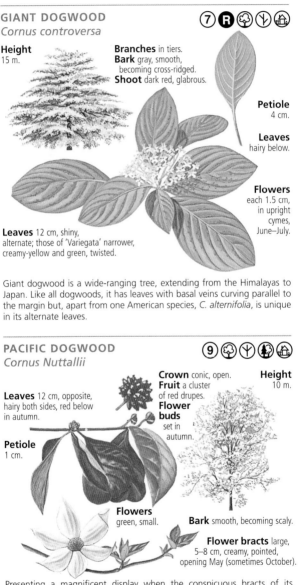

GIANT DOGWOOD
Cornus controversa

⑦ Ⓡ 🌸 🌱 🏠

Height
15 m.

Branches in tiers.
Bark gray, smooth, becoming cross-ridged.
Shoot dark red, glabrous.

Petiole
4 cm.

Leaves
hairy below.

Flowers
each 1.5 cm, in upright cymes, June–July.

Leaves 12 cm, shiny, alternate; those of 'Variegata' narrower, creamy-yellow and green, twisted.

Giant dogwood is a wide-ranging tree, extending from the Himalayas to Japan. Like all dogwoods, it has leaves with basal veins curving parallel to the margin but, apart from one American species, *C. alternifolia*, is unique in its alternate leaves.

PACIFIC DOGWOOD
Cornus Nuttallii

⑨ 🌸 🌱 🌲 🏠

Crown conic, open.
Fruit a cluster of red drupes.
Flower buds set in autumn.

Height
10 m.

Leaves 12 cm, opposite, hairy both sides, red below in autumn.

Petiole
1 cm.

Flowers
green, small.

Bark smooth, becoming scaly.

Flower bracts large, 5–8 cm, creamy, pointed, opening May (sometimes October).

Presenting a magnificent display when the conspicuous bracts of its flower-heads open, Pacific dogwood is a native ornamental from the West Coast of the United States where it reaches 30 m. Flowering dogwood (*C. florida*) has smaller leaves and always has four bracts.

FLOWERING DOGWOOD
Cornus florida

Flowers 5 mm, greenish-yellow, crowded into dense heads; subtended by four showy, white bracts, each 5 cm long to 4 cm broad.

Bracts arranged as a cross, notched at tip.

Blooms usually appear before leaves during early to mid-spring.

Stems slender, green when young, turning to purplish-brown and glabrous at maturity; globose flower buds occur at end of twigs and are flattened into a biscuit shape.

Branches and **laterals** of open grown trees often tend to occupy the same horizontal plane.

Bark charcoal-colored, broken into small, rectangular blocks.

Fruit to 15 mm, red drupe, usually occurring in clusters, ripening in September but often persisting on branches as late as mid-winter.

Leaves 10–15 cm, dark green (above), glaucous (below), deciduous, opposite, simple, ovate, entire but often ciliate margins.

Veins arc from the midrib toward margins.

Spring has come alive when Flowering dogwoods of eastern North America are in bloom. Dozens of cultivars are now being offered, including pink and red that make the spring show even more spectacular. This small tree, to 10 m tall, is a common, mid-canopy occupant of a variety of forest types from the pine flatwoods of the lower Gulf and Atlantic coasts to the mixed hardwoods of the Northeast and Midwest. The wood is used for engraver's blocks and turnings. The fruit is a major food source for migrating birds.

JAPANESE DOGWOOD
Cornus Kousa

(6) (🌳) (🍸) (🏛)

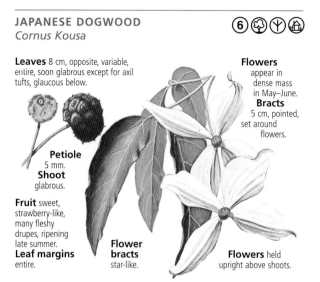

Leaves 8 cm, opposite, variable, entire, soon glabrous except for axil tufts, glaucous below.

Flowers appear in dense mass in May–June.
Bracts 5 cm, pointed, set around flowers.

Petiole 5 mm.
Shoot glabrous.

Fruit sweet, strawberry-like, many fleshy drupes, ripening late summer.
Leaf margins entire.

Flower bracts star-like.

Flowers held upright above shoots.

This dogwood is native to Japan and central China and grows to 10 m. Its branches are somewhat tiered like those of Table dogwood, from which it can be distinguished by its opposite leaves. It is notable for its brilliant autumn reds.

CORNELIAN CHERRY
Cornus mas

(4) (🌳) (🍸) (🏛)

Bark scaly.

Leaves 10 cm, variable, shiny above, with adpressed hairs on both sides.
Veins forward-curved.
Petiole 2 cm.

Height 10 m.
Crown spreading on several main stems.

Flowers in clusters 2.5 cm wide.

Fruit 1.5 cm.
Pedicel 1 cm.

Bud scales valvate.

Flowers appear before leaves.

Flowers 4 mm, with four bracts at cluster base.

This ornamental is a native of southern Europe and has long been cultivated for the bright yellow flowers, which cloak its bare branches in March and April. It is also known for its abundant fruit, which provides another attractive display in late summer. This fruit is edible and can be made into jam or syrup.

Heather Family *Ericaceae*

Members of the Heath or Heather family are mostly temperate shrubs or small trees. The family is noted for its wide variety of uses, from showy ornamentals such as Rhododendron, to edible fruits such as blueberry and cranberry, to the source of wood for pipe making.

STRAWBERRY TREE
Arbutus unedo   ⑧ 🌲 🌿 🏠

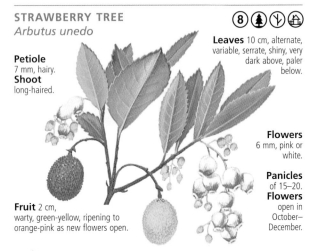

Petiole
7 mm, hairy.
Shoot
long-haired.

Leaves 10 cm, alternate, variable, serrate, shiny, very dark above, paler below.

Flowers
6 mm, pink or white.

Panicles
of 15–20.
Flowers
open in October–December.

Fruit 2 cm, warty, green-yellow, ripening to orange-pink as new flowers open.

Native to southwest Ireland and southern Europe, the Strawberry tree is a small evergreen up to 10 m high and has a dark red-brown, finely fissured bark. Its strawberry-like fruit takes a year to ripen. It can be eaten, but its insipidness is indicated by the tree's specific name *unedo* meaning "I eat (only) one."

PACIFIC MADRONE
Arbutus Menziesii   ⑨ 🌲 🌿 🌳 🌰 🏠

Leaves leathery.
Petiole
3 cm.

Bark smooth, peeling, cracked at base, orange-yellow.

Leaves to 14 cm, glossy above, very glaucous below.

Shoot green, later orange.

Flowers
3 mm, open April–May in 20 cm panicles.

Fruit 13 mm; a warty, globular berry that ripens in late summer.

Madrone is native to the Pacific Coast where it attains 30 m and is readily identified by its bark. Similar barks are carried by the Greek strawberry tree (*A. andrachne*) which has narrower leaves and *A. x andrachnoides* with serrate leaves.

SORREL TREE/SOURWOOD
Oxydendrum arboreum

⑥ 🌳 🍃 🌲 🏠

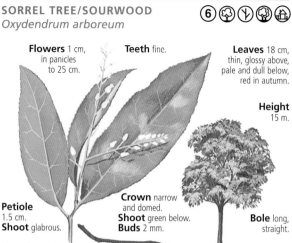

Flowers 1 cm, in panicles to 25 cm.

Teeth fine.

Leaves 18 cm, thin, glossy above, pale and dull below, red in autumn.

Height 15 m.

Petiole 1.5 cm.
Shoot glabrous.

Crown narrow and domed.
Shoot green below.
Buds 2 mm.

Bole long, straight.

Branches twisted.

Native to the eastern United States, Sorrel tree, or Sourwood, flowers into autumn with its foliage often already turning scarlet. Its name refers to the pleasantly sour taste of its leaves. The fruit capsules are whitish, 12 mm wide on long peduncles and split into five segments.

Ebony Family *Ebenaceae*

Ebony family members are noted for their very hard wood. Persimmon wood is used in bowling pins, and the fruit is edible and tasty when ripe.

PERSIMMON
Diospyros virginiana

⑤ 🌳 🍃 🌲 🏠

Bark black or dark gray.
Older bark cracked into squares.

Flowers 2 cm, open in July.

Leaves dark glossy above.

Fruit 4 cm, orange or purple.

Calyx four-lobed, persistent.

Leaves to 15 cm, waved, paler below.

Shoot slender, downy or glabrous.
Buds small.

Persimmon, from the southeastern United States, grows up to 20 m and is distinguished by its glossy leaves and astringent fruit, which is edible after exposure to autumn frosts. Date plum (*D. Lotus*), an Asian relative, has petioles only 1 cm long and 8 mm white flowers. Kaki (*D. Kaki*) has young shoots with brownish hairs.

Storax Family *Styracaceae*

The Storax family is mainly shrubs or small trees of wide distribution. This family comprises six genera mostly used as ornamentals.

JAPANESE SNOWBELL
Styrax japonicus

Leaves 8 cm, tapers both ends.

Petiole 6 mm.

Leaf margins waved. **Serration** remote.

Leaves cupped, glossier and paler below. **Apex** often droops.

Flowers 2.5 cm, white.

Fruit to 1.5 cm, in five-lobed calyx.

Shoot slightly hairy, zigzagged, speckled black.

Pedicels 2–4 cm.

Buds 4 mm, hairy, adpressed, conic, pale greenish-brown.

A native of Japan and China, Snowbell tree grows to 10 m with a dense, rounded crown of horizontal branches. Storax (*S. officinalis*) is a smaller tree with white down on the young twigs, leaves and flowers. It has ovate, cordate leaves and round fruits.

FRAGRANT SNOWBELL
Styrax Obassia

Leaves 10 cm, up to 15 cm on young trees.

Flowers in racemes of 20–25.

Leaves densely pubescent, glaucous below. **Petiole** 2 cm, encloses bud.

Flowers 2–3 cm.

Fruit 1.5 cm, tomentose.

Native to Japan, Fragrant snowbell has a gray bark and an open, upright crown that reaches 15 m. Hemsley snowbell (*S. Hemsleyana*) carries its white flowers on short, pubescent racemes. The petioles of its less downy leaves do not enclose the bud.

MOUNTAIN SILVERBELL
Halesia monticola

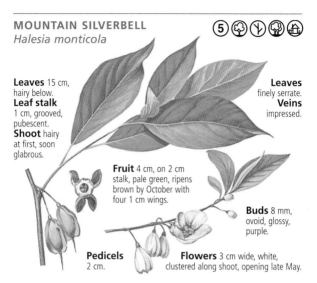

Leaves 15 cm, hairy below.
Leaf stalk 1 cm, grooved, pubescent.
Shoot hairy at first, soon glabrous.

Leaves finely serrate.
Veins impressed.

Fruit 4 cm, on 2 cm stalk, pale green, ripens brown by October with four 1 cm wings.

Buds 8 mm, ovoid, glossy, purple.

Pedicels 2 cm.

Flowers 3 cm wide, white, clustered along shoot, opening late May.

Mountain silverbell, to 25 m, is native to the mountains of the southeastern United States and is distinguished by its fruit and flowers. Carolina silverbell (*H. carolina*) is shrubbier with smaller flowers.

Loosestrife Family *Lythraceae*

The Loosestrife family of mostly tropical shrubs and trees is recognized for its ornamental value. Several of the 22 genera also produce dyes and pharmaceuticals.

CRAPE MYRTLE
Lagerstroemia indica

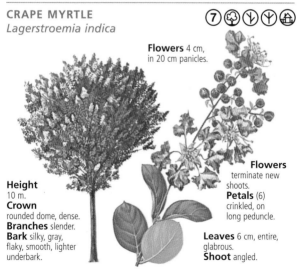

Flowers 4 cm, in 20 cm panicles.

Flowers terminate new shoots.
Petals (6) crinkled, on long peduncle.

Height 10 m.
Crown rounded dome, dense.
Branches slender.
Bark silky, gray, flaky, smooth, lighter underbark.

Leaves 6 cm, entire, glabrous.
Shoot angled.

This native of China and Japan only produces its splendid flowers in climates with long, hot summers. The flowers are usually bright pink but can be white, purple or scarlet. The buds and leaves may be set in pairs, threes or singly along the same shoot.

Olive Family *Oleaceae*

The main features of this family of about 400 trees and shrubs are the opposite, simple or pinnate leaves and the perfect or unisexual flowers with two stamens. The fruit may be a drupe, capsule or samara. Ash is the main tree genus and has fissured barks and shoots flattened between the buds. The fruit is a samara. *Olea*, *Ligustrum* and *Phillyrea* have simple leaves and a drupaceous fruit.

EUROPEAN ASH
Fraxinus excelsior

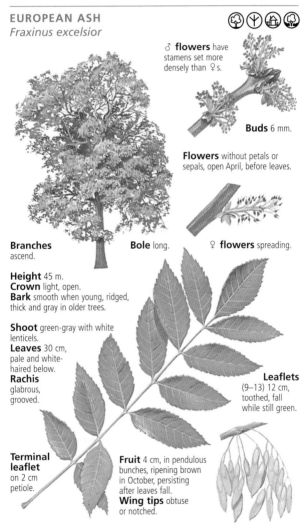

♂ **flowers** have stamens set more densely than ♀s.

Buds 6 mm.

Flowers without petals or sepals, open April, before leaves.

Branches ascend.

Bole long.

♀ **flowers** spreading.

Height 45 m.
Crown light, open.
Bark smooth when young, ridged, thick and gray in older trees.

Shoot green-gray with white lenticels.
Leaves 30 cm, pale and white-haired below.
Rachis glabrous, grooved.

Leaflets (9–13) 12 cm, toothed, fall while still green.

Terminal leaflet on 2 cm petiole.

Fruit 4 cm, in pendulous bunches, ripening brown in October, persisting after leaves fall.
Wing tips obtuse or notched.

Native throughout Europe and Asia Minor, this ash is a large forest tree that grows best on heavy, alkaline loams. While male and female flowers normally appear on separate trees, one tree may carry both sexes. The squat, black buds and smooth twigs are its best identification features. 'Pendula' is a weeping form, while 'Diversifolia' has simple leaves.

AMERICAN ASH/WHITE ASH
Fraxinus americana

Height 40 m.
Crown open, conical.
Branches stout, spreading, pendent in lower crown, often very angular.
Bole often forked, sometimes repeatedly.

Bark gray, smooth at first but becoming evenly fissured into diamond-shaped ridges, older trees deeply fissured.

Flowers open before leaves, in glabrous panicles, dioecious, without petals, looking like tassels; ♂ and ♀ on separate trees.

Leaves 30 cm. Leaflets (5–9) 12 cm, ovate or oblong-lanceolate.
Petiolule 1 cm, except on terminal leaflet, to 4 cm.

Shoot stout, soon glabrous, often bloomed, gray or brown.
Bud obtuse or rounded, broadly ovate.
Scales in four pairs, outer two-keeled, acute, hairy.

Fruit to 6 cm x 6 mm.

Base cuneate.
Apex acute.

Fruit a samara in pendent clusters of 20 cm.
Wing pointed or notched at tip.

Leaflets gray-green below.
Veins prominent, those on underside may be pubescent.
Margins either entire or serrate, with forward teeth.

Samara ripens from bright green to dull brown.
Leaves turn dull gray in autumn, rarely yellow or purple.
Samara wing decurrent.

American, or White ash, is found growing on moist soils, often near streams, and in the open, not being tolerant of much shade throughout the East from Nova Scotia to Texas. This is the most common ash, and is distinguishable from others by its larger leaves and black winter buds. Oregon ash (*F. latifolia*) has 35 cm leaves with five or seven elliptic or ovate 17 cm leaflets, sessile or nearly so, which have entire or finely toothed margins. The conic buds and shoots are hairy.

GREEN ASH/RED ASH
Fraxinus pennsylvanica ③ 🌲 🍃 🌳 🌲 🏠

Shoot round, flattened between buds, pubescent at first, later gray-brown with red tinge.
Bud 3 mm, six-scaled, rounded, acute, covered with red-brown pubescence.

Leaves 30 cm, with 7–9 (rarely 5) leaflets, obovate, oblanceolate or elliptic, dark shiny above, paler and hairy below.

Leaflets 15 cm.
Base cuneate.
Apex acuminate.
Margins serrate above middle.
Bark brown with reddish hue, scaly, fissured.

Petiolule 1–10 mm, stout, grooved, longer on terminal leaflet, dense, dark pubescence in patches.

Fruit a samara to 6 cm, oblong-lanceolate, in open, spreading glabrous panicle.
Seed round.
Wing decurrent.
Apex variable.

With a wide natural distribution throughout eastern and central North America, Green, or Red, ash grows to 20 m and is variable in habit, the pubescence on leaf and shoot, the leaflet shape, and the rounded, acute or notched samara wing.

BLACK ASH
Fraxinus nigra ② 🌲 🍃 🌳 🌲

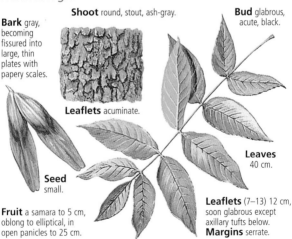

Shoot round, stout, ash-gray.

Bark gray, becoming fissured into large, thin plates with papery scales.

Bud glabrous, acute, black.

Leaflets acuminate.

Leaves 40 cm.

Seed small.

Fruit a samara to 5 cm, oblong to elliptical, in open panicles to 25 cm.

Leaflets (7–13) 12 cm, soon glabrous except axillary tufts below.
Margins serrate.

Black ash closely resembles Blue ash in that the flowers do not have calyxes or corollas. It differs in its round shoots and sessile leaflets. It is native to the Northeast, preferring wet sites, and reaches 25 m with an open, narrow crown.

FLOWERING ASH
Fraxinus Ornus

Leaflets (5–9) to 10 cm, stalked, downy below.

Teeth rounded.

Petiolule 1.5 cm.

Shoot almost glabrous, speckled with white lenticels.

Flowers in dense, 15 cm panicles; fragrant; appear in May with leaves.

Petals 5 mm, set in fours, whitish-yellow, narrow and linear.

Leaves 30 cm. **Rachis** bends, slender, grooved, pubescent at leaflet joints.

Flowering ash reaches 20 m to form a tree similar to *F. excelsior*, but distinguished from it, when not in flower, by its stalked, pubescent leaflets and gray-brown, hairy buds. It grows wild in southern Europe and western Asia and is sometimes tapped for the sugary substance which exudes from the bark.

BLUE ASH
Fraxinus quadrangulata

Leaflets (5–11) paler below, serrate.

Bud 6 mm, rounded, red-brown, slightly hairy, with six scales. **Apex** acuminate. **Base** oblique.

Shoots gray, four-angled, with four narrow corky wings, becoming round in third season.

Fruit 5 cm, a samara, oblong-ovate, loosely clustered in panicles. **Seed** flattened. **Wing** thin, decurrent, rounded, acute or notched at apex, ribbed. **Leaves** 30 cm. **Rachis** slender.

Leaflet base oblique.

Blue ash, native to a restricted area south of the Great Lakes, is usually a small tree to 15 m with a slender crown, although it occasionally reaches 40 m. The bark is irregularly divided into large plates, the light gray surface being tinged with red. It takes its name from a dye made from the inner bark.

CAUCASIAN ASH
Fraxinus oxycarpa

⑦ 🌳 🍂 🏠

Leaflets cupped.

Leaflets (7–9) 7 cm, shiny, pubescent on underside midrib vein.

Height 25 m. **Crown** narrow when young, later broadens.

Leaflets sharply serrate. **Bole** straight. **Bark** smooth, gray.

Leaves 25 cm. **Shoot** glabrous, green or brown. **Buds** set in twos or threes, coffee-colored.

This ash grows wild from southern Europe across the Caucasus to Iran and is usually encountered as the clone 'Raywood,' whose leaves turn claret in autumn. Narrow-leafed ash (*F. angustifolia*) has slender, glabrous leaflets and a rougher, dark gray bark.

VELVET ASH/ARIZONA ASH
Fraxinus velutina

⑦ 🌳 🍂 🌲 🌳 🏠

Fruit 2 cm on downy pedicel. **Wing** shorter than seed, notched.

Leaflets downy.

Buds 5 mm, velvety, six-scaled.

Shoot round, slender, velvety in first year. **Leaflets** 5 cm, thick, bluntly toothed above middle, usually fives or, less often, threes, sevens or nines.

Leaf 15 cm.

Although some forms are almost glabrous, Velvet, or Arizona ash, from the southwestern United States and Mexico, has pubescence even on its flower panicles. It can stand great extremes of temperature and reaches 10 or 15 m. The bark is broadly ridged.

OLIVE
Olea europaea

(10) (🌲) (Ⓨ)

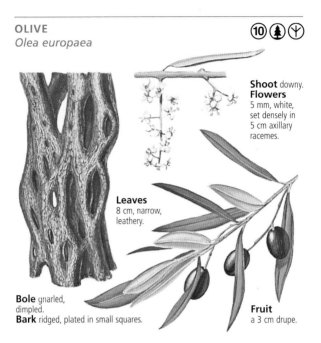

Shoot downy.
Flowers 5 mm, white, set densely in 5 cm axillary racemes.

Leaves 8 cm, narrow, leathery.

Bole gnarled, dimpled.
Bark ridged, plated in small squares.

Fruit a 3 cm drupe.

A common feature of the Californian and Mediterranean landscapes, Olive has a densely branched crown that reaches 15 m as an orchard tree, but, in the wild, is much shrubbier and has small oval leaves. If to be eaten, the fruit is harvested when green; for oil production, it is left until black and fully ripe.

GLOSSY PRIVET
Ligustrum lucidum

(8) (🌲) (Ⓨ) (🏛)

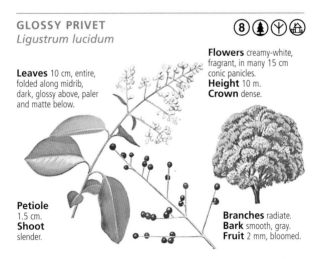

Leaves 10 cm, entire, folded along midrib, dark, glossy above, paler and matte below.

Flowers creamy-white, fragrant, in many 15 cm conic panicles.
Height 10 m.
Crown dense.

Petiole 1.5 cm.
Shoot slender.

Branches radiate.
Bark smooth, gray.
Fruit 2 mm, bloomed.

This superb Chinese evergreen is noted for its glossy and leathery leaves and the lateness of its flowers that open in late summer. Lilac (*Syringa vulgaris*) flowers in May and June and is deciduous with stout shoots ending in large pairs of green buds.

SWAMP PRIVET
Forestiera acuminata

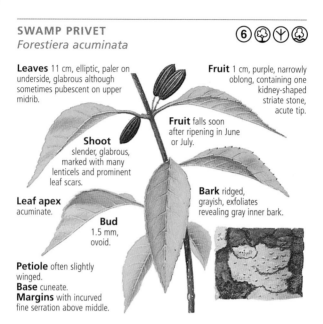

Leaves 11 cm, elliptic, paler on underside, glabrous although sometimes pubescent on upper midrib.

Fruit 1 cm, purple, narrowly oblong, containing one kidney-shaped striate stone, acute tip.

Fruit falls soon after ripening in June or July.

Shoot slender, glabrous, marked with many lenticels and prominent leaf scars.

Leaf apex acuminate.

Bud 1.5 mm, ovoid.

Bark ridged, grayish, exfoliates revealing gray inner bark.

Petiole often slightly winged.
Base cuneate.
Margins with incurved fine serration above middle.

Swamp privet is found in wet sites in the lower Mississippi region and as far east as the Georgia coast. It forms a small tree to 10 m with a spreading crown. The flowers, which have no petals, appear on short pedicels in many flowered fasicles.

FRINGE TREE
Chionanthus virginicus

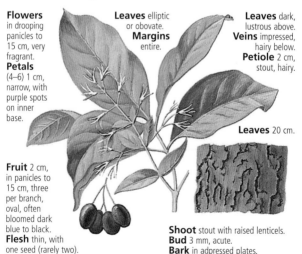

Flowers in drooping panicles to 15 cm, very fragrant.
Petals (4–6) 1 cm, narrow, with purple spots on inner base.

Leaves elliptic or obovate.
Margins entire.

Leaves dark, lustrous above.
Veins impressed, hairy below.
Petiole 2 cm, stout, hairy.

Leaves 20 cm.

Fruit 2 cm, in panicles to 15 cm, three per branch, oval, often bloomed dark blue to black.
Flesh thin, with one seed (rarely two).

Shoot stout with raised lenticels.
Bud 3 mm, acute.
Bark in adpressed plates.

This southeastern United States species grows to 10 m with a narrow, oblong crown. It is widely planted as an ornamental, being valued for its attractive star-like flowers which appear in June on the previous year's shoots below the expanding leaves.

Members of the Bombax family are tropical in origin and noted for their showy, sometimes very large, flowers. This family provides commercial kapok, as well as timber. Several species are very striking ornamentals.

RED SILK COTTON TREE
Bombax Ceiba

Flowers large, solitary and clustered near ends of branches, flowers appear before leaf emergence.
Petals 5–10 cm, bright red, recurved and fleshy.
Stamens numerous, in two whorls with the outer whorl united at the base into five bundles.

Fruit oblong, slightly angled pod to 15 cm, eventually breaking open and dispersing large quantities of seeds embedded in cotton-like fibers.
Leaves deciduous, alternate, palmately compound with 3–7 elliptic-obovate leaflets to 25 cm long.

Shoots spiny, brown, particularly when young, become grayish at maturity.

Red silk cotton trees are large, often exceeding 30 m in height and 10 m in girth. This species is native to tropical Asia and was introduced in the late 1800s to other tropical and subtropical areas. It is often seen as a landscape tree in south Florida. Its large, showy, crimson flowers emerging before the leaves make this an attractive ornamental. Bombax is derived from the Greek word for silk, which describes the cottony fibers released upon ripening of the pod. The fibers are used in India to stuff pillows. This species is often erroneously called Kapok tree. The true Kapok tree (*Ceiba pentandra*) is a related species, which rarely is used as an ornamental.

Borage Family *Boraginaceae*

The Borage family is large with over 100 genera of herbs, shrubs and trees, and is distributed worldwide. It furnishes timber, pharmaceuticals and dyes. Many members of the family are cultivated as ornamentals.

GEIGER TREE
Cordia Sebestena

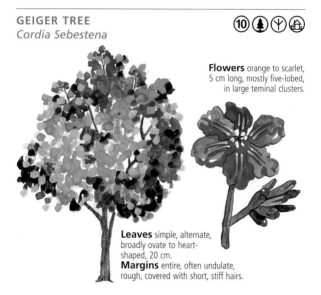

Flowers orange to scarlet, 5 cm long, mostly five-lobed, in large teminal clusters.

Leaves simple, alternate, broadly ovate to heart-shaped, 20 cm.
Margins entire, often undulate, rough, covered with short, stiff hairs.

Geiger tree, named after John Geiger, an early ship captain in the Florida Keys, is a small evergreen tree often less than 10 m tall. It is native to northern South America and the West Indies but is widely cultivated throughout the tropics and southern Florida. The tree's flowers bloom several times a year, but are showiest in the summer months. Its relative Anacahuita (*C. Boissieri*) is native to south Texas and Mexico, where it is referred to as Texas wild olive.

The Bignonia family comprises over 110 genera of mostly tropical to warm temperate trees, shrubs and vines. They are particularly noted for their showy inflorescences. Several genera, most notably Paulownia, are prized for their timber in Asia and the tropics.

PAULOWNIA/EMPRESS TREE
Paulownia tomentosa

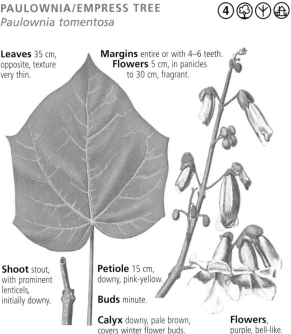

Leaves 35 cm, opposite, texture very thin.

Margins entire or with 4–6 teeth.
Flowers 5 cm, in panicles to 30 cm, fragrant.

Shoot stout, with prominent lenticels, initially downy.

Petiole 15 cm, downy, pink-yellow.

Buds minute.

Calyx downy, pale brown, covers winter flower buds.

Flowers, purple, bell-like.

A native of China, Paulownia, also called Empress tree, has a gaunt, domed crown and reaches 20 m. The flowers are often damaged over winter when fully exposed in bud. They are followed by green, ovoid, pointed capsules containing winged seeds.

INDIAN BEAN TREE
NORTHERN CATALPA
Catalpa bignonioides · Catalpa speciosa

④ ⚘ ⓨ

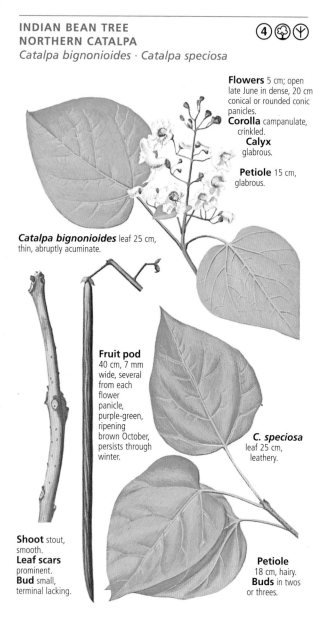

Flowers 5 cm; open late June in dense, 20 cm conical or rounded conic panicles.
Corolla campanulate, crinkled.
Calyx glabrous.

Petiole 15 cm, glabrous.

Catalpa bignonioides leaf 25 cm, thin, abruptly acuminate.

Fruit pod 40 cm, 7 mm wide, several from each flower panicle, purple-green, ripening brown October, persists through winter.

C. speciosa leaf 25 cm, leathery.

Shoot stout, smooth.
Leaf scars prominent.
Bud small, terminal lacking.

Petiole 18 cm, hairy.
Buds in twos or threes.

The catalpas are a small group of trees with large, ovate leaves and long, hanging pods. The most common, Indian bean tree, from the Gulf Coast, now widespread, forms a low, spreading tree, occasionally to 20 m. Northern catalpa, from central United States, has a conic crown and may attain 40 m, or half this height in Europe. Its flowers, to 6 cm, open earlier and the calyx is hairy. Chinese yellow catalpa (*C. ovata*) has more yellow 3 cm flowers and broadly ovate three-lobed leaves with long tips. Hybrid catalpa (*C. x hybrida*) has leaves opening purple.

DESERT WILLOW
Chilopsis linearis

⑦ 🌼 🔽 🏛 🌳

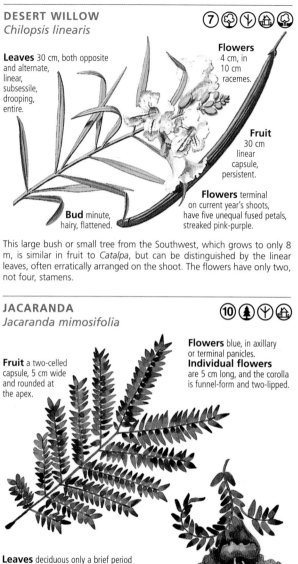

Leaves 30 cm, both opposite and alternate, linear, subsessile, drooping, entire.

Flowers 4 cm, in 10 cm racemes.

Fruit 30 cm linear capsule, persistent.

Flowers terminal on current year's shoots, have five unequal fused petals, streaked pink-purple.

Bud minute, hairy, flattened.

This large bush or small tree from the Southwest, which grows to only 8 m, is similar in fruit to *Catalpa*, but can be distinguished by the linear leaves, often erratically arranged on the shoot. The flowers have only two, not four, stamens.

JACARANDA
Jacaranda mimosifolia

⑩ 🌲 🔽 🏛

Fruit a two-celled capsule, 5 cm wide and rounded at the apex.

Flowers blue, in axillary or terminal panicles.
Individual flowers are 5 cm long, and the corolla is funnel-form and two-lipped.

Leaves deciduous only a brief period in spring, to 50 cm long, opposite, bipinnately compound with many 1 cm oblong, pubescent leaflets.

Jacaranda is a signal of spring with its profuse bluish blooms. This native of South America is widely used as a street tree in the warmer parts of Florida and southern California. It is a small tree, to 10 m. In parts of South America, the name Jacaranda is often applied to different trees, including that which produces the highly prized Brazilian rosewood lumber, which is *Dalbergia nigra* and not related to this species.

237

AFRICAN TULIP TREE
Spathodea campanulata

Flowers large, 15 x 8 cm, showy orange-red clusters at ends of the branches.
Individual flowers have a bell-shaped, two-lipped corolla emerging from a spathe-like calyx.

Fruit a boat-shaped capsule 20 x 5 cm across, contains many papery seeds.

Leaves evergreen, opposite, sometimes in threes, odd-pinnately compound; individual leaves may reach 50 cm long with dark green ovate leaflets 10 cm long.

Flower buds resemble a cluster of small fingers arranged in circular fashion on the branch tips; when squeezed, the buds will send out a small stream of water.

Native to equatorial Africa, this 20 m tree is cultivated throughout the warm tropics, particularly southern Florida, for its spectacular flowers and flowering habit. The tree may bloom two or three times a year, and blooming may last a month or more. The wood is light and brittle and used by African natives for making drums.

SILVER TRUMPET TREE / TREE OF GOLD
Tabebuia argentea

Branches often form a curved pattern.
Bark fissured, corky.

Flowers showy, yellow, in dense heads at the ends of branches.
Corolla trumpet-shaped, 5 cm, slightly two-lipped, blooming occurs in late winter or early spring.

Leaves opposite, palmately compound with 5–7 oblong leaflets, 15 cm with dense silvery scales.

Fruit 10 cm linear capsule, smooth, gray with black lines.

Trumpet trees are native to the New World tropical and subtropical areas and represented by 100 or more species. Although generally classed as evergreen, in subtropical areas it may lose its leaves briefly just before flowering. Most have showy flowers and blooming occurs in late winter or early spring. A dozen or so are used as ornamental shade and street trees in southern Florida. Some species produce valuable timber while the bark of others has medicinal properties.

The palms are one of the few monocot families to produce a tree form. Palms have been cultivated since ancient times as a source of food and fiber. The wood of palm trees is very durable and the fronds, or leaves, are a common thatching material for many roofs in the tropics. Coconut palm produces one of the largest leaves and seeds in the plant kingdom, and its fruit is not only a food staple, but also an important source of vegetable oil.

CHUSAN PALM / WINDMILL PALM
Trachycarpus Fortunei

⑧ Ⓡ 🌲 🌱 🏠

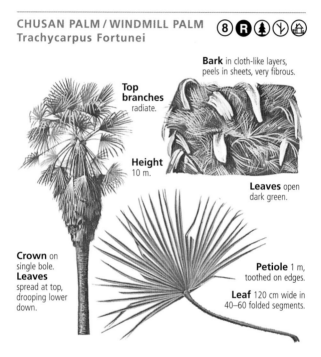

Bark in cloth-like layers, peels in sheets, very fibrous.

Top branches radiate.

Height 10 m.

Leaves open dark green.

Crown on single bole.
Leaves spread at top, drooping lower down.

Petiole 1 m, toothed on edges.

Leaf 120 cm wide in 40–60 folded segments.

Chusan palm, also called Windmill palm, from central China, is the palm most tolerant of cold. It is remarkable for its cloth-like bark. Like all true palms, it has only a single growing point and so never branches.

ROYAL PALM
Roystonea regia

⑨ 🌲 🌴 🌿 🏠

Height 30 m.
Crown apical cluster of foliage.
Bole long, often swollen at middle.

Bark blotchy in color, broken into small, irregular plates.
Leaf rachis hemispherical, unarmed, scaly, clasping stem at base.
Leaves 3–6 m, closely pinnate, arched.

Fruit 1.3 cm drupe, blue-black, subsessile, thin loose outer coat.

Leaflets 1 m, up to 3 cm wide at base but tapering toward apex, numerous, with glandular spots below, many parallel veins.

Native from southern Florida throughout central America, this palm is widely planted in humid subtropical regions as an ornamental, often being used in avenues of trees. The bole, often swollen halfway up, is diagnostic, and the small, white flowers are clustered in spadices (spikes with fleshy axes).

DATE PALM
Phoenix dactylifera

⑩ 🌲 🌴 🌿 🏠

Young leaves erect.
Older leaves arched, pendent.
Leaves 6 m, pinnate, with many pairs of feathery leaflets.
Leaflets 50 cm, gray-green, glaucous below, often drooping.
Apex long, acute.

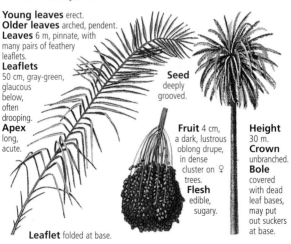

Seed deeply grooved.

Fruit 4 cm, a dark, lustrous oblong drupe, in dense cluster on ♀ trees.
Flesh edible, sugary.

Height 30 m.
Crown unbranched.
Bole covered with dead leaf bases, may put out suckers at base.

Leaflet folded at base.

This fruit tree is widely cultivated in the hot, dry regions of Florida and California, which resemble its native north Africa and western Asia. Small, yellowish flowers are produced in panicles but, being dioecious, artificial pollination is used.

CANARY ISLAND DATE PALM / PINEAPPLE PALM

⑩ 🌲 🌴 🌿 🏠

Phoenix canariensis

Leaves to 7 m, erect, arching, pinnate, evergreen.
Leaflets 50 cm, narrow, straight, folded at base.
Margins turned upward.
Apex acuminate, with very long, tapered point.

Crown of broad, arching leaves.

Height 20 m.

Fruit yellow, with long 1 m peduncle.

Rachis very stout, with two long green spines at base of leaflets.
Leaf persists hanging on tree when dead.

Fruit sessile.

Fruit 2 cm, an ovoid or rounded drupe.

Flesh dry, inedible.

Bole very stout, often widening near top and at base where aerial roots may protrude, rough, covered with pale brown leaf bases.

Sometimes called Pineapple palm because of the appearance of its bole, this species can be distinguished from the similar Date palm by its thicker stem, wide, stiffer leaflets and the dry, inedible fruit. It is named after its native islands.

COCONUT PALM
Cocos nucifera

(10) (🌲) (🌴) (🌿) (🏠)

Leaves pinnate up to 7 m long, individual pinnae up to 1 m.
Petiole stout, unarmed along the margin, attached to stem by fibrous sheath.

Height 25 m.

Stems singular, often curving unbranched, show remnants of sheath scars.

Fruits drupaceous.
Nuts large, to 30 cm, covered with a fibrous mesocarp, hard bony endocarp.

Flowers monoecious, small, greenish and many occurring on the same tree on a branched inflorescence to 1 m long.

Coconut palm is widely cultivated throughout the tropics, including south Florida, and used as ornamentals. The seeds are a principal source of vegetable fat, and have great economic importance in many tropical countries. The endosperm is used in many confectioneries, and the husk is a source of fiber. In Africa, the base of the inflorescence is tapped, and the milky sap is collected to yield a naturally fermented beverage known as palm wine.

EUROPEAN FAN PALM
Chamaerops humilis

(9) (🌲) (🌴) (🏠)

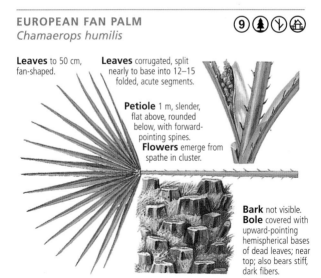

Leaves to 50 cm, fan-shaped.

Leaves corrugated, split nearly to base into 12–15 folded, acute segments.

Petiole 1 m, slender, flat above, rounded below, with forward-pointing spines.
Flowers emerge from spathe in cluster.

Bark not visible.
Bole covered with upward-pointing hemispherical bases of dead leaves; near top; also bears stiff, dark fibers.

In its native habitat on the shores of the western Mediterranean, this palm may occur as a dwarf shrub or a small tree to 6 m, but in cultivation in subtropical North America, it can grow to 10 m. The small yellow flowers, in clusters, are followed by brown or yellow rounded fruits to 4 cm.

CALIFORNIA FAN PALM / DESERT PALM
Washingtonia filifera

⑧ 🌲 🌴 🏠

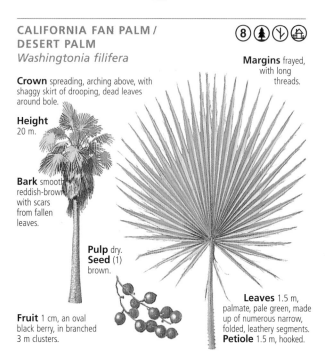

Crown spreading, arching above, with shaggy skirt of drooping, dead leaves around bole.

Height 20 m.

Bark smooth reddish-brown with scars from fallen leaves.

Pulp dry. **Seed** (1) brown.

Fruit 1 cm, an oval black berry, in branched 3 m clusters.

Margins frayed, with long threads.

Leaves 1.5 m, palmate, pale green, made up of numerous narrow, folded, leathery segments.
Petiole 1.5 m, hooked.

Widely planted as a street ornamental, this is one of the largest palms, and is distinctive for the way its leaves arise erect and end up as a dead frill around the trunk. It differs from many palms in its smooth bark without fibrous threads.

MEXICAN FAN PALM
Washingtonia robusta

⑨ 🌲 🌴 🏠

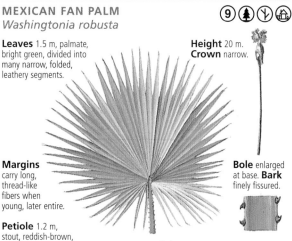

Leaves 1.5 m, palmate, bright green, divided into many narrow, folded, leathery segments.

Height 20 m.
Crown narrow.

Margins carry long, thread-like fibers when young, later entire.

Bole enlarged at base. **Bark** finely fissured.

Petiole 1.2 m, stout, reddish-brown, leaves scar.

Petiole with marginal hooked spines.

Mexican fan palm is similar to California fan palm, but has a narrower crown, less smooth bark and loses the marginal fibers as the leaves mature. It is also native to California, now widely planted across the Gulf states, but prefers temperate coastal sites.

FLORIDA THATCH PALM
Thrinax parviflora

⑩ 🌲 🌳 🏠

Leaves 1 m across, to 60 cm long, fan-shaped, divided nearly to the center into many linear, folded segments with long-pointed apexes.

Height 10 m.
Crown a rounded apical cluster of foliage.
Petiole 1.5 m, green, reddish near stem, broad, flattened, with winged margin.

Bole slender, slightly tapering toward crown, commonly covered with dead leaf bases.
Bark pale gray, barely visible.

Leaves shiny yellow-green above, silvery-white below, hairy when young.

The thatch palms are a group of small trees found mainly in the Caribbean. Florida thatch palm, one of four native to the south of that state, is the most common, and is also known as the Jamaica thatch and Palmetto palm. The fragrant yellow flowers appear in a raceme.

CABBAGE PALMETTO
Sabal palmetto

⑧ 🌲 🌳 🏠

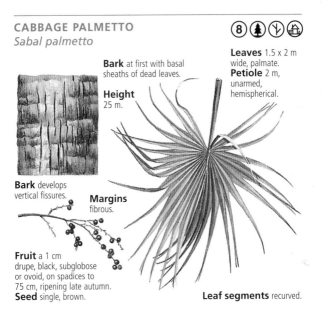

Bark at first with basal sheaths of dead leaves.

Leaves 1.5 x 2 m wide, palmate.
Petiole 2 m, unarmed, hemispherical.

Height 25 m.

Bark develops vertical fissures.

Margins fibrous.

Fruit a 1 cm drupe, black, subglobose or ovoid, on spadices to 75 cm, ripening late autumn.
Seed single, brown.

Leaf segments recurved.

Native to Florida and up the coast to South Carolina, Cabbage palmetto grows to 25 m with a thatch of dead leaves below its crown like California fan palm, though differing in its unarmed petioles. The bark becomes smooth with age.

Agave Family *Agavaceae*

The Agave family is an important source of fiber (sisal) and many ornamentals. It is commonly distributed in warm, dry climates. One genus, *Agave*, provides a sap that is fermented into tequila and mescal, without which a margarita would be a very ordinary drink.

CABBAGE PALM
Cordyline australis

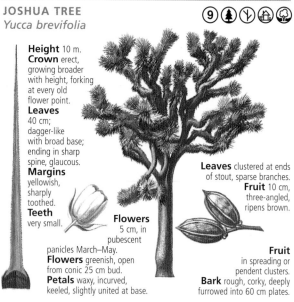

Leaves 90 cm, lanceolate, pointed tip, erect, later drooping, persisting dead.

Height 10 m.

Branches erect, spreading.
Crown on large, straight bole.

Bark grayish, fissured into small, corky ridges.

Cabbage palm, from New Zealand, is hardy on warm coasts. Leaves are arranged spirally in tufts on shoots. The fragrant, creamy-white flowers are carried in terminal panicles up to 1 m high and are followed by numerous 6 mm bluish-white berries.

JOSHUA TREE
Yucca brevifolia

Height 10 m.
Crown erect, growing broader with height, forking at every old flower point.
Leaves 40 cm; dagger-like with broad base; ending in sharp spine, glaucous.
Margins yellowish, sharply toothed.
Teeth very small.

Leaves clustered at ends of stout, sparse branches.
Fruit 10 cm, three-angled, ripens brown.

Flowers 5 cm, in pubescent panicles March–May.
Flowers greenish, open from conic 25 cm bud.
Petals waxy, incurved, keeled, slightly united at base.

Fruit in spreading or pendent clusters.
Bark rough, corky, deeply furrowed into 60 cm plates.

This southwestern United States species, a native of the Mohave Desert, was named by the early Mormons who thought its habit resembled a man reaching out his arms to heaven. It is the tallest of several Yuccas from the South although it has the shortest leaves.

Acuminate Tapering to a narrow point.

Acute Angled sharply to a point.

Adpressed Closely pressed to an adjoining part of the plant, such as a bud against a twig or shoot (Hornbeam).

Alternate Leaves arranged singly along and on both sides of a stem.

Ament A scaly or bracted spike of unisexual flowers, a catkin, usually deciduous in one piece.

Angiosperm (*Angiospermae*), one of the two main divisions of seed bearing plants (the other being Gymnosperms). Angiosperms produce flowers and reproduce by seeds borne in a closed carpel, or female flower part.

Aril Fleshy outer covering of a seed (Yew).

Assurgent Ascending.

Auricles Ear-like appendages at the base of a leaf (Pedunculate oak).

Awl-like leaves Leaves tapering to a slender, sharp point.

Axil Upper angle formed between a leaf and a twig, or a twig and a shoot, or the junction between two veins.

Axil tufts Pubescence in axil.

Bipinnate A type of pinnate leaf whose leaflets are themselves pinnate (Honey locust).

Blade Greatest part of a leaf, the part other than the leaf stalk.

Bloom Powdery or waxy sheen of a shoot or leaf (Eucalyptus), or fruit, which can easily be rubbed away.

Bole Trunk or stem of a tree.

Bract Modified leaf associated with a flower. In some trees, they are more conspicuous than the flowers themselves; in conifers bract scales often extend beyond the edge of the fertile scales.

Buttress Strengthened part of a bole or root that assists in supporting a tree (Beech).

Calyx Aggregate of sepals subtending a flower.

Carpel Single unit of a flower comprising the stigma, style and ovary.

Catkin Dense, usually long and pendent, group of flowers.

Chambered Pith of a shoot that is broken up by hollow spaces.

Ciliate Having a hairy fringe on margins.

Columnar-conic Shape of a habit which is narrow and straight-sided at its base and then becomes pyramidal.

Compound Leaves comprised of several separate leaflets.

Coppicing The practice of cutting back trees, such as willows, to their stumps in order to promote growth of new shoots.

Cordate Heart-shaped; used especially in reference to leaves where the leaf bases curve away from the leaf stalk (Linden).

Corymb Domed or flat-topped flower cluster with the external flowers opening first.

Crenate Serration which has broad, rounded teeth.

Crown Upper part of the tree; the branches and foliage.

Cultivar Variety of tree selected in cultivation.

Cuneate Wedge-shaped base of a leaf tapering into a leaf stalk (Cork oak).

Cupule Circle of bracts which become cup-shaped and enclose fruit such as an acorn.

Cyme Flat-topped flower cluster, the central flowers opening first.

Deciduous Falling at the end of a growth period.

Decurrent Extending in a downward direction, as a leaf blade or petiole ridge along a stem.

Decussate Alternating right-angled pairs of leaves or scales.

Dehiscent Opening by slits or valves.

Deltoid Equilaterally triangular with the broad end close to the attachment to the petiole.

Dioecious Having male and female flowers on separate trees.

Drupe Fruit containing a single seed in the form of a stone.

Entire Margin without either teeth or lobules.

Exserted Extending.

Fascicle Bundle or cluster.

Fastigiate Tree habit which has very upswept, almost erect branches (Lombardy poplar, Cypress oak).

Fluted With alternate ridges and grooves (Dawn redwood).

Glabrous Smooth, not hairy.

Glaucous Covered with a blue-gray or whitish bloom.

Globose Irregularly spherical.

Gymnosperm (*Gymnospermae*), one of the two main divisions of seed bearing plants. Such plants do not produce flowers but reproduce by seeds borne naked, on an open sporophyll, or special bract, most often in the form of a cone.

Habit General appearance of a tree, usually from a distance.

Hilum Paler, basal seed scar of a nut (Yellow buckeye).

Hybrid Species arising from the cross fertilization of two members of the same genus in which case the generic and specific names are separated by an 'x' (*Tilia x euchlora*) or (far less commonly) the members of two genera when the 'x' usually precedes the generic name (*Cupressocyparis x Leylandii*).

Illobulate Entire, not bearing lobes.

Imbricate Overlapping like roof tiles.

Impressed vein Vein set below surface of leaf (American hornbeam).

Inflorescence Floral part of a plant.

Involucre Circle of bracts developed to cover a fruit (Beech).

Keeled With a central ridge like a keel of a boat.

Lanceolate Shaped like the blade of a spear, as most willow leaves (Black willow).

Layering The ability of a tree to regenerate by a branch touching the ground where it roots and forms a new plant.

Leader Leading shoot of tree and one of the youngest; may droop and thereby be an identification feature.

Leaf scar Imprint left on a twig or shoot by a fallen leaf.

Lenticel Raised corky growth on a twig or a shoot which admits air to the interior of the branch.

Lobe Rounded section of a leaf, divided by sinuses.

Lobulate Bearing small lobes.

Margin Leaf edge.

Midrib Central vein of a leaf.

Monoecious Having both male and female flowers on the same tree.

Oblique Unequal-sided base of a leaf, as in most elms.

Obovate Ovate with the widest part beyond the middle of the leaf.

Obovoid Ovoid and largest beyond the middle.

Operculum Cap of fused petals that covers flower bud of Eucalyptus, falls as flower opens.

Opposite Set in pairs at the same level each side of the twig or shoot.

Orbicular Almost circular-shaped leaf.

Ostiole A pore or small circular opening.

Ovate Leaf that is egg-shaped in outline, widest below the middle.

Ovule Part of the plant that becomes the seed after fertilization.

Palmate Leaf that has lobes or leaflets radiating from one simple point, like the fingers of a hand; also applies to a leaf's venation pattern.

Panicle Compound inflorescence whose flowers branch from a central stem.

Pectinate 2-ranked arrangement of leaves either side of a central shoot in the nature of the teeth of a comb.

Peduncle Flower stalk.

Peltate Shield-shaped.

Perfect Having male and female organs combined in one flower and not as separate flowers.

Petiole Leaf stalk.

Petiolule The stalk attaching leaflets to a central rachis.

Pinna Leaflet or primary division of a pinnate leaf.

Pinnate Compound leaf with leaflets arranged regularly each side of a rachis.

Pith Softer, central section of a shoot's stem.

Pneumatophores Special aerial root that provides air to roots on waterlogged sites (Bald cypress).

Pollarding The practice of lopping trees at about 3 m above the ground in order to encourage further growth.

Pome Fruit of several carpels enclosed in thick flesh (Crab apple).

Puberulous Minutely pubescent.

Pubescence Covering of soft and short hairs.

Pulvinus Swelling, cushion or pad at the base of a stem, leaf or leaflet, as in some conifers and members of the Legume family.

Raceme Inflorescence of stalked flowers growing from a rachis.

Rachis Central stalk of a compound (pinnate) leaf or inflorescence.

Recurved Curving backward or downward.

Reflexed Curving abruptly backward or downward.

Reticulate Net-like or net-shaped.

Samara Winged fruit (Maple).

Serrate Toothed.

Sessile Non-stalked.

Sheath Tubular envelope enclosing a bunch of fascicle leaves (Pine).

Simple Leaf consisting of one single blade (Tulip tree).

Sinuate Strongly waved.

Sinus Recess between lobes.

Stipule Appendage usually at the base of a petiole.

Stomata Orifices in a leaf used to let air into the leaf.

Style The usually slender part of a pistil, rising from the ovary and tipped by the stigma.

Subsessile With a minute stalk.

Ternate Set in threes.

Tomentose Having a dense, wooly pubescence.

Trifoliate Leaf comprising three leaflets.

Truncate Abrupt end to a leaf base or tip.

Umbel Inflorescence with pedicels all arising from the same point.

Umbo Raised center of the scale of a pine cone.

Valvate Meeting at edges like a clam's shell, not overlapping.

Valve Section into which a fruit capsule splits.

Venation Pattern of veins. Vein Strands of vascular tissue visible on leaf surfaces.

Vein axils Upper angle between two veins.

Whorl The circular arrangement of plant parts (leaves, buds, branches, flower parts) arising from a single point, or node.

Index

Entries refer to spp, vars and cvs described in detail and illustrated;
for related trees see genus or nearest sp entry.

Conversion Tables

The tables below will enable you to convert the metric measurements given in the book into imperial units. Use the first table for buds and small flowers or fruit, the second for leaves and larger fruits, and the third for the overall size of the tree.

Remember that all the measurements given in the book are maxima; features on trees illustrated may be smaller.

Millimeters to Inches

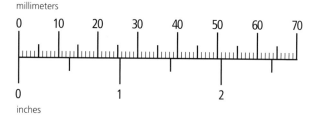

Centimeters to Inches

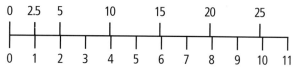

Meters to Feet

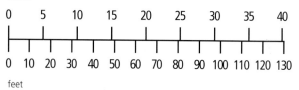

Acknowledgments

The authors and publishers would like to thank the following people and organizations for their help:

Alf Westall and Malcolm Scott, Bedgebury National Pinetum, Kent; Alan Mitchell, The Forestry Commission, Alice Holt Lodge, Farnham, Surrey; Jim Keesing and Charles Erskine, The Royal Botanic Gardens, Kew; Ivan Hicks, West Dean Estates, Chichester, Sussex; A. Chris Nelson and Richard Bryant, International Paper, Southlands Forest, Bainbridge, Georgia; Dr. John Olsen, professor of biology and associate dean of academic affairs, Rhodes College, Memphis, Tennessee; Edward A. Cope, extension botanist, Bailey Hortorium, Cornell University, Ithaca, N.Y.; Dr. Mark H. Hughes, manager terrestrial and aquatic biology, International Paper

Artwork:
Joseph Rattan: 14-26, 35, 48, 67, 81, 101, 106, 125, 133, 143, 145, 153, 156, 164, 177, 180, 182, 188-189, 214, 217, 220, 233-234, 237-239, 243;
Olivia Beasley: 30-31, 37-38, 41-47, 49-59, 62-66, 68-72;
John Davis: 93-100, 119-122, 128-131, 132-133, 160-176;
John Michael Davis: 29, 34, 36, 39-40, 60-61, 73-89, 150-155, 157-159, 178-179, 181, 183-187, 189-208;
Annabel Milne and Peter Stebbing: 10-12, 14-26, 32-33, 90-92, 209-219, 221-232, 235-237, 240-146;
David Moore: 102-105, 107-116, 134-142, 144, 146-149;
Paul Wrigley: 117-118, 123-127, 131-132

Designers: Jennifer Frink, 2006 edition; Joseph Rattan, 2003 edition; Jacqueline Moore, 1980 edition

Cover photo: Digital Vision/Getty Images

First published 1980 under the title *The Pocket Guide to Trees* by Mitchell Beazley (an imprint of Octopus Publishing Group Ltd.), 2-4 Heron Quays, Docklands, London E14 4JP
© Mitchell Beazley International Ltd 1980, reprinted 1990, 1992, 1996
2003 edition *The Pocket Guide to Trees,* copyright © International Paper Company, 2003

Printed and bound by R.R. Donnelley & Sons, Shenzhen, China.

ISBN 0-7922-5310-8